UNDERSTANDING GAME SCORING

The Evolution of Compositional
Practice for and through Gaming

Mack Enns

Routledge
Taylor & Francis Group

LONDON AND NEW YORK

First published 2022
by Routledge
2 Park Square, Milton Park, Abingdon, Oxon OX14 4RN

and by Routledge
605 Third Avenue, New York, NY 10158

Routledge is an imprint of the Taylor & Francis Group, an informa business

British Library Cataloguing-in-Publication Data
A catalogue record for this book is available from the British Library

Library of Congress Cataloging-in-Publication Data
Names: Enns, Mackenzie, author.
Title: Understanding game scoring: the evolution of compositional practice for and through gaming / Mackenzie Enns.
Description: [1.] | Abingdon, Oxon; New York: Routledge, 2021. |
Series: Perspectives on music production | Includes bibliographical references and index.
Identifiers: LCCN 2021029237 (print) | LCCN 2021029238 (ebook)
Subjects: LCSH: Video game music—Instruction and study. | Video game music—Production and direction. | Composition (Music)—Collaboration.
Classification: LCC MT64.V53 E65 2021 (print) | LCC MT64.V53 (ebook) |
DDC 781.5/4—dc23
LC record available at https://lccn.loc.gov/2021029237
LC ebook record available at https://lccn.loc.gov/2021029238

ISBN: 978-0-367-49283-0 (hbk)
ISBN: 978-0-367-49281-6 (pbk)
ISBN: 978-1-003-04546-5 (ebk)

DOI: 10.4324/9781003045465

Typeset in Bembo
by codeMantra

CONTENTS

FIGURES

TABLES

PREFACE

This work is an adaptation of my PhD dissertation, "Understanding Game Scoring: Software Programming, Aleatoric Composition and Mimetic Music Technology" (2019). After teaching courses in my field for one year, I can firmly say that there remains much to explore in the study of the composition, programming and design of music for video games. Students in my courses have shown me that games can inspire musicians and composers to think differently about music, and form new musical strategies to accommodate different game designs and technologies. I have seen that the interactive context of gaming is especially interesting for students to score, as they seek different aesthetic goals while envisioning a participatory experience of their music. While there remains more to be said about game scoring, I hope for this book to be a guide for the reader in understanding what makes the practice inspiring, creatively fulfilling and unique.

1

AN INTRODUCTION TO GAME SCORING

Have you ever turned a video game into a musical instrument? That is, have you ever decided to — temporarily — change your competitive goals to musical ones, while playing a game? My guess is that I am not alone in indulging in this activity, because gaming is a *mimetic* art form that involves different modes of cognitive and sensory interaction. One of these modes of interaction is musical, but the musical experience of gaming is different from traditional music listening, and the way video game music composers or "game scorers" write music for games is different from traditional musical scoring activities.

In this book, I study the act of composing music for — and *through* — gaming, or what I refer to as "game scoring." As with film scoring, game scoring supports and elucidates the visual aspects of a broader narrative medium — in this case, video games. However, any further resemblances between game scoring and film scoring are illusory, in my opinion.[1] A host of unique technical and aesthetic priorities and concerns faces game scorers today. Most obviously, game scores must remain flexible and interactive in response to gameplay. They are only finally "realized" — that is, game scores only ever exist as something other than imperceptible digital bits — through gameplay. Game scorers also compose for particular sound hardware configurations, and so their compositional activity is structured in its entirety by the limited set of aesthetic possibilities each console's particular audio processing Unit (APU) affords. If it cannot be programmed into a console's APU, it simply cannot exist as part of a game score. As such, game scoring most closely resembles software programming.[2]

Actually, game scoring *is* software programming. This does not mean, though, that it is therefore somehow aesthetically impoverished, being so limited by the dictates of a single variety of modern consumer electronics. In fact, since game scoring is structured in its entirety by gaming technology, it constitutes a unique compositional mode that should be understood as a variety of so-called "aleatoric composition."[3] Aleatoric composition includes all compositional activity in which one or more musical elements are left to chance, as well as compositions in which some degree of improvisational freedom is afforded to performers. *Musikalisches Würfelspiel* ("musical dice game"), for instance, qualifies as aleatoric because

DOI: 10.4324/9781003045465-1

it uses dice to randomly "generate" music from pre-composed options.[4] In this case, the chance operation involved in the music's composition is a roll of the dice, and the element of composition that chance determines is the order in which the pre-composed sections of the piece are performed.[5] Similarly, any composition with improvisatory sequences is at least partially aleatoric. For example, Ornette Coleman's *Free Jazz* (1961) was the first album-length improvisation, making it at least partially aleatoric.

Game scoring includes both of these "types" of aleatoric composition. That is, a game score involves both chance operations *and* a degree of improvisation. In fact, game scoring is a peculiar type of composition because the "performer" of a game score is not a musical performer but a "ludal" one — a "gamer" apparently involved in a non-musical activity. Sound, visuals and controls, or "haptics," inform the gamer's gameplay choices, and so game scores are open to improvisatory and chance operations that only the combination of these elements enable. In other words, game scorers arguably *collaborate* with players to produce the final score for a game. In *Super Mario Bros.* (1985), for instance, the thematic content of each composition's conclusion is determined by whether or not players successfully complete a level. If players "beat" a level, the score triggers the "Flagpole Fanfare" theme, a triumphant ascending melody (see Figure 1.1). Players who fail to conquer that same level, on the other hand, hear the "Death Sound," a comedic descending riff instead (see Figure 1.2).[6] Thus, whether or not the "Flagpole Fanfare" theme ever sounds, and how often, is up to the gamer.

To be clear, my definition of "game scoring" encompasses the organization of sound, its encoding as software via programming and, most importantly, its *actualization* through gameplay. I make this distinction to emphasize the difference between what I call "game scores," which are actively created through gameplay, and video game soundtracks. I will explore this difference in greater detail in Chapter 5 of this book.

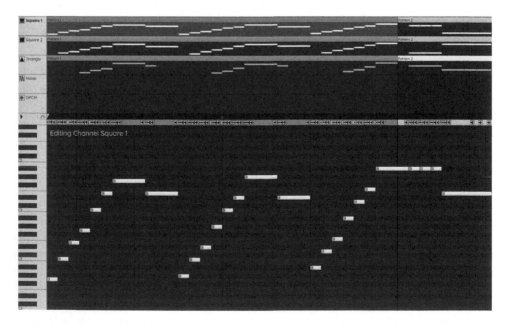

FIGURE 1.1 The "Flagpole Fanfare" theme, heard when a player successfully completes a level in *Super Mario Bros.* The ascending melody has a triumphant or victorious thematic content.

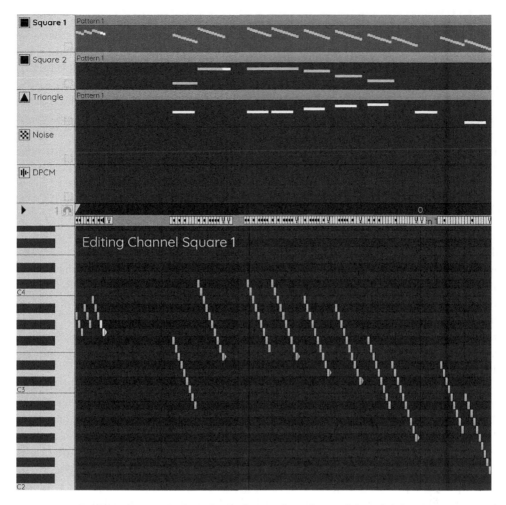

FIGURE 1.2   The "Death Sound" that plays when a player loses a life and fails to "beat" a level. The descending riff evokes disappointment, but is notably shorter than the "Flag-pole Fanfare" theme and adds a comedic element through syncopated percussion. The "Death Sound" in *SMB* is archetypal for its effectiveness in encouraging the player to attempt the level again, even after "dying" multiple times.

As a means of concretizing the theoretical terrain I intend to cover in this book, I offer the following case study, specifically, of Richard Vreeland's game score for the 2012 Xbox Live Arcade "puzzle-platform" game *FEZ*. This theoretical terrain is drawn largely from work by Whalen (2004) and Collins (2013), both of whom pose salient questions about the interactive nature of game scoring. Whalen's (2004: 2) "Play Along – An Approach to Videogame Music" relates the concept of player immersion to game scoring:

> The interactive element of videogames [sic] requires its own analysis [...] Cognitive theories of perception and questions of immersion versus engagement as a means of understanding 'flow' or pleasurability in games allows for a richer understanding of the complex communication involved in videogame [sic] music.[7]

Collins (2013) suggests that new media, such as video games, provide instances of interactive sound that are unique for their diffused sources of composition. In interactive sound design, she argues, not only does the composer have a hand in the compositional process, but also the designer, programmer and even the gamer. Collins' (2013) argument is useful as a basis for a study of game scoring, and so will provide a model for my "ludo-musicological" analysis of game scoring. Ludo-musicology is a relatively new field of research which focuses exclusively on video game music, as opposed to music composed for the non-performative visual arts or non-interactive film, for instance. As Collins (2013) notes, and as I will now demonstrate, it is the "performative" and "interactive" aspects of video games that create the unique challenges and concerns that game scorers must address through their work.

Disasterpeace and *FEZ*: a case study of game scoring

In what follows, I examine some aspects of the compositional process Richard Vreeland — also known as Disasterpeace — undertook to compose his celebrated score for *FEZ*, a puzzle-platformer video game released for Xbox Live Arcade in 2012. All of what follows, including screenshots of and technical information about the music system for *FEZ*, is drawn from a conference presentation entitled "Philosophy of Music Design in Games," given by Vreeland himself at the 2012 Game Audio Network Guild Summit.[8] This case study is by no means an exhaustive examination. Here I simply examine some aspects of game scoring, and demonstrate that they resemble software programming more than anything traditionally described by the moniker of "music composition."

FEZ was developed by the independent software company Polytron Corporation, which includes the game's creator and designer Phil Fish, and its programmer Renaud Bédard. They were responsible for most of the development of the game: Fish determined the creative vision for the project by designing its gameplay mechanics and visual style, while Bédard made that vision a reality through programming. It was only until after the game's gameplay and visuals were designed and programmed that Vreeland was invited to compose and produce the game's celebrated score. Therefore, his task was to compose music that elucidates a pre-conceived visual world with its own spatial limitations, mechanics, aesthetics and logic, and to provide a score to represent, complement and sonically realize that world.

The world of *FEZ* is highly dynamic. Its "levels" consist of non-Euclidean[9] spaces known as "Rooms." At the outset of the game, Gomez, the game's "protagonist," is a two-dimensional creature who lives in a two-dimensional world. Much like the Mario Bros., the protagonists in the classic 8- and 16-bit *Super Mario Bros.* "platformer" series, Gomez has impressive jumping abilities that serve as the main element of gameplay in a world composed of various types of platforms. Eventually, after a short "tutorial" introduction, Gomez encounters a mysterious being known as the Hexahedron, who grants him a "magical fez hat" that allows him to perceive a third dimension, and that allows players to rotate the gameplay perspective at will, ninety degrees at a time. As players direct Gomez to experiment with his new abilities, the Hexahedron unexpectedly fractures and explodes, causing the game to glitch, freeze and reboot, complete with a Basic Input/Output System, or (BIOS) screen. Gomez awakens in his room with his ability to perceive and manipulate a third dimension intact, and is charged with the task of recovering the scattered fragments of the Hexahedron before the world is torn apart.

Even after Gomez acquires the ability to perceive the third dimension, gameplay in *FEZ* remains largely two-dimensional. Depth, or the Z-axis, is only visible to the player in the rotation of perspectives, and is not a factor in the actual obstacles and chasms that Gomez must traverse. The player must manipulate these perspectives to explore the world of *FEZ* and collect 32 cubes in the form of "cube bits," "whole cubes" or "anti-cubes." In so doing, Gomez performs actions that would normally be impossible in a truly three-dimensional world. For example, players may rotate the perspective so that a platform Gomez is standing on moves to the other side of the screen, even though Gomez himself has not moved at all. Figures 1.3 and 1.4 are gameplay screenshots from *FEZ* that exemplify this mechanic:

Players of *FEZ* must conceive of space in a different way than usual in order to navigate its world. One of the first people who was allowed to explore this world was Rich Vreeland, though, of course, he did so in silence. Not only did Vreeland have to conceive of space differently in this initial run-through of *FEZ*, but he was also forced to conceive of music composition in a new way. The incorporation of the music system into *Fezzer*, the game's programming system developed by Renaud Bédard, allowed for this new compositional approach. Moreover, *Fezzer* was no less dynamic than the world it was used to create: as he composed, Vreeland was invited to propose ideas for the music system that Bédard would then implement into his programming. The music system they eventually developed took the form of various tools and techniques integrated into *Fezzer* itself, and so the production and composition of the score for *FEZ* was inextricably linked with the development of gameplay and design. The three tools and techniques from *Fezzer* that I will explain now are (i) the sequence context menu; (ii) the scripts browser; and (iii) the main composition sequencer. These are names that I have given to these tools and techniques, and not what Vreeland or Bédard may have called them.

FIGURE 1.3 Gomez atop a tree, unable to reach a higher ledge.

FIGURE 1.4 Gomez atop the same tree as Figure 1.3 with the perspective rotated once, ninety degrees clockwise. He is now able to ascend the tower.

Music system overview: sequence context menu

Fezzer allows the user to physically explore every aspect of *FEZ* as an omniscient observer. Manipulation of perspectives is not necessary here as the user can already view any area in three dimensions. Right-clicking on any element in the game world, such as the block in Figure 1.5, prompts the sequence context menu. The sequence context menu is a tool for the assignment of sounds to physical elements within the game. It is used for either sound effects

FIGURE 1.5 The sequence context menu in *Fezzer*. One of the appearing and disappearing blocks in one of the Music Rooms is right-clicked, prompting the context menu.[10]

or music given the scenario, or both as in the instance of Figure 1.5. The "Sequence…" button allows the user to load a sample piece of music or sound effect into the menu. In the above example, Vreeland has loaded "3×03" and "3×04" into the context menu as usable sound elements. These refer to the bright and bit-crushed synth arrays that coincide with the appearance and disappearance of bright red blocks in the Music Rooms.

This particular example involved considerable collaboration between Bédard and Vreeland. The programmer had to adapt the gameplay to the rhythm of the music written by the composer. The blocks thus not only appear with the synth arrays, but appear on beat with the level's score. Vreeland (2012) said that this process involved thinking about music in terms of "proximity rather than order," or in terms of spatiality rather than temporality. The ability to visualize the implementation of music in *Fezzer* was indispensable in Vreeland's (2012) composition process, as he could now think about "which notes do I want to happen near other notes so that they sound pleasing." The word "near" in Vreeland's quote does not denote a nearness in time, but in (spatial) proximity between elements in the world of *FEZ*. Bédard's music system allows for a spatial conception of music through its incorporation into the programming software itself. Right-clicking an element and assigning it a sound may seem like a simple task, but it also prompts a new way of thinking about music production and composition.

Music system overview: scripts browser

Unlike the sequence context menu, the scripts browser window in *Fezzer* affects an entire room rather than just any one single element. Scripts are programs that are written for a specific run-time environment — which can also be a program, such as a game — that can read and execute tasks in an automated fashion. In other words, scripts are sets of tasks that can be performed by programs that can interpret them; hence, *Fezzer* deals with its own specific type of scripts. The general nature of this definition points towards the wealth of possibilities with scripts, as they can perform almost any function so long as the host program can interpret them.

The scripts browser window in *Fezzer* consists of a table that lists each script's "Id," "Name," "Trigger," "Condition" and "Action." The "Id" of a script is simply an identifying number, while the "Name" column serves largely the same function. In Figure 1.6, I assume that Vreeland left the "Id" and "Name" fields at their default values. The "Trigger" of a script is generally self-explanatory as that which sets the execution of a script in motion, but its implementation becomes more complicated in specific cases. Figure 1.6 shows a scripts browser window with scripts for one of the Music Rooms, which incorporates altitude-sensitive musical elements. As Gomez ascends higher in the Music Rooms in *FEZ*, as in Figure 1.7, different musical elements are added to and subtracted from the mix. Each trigger therefore indicates an altitude, signified by the "Volume[x]" condition.

Furthermore, there is another condition that signifies whether Gomez is higher or lower than the specified altitude. For example, script four has "Volume[5], GoHigher" as its trigger value, and so any time Gomez goes higher than an altitude of "5," the script is triggered. The numbers that denote altitude are arbitrarily assigned to invisible blocks that are positioned by Bédard in the Music Room. The "Condition" column of the scripts browser allows for any other conditions to be entered, such as time of day or perhaps the amount of cube bits Gomez has acquired. In Figure 1.6, no extra conditions are necessary, and so the

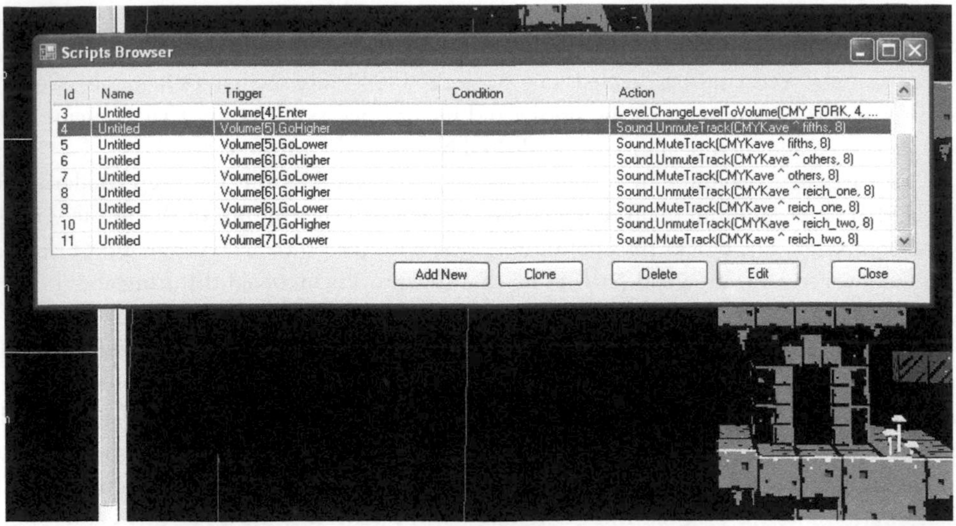

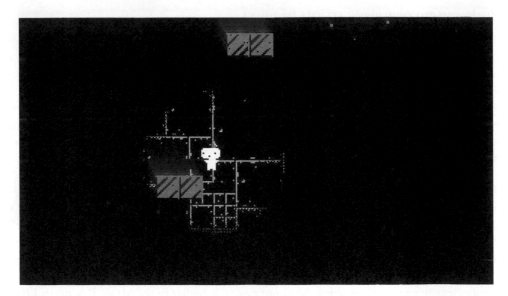

FIGURE 1.6 The scripts browser window in *Fezzer*. This example is again from one of the Music Rooms, but the window may be pulled up in any area, as with the sequence context menu.[11]

FIGURE 1.7 Gomez ascends the first Music Room by jumping to bright red blocks as they appear.

column remains unused. Finally, the "Action" column refers to what action will be taken when the trigger's conditions are met.

It may be helpful here to reiterate the flexibility of scripts, and note that they are governed by their own scripting language. "Volume[x]" refers to altitude in the trigger field, rather than the volume of a sound, for example. The "Action" column uses this same scripting language in the form of "[Target type].[Action][Target type 2]([Name], [Number of bars]," where "Target type" is the type of element being acted upon, "Action" is the action to be taken, "Target type 2" is the sub-type of element being acted upon, "Name" is the name of that element and "Number of bars" is simply the length of the element. Script four, for instance, performs the unmute function on the loop "CMYKave ^ fifths," that is 8 bars long.

If Gomez ascends higher than the altitude marked by an invisible block as "5," a new musical element will therefore enter the mix, and it will remain there unless Gomez descends lower than the marked altitude. When this happens — that is, when Gomez descends below the designated altitude — gamers hear the opposite effect: the loop is muted again. In this sense, Vreeland's "composition" for the game is actually interactive, what Vreeland calls "Music Gameplay." Progress in the Music Rooms is signified by the score, which rewards players with more elements of music as they approach the summit.

Music system overview: main composition sequencer

The main composition sequencer window is used mostly to determine the timing logic of the elements in one of Vreeland's "songs." Like the scripts browser, the main composition sequencer can make changes that affect an entire level, but also, like the sequence context menu, it can be used to tweak single musical elements. The theme name can be entered or re-entered at the top of the window. The "Overlay Loops" list box displays all the loops that can be in a level's theme, which can be added, removed and reordered with the buttons at the bottom.

Although it is not evident in Figure 1.8, I assume that you can select and manipulate more than one loop at a time for faster workflow. Vreeland's naming style for his loops can be seen in the above example, and takes the form of "[Theme Name] ^ [Mode]_[Musical Element]_[Amount of bars]bars." All the information of a given loop is in the file name, and so there is no guesswork necessary to determine which loop is which. It is notable that the "Musical Element" field does not adhere to any specific type of musical aspect, but instead serves solely to help programmers identify the loop. In some cases, it identifies a type of instrument featured, as in "Bass," while in other cases it identifies a melodic phrase in relation to others, such as "antecedent" and "consequent."

The "Selected Loop Properties" area serves most of the functionality of the main composition sequencer window. The "Loop Filename" is visible at the top, with a browse button beside the text field. The "Trigger between after every…" area has two text fields, with scroll arrow buttons, where a range of bars may be entered. In Figure 1.8, the theme "Cycle" is split into many overlay loops that play in the Puzzle Rooms according to the settings entered here. The "Trigger" section, for instance, denotes where the selected loop will play, within a given range if desired. These options make the actual music heard during gameplay slightly unpredictable, or aleatoric, as loops may come and go anytime within these set ranges.

Below, the "Fractional time" checkbox allows for irregular time signatures to be used in enabling loops. The "…and loop between…" section includes another pair of text fields with scroll arrow buttons. These can be set to a range of the amount of times the selected loop will play — another instance of aleatoric composition involving chance operations. The length of the selected loop may be entered in the "The loop is…" field, or it may be automatically supplied by the "Detect" button. Vreeland's naming style incorporates the length of the loop in bars, and so it is likely that he never uses the "Detect" button. The "Delay first trigger by…" field can be set to denote the number of bars after which the loop

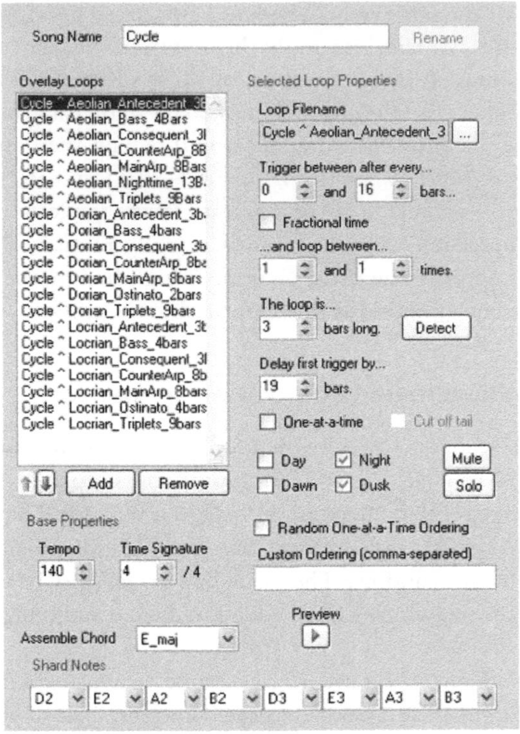

FIGURE 1.8 The main composition sequencer window. This example is from work on one of the Puzzle Rooms, which uses the "Cycle" theme.[12]

is played the first time. In this case, loops may be staggered in order to adhere more to the logic of a traditional song form.

The "One-at-a-time" checkbox is oddly placed, as its setting applies to the entire theme's "system," instead of just the selected loop. This setting works in conjunction with the "Custom Ordering" text field below it, and allows the user to restrict the theme to play only one loop at any given time, while the "Custom Ordering" field dictates the order of those loops. Alternatively, "Random One-at-a-Time Ordering" precludes the need for a custom order, as it plays loops one at a time at random. The "Mute," "Solo" and "Preview" buttons are used to preview the theme or selected loop within the main composition sequencer window. Finally, the time of day checkboxes "Day," "Night," "Dawn" and "Dusk" may be checked to specify when the selected loop may play according to the game's time system.

The "Base Properties" section of the composition sequencer allows for theme-wide changes to be made to the tempo and time signature. As with many settings in this window, these are musical elements that would normally be set early in the compositional stages of writing music. In non-interactive sources of music such as records, the tempo and time signature are ordinarily set early in composition because they can dramatically change the form of the piece. This process follows a more traditional approach to composition because it is built upon the notion of a piece's "essence" that can be represented as notation (or sheet music). In *FEZ*, the "essence" of the music is in gameplay, as it were, because it is inextricably linked to it. Settings such as tempo and time signature must therefore remain malleable even late into the composition process. Alternatively, perhaps a better way to express this difference would be simply to say that the composition process must remain extended and "open," right until the video game itself is complete.

The bottom section of the main composition sequencer actually deals with sound effects, as Vreeland wanted the eight cube bits that make up a full cube to have corresponding sounds that make up a full musical scale. The "Assemble Chord" drop-down menu allows the user to choose the chord to be assembled, while each drop-down menu in the "Shard Notes" area allows the user to choose a note for each cube bit to play.

Game scoring as a unique mode of musical composition

It should be clear by now that "game scoring" is an entirely unique compositional activity, especially insofar as it incorporates software programming (coding) into the creative process. In fact, game scoring *is* software programming — nothing more, nothing less. The game scorer's choices are limited by whatever gaming technology is available for them to use, after all, and the "programmability" of their musical ideas supersedes any particular aesthetic ideation.[13] Moreover, game scores are unique in that they must allow for an unprecedented level of musical flexibility, given the high degree of interactivity the medium encompasses. As noted, game scoring *necessarily* constitutes "aleatoric" compositional activity, the final score being determined as much through gameplay as traditional composition.[14]

How exactly is game scoring distinct from scoring for other media? Before I can explain how I will answer this question, I will first have to consider scoring for non-interactive media. Ironically, film seems to be a suitable medium to begin this comparison, but to elucidate the more subtle peculiarities of game scoring better, I choose to analyze a medium that analysts, casual listeners and even gamers chronically confuse with actual game scores: video game soundtracks. Video game soundtracks are officially released, and licensed, as recordings that excerpt music heard through gameplay. The music contained on a video game soundtrack, however, differs from game scores in that it is fixed and subject only to playback and equalization via the playback machine. Moreover, it is composed through a terminable scoring process, unlike game scores, which are composed through gameplay.

Video game soundtracks are not open to aesthetic changes as a result of distinct gameplay experiences. They feature the same formal contours each time they are played. Video game soundtracks are, in other words, ontologically "closed."[15] In effect, they are "idealized" versions of game scores, and in many cases they remain impossible to reproduce through gameplay. Game scoring, on the other hand, remains ontologically "open." It depends entirely on, and remains completely responsive to gameplay, and so no single definitive game score can ever actually be said to exist.

Methodology and outline

This book includes six chapters in total. In Chapter 1, I have offered a critical orientation to studying game scoring as software programming. I conducted a case study of the score for *FEZ* (2012) to concretize the theoretical terrain I cover in Chapters 2 through 5. I should note that a major goal of this book is to develop a working methodology for the study of game scores. The methodology I hope to construct will roughly do the following:

1. Examine the musical ability of the gaming technology (i.e., the sound hardware configuration) used to produce the game score.
2. Examine compositional strategies undertaken in response to the musical ability (and limitations) of the gaming technology used to produce the game score.
3. Produce game scores (play the video game).
4. Examine game scores for all musical outcomes, and analyze the gameplay states that "trigger" these outcomes.
5. Relate (1) and (2) to (4) by examining the compositional activity involved in gameplay itself (with a focus on chance operations and any degree of performer freedom involved therein).

In Chapter 2, I will extend my discussion of the context of game scoring by considering the interactive elements of gaming that are not present in older forms of multimedia. I will explore the implications of an interactive context for game scoring research through a case study of music for *The Legend of Zelda* (1987). Though the score for *Zelda* exemplifies functions similar to those of scores for animation, opera and film alike, its large-scale structure, and thus overall affect, is dependent on gameplay. The same is true of all game scores, and so I suggest that the context for game scoring, that is, gameplay — activity that is both narrative and ludal — requires a different mode of analysis. As Collins (2013) explains, gamers have a different kind of relationship to game scores because they help create, or activate them through haptic input. The same can be said for playing a musical instrument, though gamers are largely concerned with ludal goals, rather than musical ones. Game scores are shaped by non-musical factors, and so my case study for *Zelda* will focus on the relationship between video game music and gameplay.

To support my discussion in Chapter 2, I will also offer and explore three game scoring "categories" based on gameplay contexts: Title Music, Source Music and Results Music. These categories are the first of several that I will offer in each chapter of this book, as part of a game scoring "taxonomy" that covers the most common contexts for music in games. In Chapter 2, I include a discussion of Title, Source and Results Music because they pertain to large-scale musical structures in game scores, which are nonetheless experienced differently by each player.

In Chapter 3 of this book, I explore how game scoring is structured entirely by gaming technology, and in turn how it remains distinct from other kinds of scoring activities. I demonstrate this configuration first through a case study of the Nintendo Entertainment System (NES) APU, wherein I survey the musical possibilities and limitations of this gaming hardware technology. I choose the NES APU as the subject of my case study because it has relatively simple musical abilities, and so is instructive. The same is true of all my case studies, such as the choice of *Super Mario Bros.* levels in Chapter 5, for instance. With these findings, I am able to discuss specific compositional strategies NES game scorers developed in response to the technology of the NES APU. These responses reveal how NES game scoring is structured by NES technology, and, more importantly, how game scoring in general is structured by gaming (hardware) technology. Finally, in Chapter 3, I introduce three further game scoring categories, that are particularly susceptible to changes in game hardware, to support my discussion of gaming technology's bearing on game scoring activity: Logo Jingles; Loading Music; and Voice Acting and Vocals.

In Chapter 4, I explore how game scoring is also structured by software-programming-as-gaming-technology, or, more simply, game design. Here I will continue to examine specific contexts for music and sound in games, namely, common components and musical requirements of game scores, to demonstrate how game scoring is structured by game design. I will focus on components of game scores that exist across gaming genres, in an effort to avoid a genre-based approach to studying video game music, and to preserve breadth in my work. The "taxonomy" that arises from this chapter (and others) will be useful in Chapter 5, where I discuss game scoring as aleatoric composition, and how these components react and relate to each other in players' scores for games.

In Chapter 5, I examine game scoring's unique constitution as a kind of aleatoric compositional activity. I will first provide a brief case study of a canonic aleatoric composition, namely, *TV Köln* (1958) by John Cage, in order to survey the aleatoric tradition, which developed long before the release of the first video game. Here I outline the basic tenets of aleatoric music, such as the surrender of composer control, through specific reference to Cage's piece. Importantly, *TV Köln* — as well as much of the aleatoric repertoire — includes a recognition and integration of sounds that analysts would normally consider "extramusical sound effects." I use these precedents to model my consideration of sound effects as a component of a game score just as crucial as its "music." Game scorers must recognize, integrate, and in many cases "compose" sound effects as they work, and game scores are marked by many instances of such sounds.

With a basic understanding of the aleatoric tradition laid out, I am then able to analyze "performances" of aleatoric music in video games. This analysis will involve a case study of "World 6-2," one "level" of *Super Mario Bros.* for NES. I analyze game scores produced by my own gameplay, and I expect to find many "chance operations" and opportunities for "performer freedom" in my scores for this level. I discuss these and the aleatoric nature of game scoring through a comparison of my game scores for World 6-2 to the officially-released soundtracks for *Super Mario Bros.*

Finally, in Chapter 5, I will also extend my discussion of game scoring as aleatoric composition by offering the remaining categories of my taxonomy, namely, Menu Sound Effects, Menu Music, Status Music and Gameplay Sound Effects. These categories will help demonstrate how game scorers employ aleatoric techniques throughout games, and even in "non-gameplay" scenarios, such as menu screens. In fact, the hierarchical structures of game menu systems are ideal venues for composers to map aleatoric musical gestures, as I will explain in this section.

In Chapter 6, I provide a brief summary of my findings, and I suggest some future directions for continuing research on game scoring as a unique compositional activity. I conclude by considering the significance of my work to the field of ludo-musicology and its implications for future research on game scoring.

Notes

1 Much academic work has applied film scoring concepts to game scoring analyses. For example, many researchers analyze video game music through concepts developed in film studies, such as "diegetic" and "non-diegetic" sound. See, for instance: Berndt et al. (2006); Bessell (2002); Boyd (2003); Bridgett (2010); Chan (2007); Collins (2007a–d); d' Escrivan (2007); Deutsch (2003); Furlong (2004); Hart (2015); Hoover (2010); Jørgensen (2004, 2006, 2007b, 2008a); Kanamori, Yoneda, and Yamada (2012); Lerner (2014a, 2014b); Munday (2007); Roberts (2014); Sadoff (2013); Toprac and Abdel-Meguid (2010); Wilhelmsson and Wallén (2010); and Wood, Harper and Doughty (2009), among others. Other scholars have begun to question the usefulness of such concepts in game scoring analyses, including, but not limited to: Berndt (2011); Jørgensen (2007a, 2010); Kamp (2014, 2016); and Kassabian (2013).

2 The field of computer science is, of course, better-equipped to examine programming in video games, and researchers who choose to analyze game scoring as software programming come almost exclusively from this field. Some offer general guidelines for sound and music design in video games, such as: Alves and Roque (2011); Baccigalupo (2003); Berndt and Hartmann (2007, 2008); Berndt et al. (2006); Boer (2003); Borchers and Mulhauser (1998); Childs IV (2007); Ekman and Lankoski (2009); Farnell (2007); Friberg and Gärdenfors (2004); Hoffert (2007); Hug (2011); Huiberts (2010, 2011); Lendino (1998); Lieberman (2006); Liljedahl (2011); Marks (2009); Mullan (2010); Murphy and Neff (2010); Sanger (2003); Sanders and Cairns (2010); Toprac and Abdel-Meguid (2010); Villareal III (2009); Weske (2002); and Wilde (2004), among others. Some computer science researchers propose or analyze specific game music programming systems, such as: Aav (2005); Fay (2004); and Knight (1987), among others. Still others seek to understand and organize the relationships between audio and gameplay, and construct game scoring "ecologies." See, for example: Droumeva (2011); Farnell (2011) Grimshaw (2007); Grimshaw and Schott (2007); Havryliv and Vergara-Richards (2006); Holtar, Nelson and Togelius (2013); Wilhelmsson and Wallén (2010); and Wooller et al. (2005), among others.

3 Work which relates video game music to aleatoric composition includes: Collins (2009); Lieberman (2006); Philips (2014); Rayman (2014); Summers (2011); Paterson et al. (2011); Young (2012); Paul (2013); Custodis (2013); Pannerden et al. (2011); d'Escrivan (2007); Hermans (2013); and Mitchell (2014b).

4 The word "aleatory" or "aleatoric" is derived from the Latin word *alea*, which actually means "dice."

5 For example, see: *Der Allezeit Fertige Menuetten- und Polonaisencomponist* (German for "The Ever-Ready Minuet and Polonaise Composer") (1757) composed by Johann Philip Kirnberger; *Einfall Einin Doppelten Contrapunct in der Octave von sechs Tacten zu Machen ohne die Regeln Davon zu Wissen* (German for "A method for making six bars of double counterpoint at the octave without knowing the rules") (1758) composed by C.P.E. Bach; and *Table pour Composer des Minuets et des Trios à la Infinie; avec deux dez à Jouer* (French for "A table for composing minuets and trios to infinity, by playing with two dice") (1780).

6 All score figures for Nintendo Entertainment System games are obtained by the author using *FamiStudio*, a Nintendo Sound Format (NSF) audio workstation, unless otherwise noted.

7 Mihaly Csikszentmihalyi (1990) defines "flow" as a state of complete involvement or immersion in an activity. To achieve a flow state, there must be a balance between the challenge of the task and the skill of the performer. If the task is too easy or too difficult, flow cannot occur. Game developers desire the cultivation of "flow" in the gamer because it is a pleasurable state.

8 Screenshots of *FEZ* gameplay are created by the author, from the PC version of the game.

9 Non-Euclidean space is space which cannot be measured by Euclidean geometry, which is the study of flat space. Non-Euclidean geometries introduce fundamental changes to our concept of space, as in *FEZ*.

10 Vreeland (2012).

11 Ibid.

12 Ibid.

13 That is, as Jay Hodgson (2006: 15) puts it, "technology replaces ontology" in game scoring.

14 Aleatoric music is music in which some element of the composition is left to chance, and/or some degree of freedom is afforded its performer. For more on this, see Antokoletz (2014).

15 I use the term "ontological" here as Martin Heidegger uses it, who notes that "ontological inquiries in philosophy are concerned with [being]" (qtd. in Munday [2009]: "Ontology"). Thus, an ontological inquiry into popular music scoring would analyze where such a process exists. Such an inquiry would reveal that the process only exists and terminates in the production of the record. It is ontologically closed because scoring does not continue in the playback of said record.

References

Aav, Sebastian. 2005. "Adaptive Music System for DirectSound." Master's Thesis, University of Linköping, Campus Norrköping.

Alves, Valter, and Licinio Roque. 2011. "Guidelines for Sound Design in Computer Games." In *Game Sound Technology and Player Interaction: Concepts and Developments*, edited by Mark Grimshaw, 362–83. Hershey, PA: IGI Global.

Antokoletz, Elliott. 2014. *A History of Twentieth-Century Music in a Theoretic-Analytical Context*. Taylor & Francis. https://books.google.ca/books?id=qrkTAwAAQBAJ.

Baccigalupo, Claudio. 2003. "Design and Production of Audio Technologies for Video Games Development." Master's Thesis, Universita degli Studi di Milano.

Berndt, Axel. 2011. "Diegetic Music: New Interactive Experiences." In *Game Sound Technology and Player Interaction: Concepts and Developments*, edited by Mark Grimshaw, 60–76. Hershey, PA: IGI Global.

Berndt, Axel, and Knut Hartmann. 2007. "Strategies for Narrative and Adaptive Game Scoring." In *Audio Mostly 2007-2nd Conference on Interaction with Sound*, 141–47. Ilmenau: Fraunhofer Institute for Digital Media Technology.

———. 2008. "The Functions of Music in Interactive Media." *Proceedings of Interactive Digital Storytelling (ICIDS)*, 126–31. Springer-Verlag Berlin Heidelberg, University of Applied Sciences Erfurt, Germany.

Berndt, Axel, Knut Hartmann, Niklaus Rober, and Maic Masuch. 2006. "Composition and Arrangment Techniques for Music in Interactive Immersive Environments." In *Proceedings of Audio Mostly 2006*, 53–59. Interactive Institute/Sonic Studio, Pitea, Sweden.

Bessell, David. 2002. "What's That Funny Noise? An Examination of the Role of Music in *Cool Boarders 2*, *Alien Trilogy* and *Medievil 2*." In *Screenplay: Cinema/Videogames/Interfaces*, edited by Geoff King and Tanya Krzywinska, 136–44. London and New York: Wallflower.

Boer, James. 2003. *Game Audio Programming*. Monograph. Hingham, MA: Charles River Media.

Borchers, Jan, and Max Mulhauser. 1998. "Design Patterns for Interactive Musical Systems." *IEEE Multimedia* 5 (3), 36–46.

Boyd, Andrew. 2003. "When Worlds Collide: Sound and Music in Film and Computer Games." *Gamasutra*. http://www.gamasutra.com/view/feature/131310/when_worlds_collide_sound_and_.php.

Bridgett, Rob. 2010. *From the Shadows of Film Sound: Cinematic Production and Creative Process in Video Game Audio: Collected Publications 2000–2010*. Monograph. Self Published.

Chan, Norman. 2007. "A Critical Analysis of Modern Day Video Game Audio." Undergraduate Thesis, University of Nottingham.

Childs IV, G.W. 2007. *Creating Music and Sound for Games*. Monograph. Boston, MA: Thompson Course Technology.

Collins, Karen. 2005. "From Bits to Hits: Video Games Music Changes Its Tune." *Film International* 12: 4–19.

———. 2006. "Loops and Bloops: Music on the Commodore 64." *Soundscape: Journal of Media Culture* 8 (1). http://www.icce.rug.nl/~soundscapes/VOLUME08/Loops_and_bloops.shtml.

———. 2007a. "An Introduction to the Participatory and Non-Linear Aspects of Video Game Audio." In *Essays on Sound and Vision*, edited by John Richardson and Stan Hawkins, 263–98. Helsinki: Helsinki University Press.

———. 2007b. "Flat Twos and the Musical Aesthetic of the Atari VCS." *Popular Musicology Online* 1 (1).

———. 2007c. "In the Loop: Confinements and Creativity in 8-Bit Games." *Twentieth-Century Music* 4 (2): 209–27.

———. 2007d. "Video Games Killed the Cinema Star." *Music, Sound and the Moving Image* 1 (1): 15–20.

———, ed. 2008a. *From Pac-Man to Pop Music: Interactive Audio in Games and New Media*. Aldershot, Hampshire and Burlington, VT: Ashgate.

———. 2008b. *Game Sound: An Introduction to the History, Theory and Practice of Video Game Music and Sound Design*. Monograph. Cambridge, MA and London: MIT Press.

———. 2008c. "Grand Theft Audio? Popular Music and Interactive Games." *Music and the Moving Image* 1 (1), 35–48.

———. 2009. "An Introduction to Procedural Audio in Video Games." *Contemporary Music Review: Special Issue on Generative Audio* 28 (1): 5–15.

———. 2013. "Implications of Interactivity: What Does It Mean for Sound to Be 'Interactive'?" In *The Oxford Handbook of New Audiovisual Aesthetics*. Oxford Handbooks Online.

http://www.oxfordhandbooks.com/view/10.1093/oxfordhb/9780199733866.001.0001/oxfordhb-9780199733866.

————. 2014a. "A History of Handheld and Mobile Video Game Sound." In *The Oxford Handbook of Mobile Music Studies*, edited by Sumanth Gopinath and Jason Stanyek, Vol. 2, 383–401. Oxford: Oxford UP.

————. 2014b. "Breaking the Fourth Wall? User-Generated Sonic Content in Virtual Worlds." In *The Oxford Handbook of Virtuality*, edited by Mark Grimshaw, 351–363. Oxford: Oxford UP.

Collins, Karen, Holly Tessler, Kevin Harrigan, Michael J. Dixon, and Jonathan Fugelsang. 2011. "Sound in Electronic Gambling Machines: A Review of the Literature and Its Relevance to Game Sound." In *Game Sound Technology and Player Interaction: Concepts and Developments*, edited by Mark Grimshaw, 1–21. Hershey, PA: IGI Global.

Collins, Karen, and Leonard J. Paul, eds. 2008. "An Introduction to Granular Synthesis in Video Games." In *From Pac-Man to Pop Music: Interactive Audio in Games and New Media*, edited by Karen Collins, 135–49. Aldershot, Hampshire and Burlington, VT: Ashgate.

Csikszentmihalyi, Mihaly. 1990. *Flow: The Psychology of Optimal Experience*. New York City: Harper & Row.

Custodis, Michael. 2013. "Playing with Music–Featuring Sound in Games." In *Music and Game: Perspectives on a Popular Alliance*, edited by Peter Moormann, 159–70. Wiesbaden: Springer.

D'Escrivan, Julio. 2007. "Electronic Music and the Moving Image." In *The Cambridge Companion to Electronic Music*, edited by Nick Collins, 156–70. Cambridge: Cambridge University Press.

Deutsch, Stephen. 2003. "Music for Interactive Moving Pictures." In *Soundscape: The School of Sound Lectures 1998–2001*, edited by Larry Sider, Diane Freeman, and Jerry Sider, 28–34. London and New York: Wallflower.

Droumeva, Milena. 2011. "An Acoustic Communication Framework for Game Sound: Fidelity, Verisimilitude, Ecology." In *Game Sound Technology and Player Interaction: Concepts and Developments*, edited by Mark Grimshaw, 131–52. Hershey, PA: IGI Global.

Ekman, Inger, and Petri Lankoski. 2009. "Hair-Raising Entertainment: Emotions, Sound, and Structure in *Silent Hill 2* and *Fatal Frame*." In *Horror Video Games: Essays on the Fusion of Fear and Play*, edited by Bernard Perron, 181–99. Jefferson, NC: McFarland.

Farnell, Andy. 2007. "An Introduction to Procedural Audio and Its Application in Computer Games." Self Published.

————. 2011. "Behaviour, Structure and Causality in Procedural Audio." In *Game Sound Technology and Player Interaction: Concepts and Developments*, edited by Mark Grimshaw, 313–39. Hershey, PA: IGI Global.

Fay, Todd M. 2004. *DirectX 9 Audio Exposed: Interactive Audio Development*. Plano, TX: Wordware.

Friberg, Johnny, and Dan Gärdenfors. 2004. "Audio Games:

Furlong, Cian. 2004. "Computer Game Music — Multifunctional Medium." Undergraduate Thesis, University College Dublin.

Grimshaw, Mark. 2007. "The Acoustic Ecology of the First-Person Shooter." PhD Dissertation, University of Waikato.

Grimshaw, Mark, and Gareth Schott. 2007. "Situating Gaming as a Sonic Experience: The Acoustic Ecology of First-Person Shooters." In *Proceedings of DIGRA, Digital Games Research Association*. Tokyo.

Hart, Iain. 2015. "Hard Boiled Music: The Case of L.A. Noire." *Screen Sound* 5: 19–35.

Havryliv, Mark, and Emiliano Vergara-Richards. 2006. "From Battle Metris to Symbiotic Symphony: A New Model for Musical Games." University of Wollongong Research Online.

Hermans, Philip. 2013. "Cooperation and Competition in Music Composition." Master's Thesis, Dartmouth College.

Hodgson, Jay. 2006. "Navigating the Network of Recording Practice: Towards an Ecology of the Record Medium." PhD Dissertation, University of Alberta.

Hoffert, Paul. 2007. *Music for New Media: Composing for Videogames, Web Sites, Presentations, and Other Interactive Media*. Monograph. Boston, MA: Berklee Press.

Holtar, Nils I., Mark J. Nelson, and Julian Togelius. 2013. "Audioverdrive: Exploring Bidirectional Communication Between Music and Gameplay." In *Proceedings of the 2013 International Computer Music Conference*. Ann Arbor, MI: Michigan Publishing.

Hoover, Tom. 2010. *Keeping Score: Interviews with Today's Top Film, Television and Game Music Composers*. Monograph. Boston, MA: Course Technology.

Hug, Daniel. 2011. "New Wine in New Skins: Sketching the Future of Game Sound Design." In *Game Sound Technology and Player Interaction: Concepts and Developments*, edited by Mark Grimshaw, 384–415. Hershey, PA: IGI Global.

Huiberts, Sander. 2010. "Captivating Sound: The Role of Audio for Immersion in Computer Games." PhD Dissertation, Utrecht School of the Arts.

———. 2011. "Listen! – Improving the Cooperation between Game Designers and Audio Designers." In *Proceedings of DiGRA 2011 Conference: Think Design Play*. Hilversum, Netherlands.

Jørgensen, Kristine. 2004. "Sounds and Sources in Sacred." In *Proceedings from Cosign 2004*. Split, Croatia.

———. 2006. "On the Functional Aspects of Computer Game Audio." In *Proceedings of the Audio Mostly Conference*. Interactive Institute/Sonic Studio, Pitea, Sweden.

———. 2007a. "On Transdiegetic Sounds in Computer Games." *Northern Lights: Film & Media Studies Yearbook* 5 (1). doi:10.1386/nl.5.1.105_1.

———. 2007b. "'What Are These Grunts and Growls Over There?' Computer Game Audio and Player Action." PhD Dissertation, Copenhagen University.

———. 2008a. "Audio and Gameplay: An Analysis of PvP Battlegrounds in World of Warcraft." *Game Studies* 8 (2). http://gamestudies.org/0802/articles/jorgensen.

———. 2010. "Time for New Terminology? Diegetic and Non-Diegetic Sounds in Computer Games Revisited." In *Game Sound: Game Sound Technology and Player Interaction: Concepts and Developments*, edited by Mark Grimshaw, 78–97. Hershey, PA: IGI Global.

Kamp, Michiel . 2014. "Musical Ecologies in Video Games." *Philosophy & Technology* 27 (2): 235–49.

———. 2016. "Suture and Peritexts: Music beyond Gameplay and Diegesis." In *Ludomusicology: Approaches to Video Game Music*, edited by Michiel Kamp, Tim Summers, and Mark Sweeney, 73–91. Sheffield; Bristol, CT: Equinox.

Kanamori, Shinya, Ryo Yoneda, and Masashi Yamada. 2012. "Congruency between Music and Motion Pictures in the Context of Video Games: Effects of Emotional Features in Music." Thessaloniki, Greece.

Kassabian, Anahid. 2013. "The End of Diegesis as We Know It?" In *The Oxford Handbook of New Audiovisual Aesthetics*, edited by John Richardson, Claudia Gorbman, and Carol Vernallis. Oxford Handbooks Online. http://www.oxfordhandbooks.com/view/10.1093/oxfordhb/9780199733866.001. 0001/oxfordhb-9780199733866.

Knight, Tim. 1987. *Mastering Sound and Music on the Atari ST*. Monograph. Berkeley, CA: Sybex.

Lendino, James. 1998. "Scoring for the Modern Computer Game." In *Proceedings of the International Computer Music Conference*. San Francisco, CA: International Computer Music Association.

Lerner, Neil. 2014a. "Mario's Dynamic Leaps: Musical Innovations and the Specter of Early Cinema in Donkey Kong and Super Mario Bros." In *Music in Video Games: Studying Play*, edited by Kevin J. Donnelly, William Gibbons, and Neil Lerner, 1–29. New York: Routledge.

———. 2014b. "The Origins of Musical Style in Video Games." In *The Oxford Handbook of Film Music Studies*, edited by David Neumeyer, 319–49. Oxford: Oxford UP.

Lieberman, David. 2006. "Game Enhanced Music Manuscript." In *Proceedings of the 4th International Conference on Computer Graphics and Interactive Techniques in Australasia and South East Asia*, edited by Stephen Spencer, 245–50. New York City: Association for Computing Machinery.

Liljedahl, Mats. 2011. "Sound for Fantasy and Freedom." In *Game Sound Technology and Player Interaction: Concepts and Developments*, edited by Mark Grimshaw, 22–43. Hershey, PA: IGI Global.

Marks, Aaron. 2009. *The Complete Guide to Game Audio for Composers, Musicians, Sound Designers, and Game Developers*. Burlington, MA and Oxford: Focal Press.

Mitchell, Helen R. 2014a. "Fear and the Musical Avant-Garde in Games: Interviews with Jason Graves, Garry Schyman, Paul Gorman and Michael Kamper." *Horror Studies* 5 (1): 127–44.

———. 2014b. "Let's Mix It Up: Interviews Exploring the Practical and Technical Challenges of Interactive Mixing in Games." In *The Oxford Handbook of Interactive Audio*, edited by Karen Collins, Bill Kapralos, and Holly Tessler, 479–97. Oxford: Oxford UP.

Mullan, Eoin. 2010. "Physical Modelling for Sound Synthesis." In *Game Sound Technology and Player Interaction: Concepts and Developments*, edited by Mark Grimshaw, 340–60. Hershey, PA: IGI Global.

Munday, Rod. 2007. "Music in Video Games." In *Music, Sound and Multimedia: From the Live to the Virtual*, edited by Jamie Sexton, 51–67. Edinburgh: Edinburgh UP.

Munday, Roderick. 2009. "Glossary of Terms in Heidegger's *Being and Time*." *Visual Memory*. http://www.visual-memory.co.uk/b_resources/b_and_t_glossary.html.

Murphy, David, and Flaithrí Neff. 2010. "Spatial Sound for Computer Games and Virtual Reality." In *Game Sound Technology and Player Interaction: Concepts and Developments*, edited by Mark Grimshaw, 340–60. Hershey, PA: IGI Global.

Pannerden, Than van Nispen tot, Sander Huiberts, Sebastiaan Donders, and Stan Koch. 2011. "The NLN-Player: A System for Nonlinear Music in Games." In *Proceedings of the International Computer Music Conference 2011*. University of Huddersfield.

Paterson, Natasa, Katsiaryna Naliuka, Tara Carrigy, Mads Haahr, and Fionnuala Conway. 2011. "Location-Aware Interactive Game Audio." *Audio Engineering Society Conference: 41st International Conference: Audio for Games*. Dublin: Trinity College.

Paul, Leonard J. 2013. "Droppin'Science: Video Game Audio Breakdown." In *Music and Game: Perspectives on a Popular Alliance*, edited by Peter Moormann, 63–80. Wiesbaden: Springer.

Rayman, Joshua. 2014. "Experimental Approaches to the Composition of Interactive Video Game Music." Master's Thesis, University of East Anglia.

Roberts, Rebecca. 2014. "Fear of the Unknown: Music and Sound Design in Psychological Horror Games." In *Music in Video Games: Studying Play*, edited by Kevin J. Donnelly, William Gibbons, and Neil Lerner, 138–50. New York: Routledge.

Sadoff, Ronald H. 2013. "Scoring for Film and Video Games: Collaborative Practices and Digital Post-Production." In *The Oxford Handbook of Sound and Image in Digital Media*, edited by Carol Vernallis, Amy Herzog, and John Richardson, 663–81. Oxford: Oxford UP.

Sanger, George. 2003. *The Fat Man on Game Audio: Tasty Morsels of Sonic Goodness*. Monograph. Indianapolis, IN: New Riders Games.

Summers, Tim. 2011. "Playing the Tune: Video Game Music, Gamers, and Genre." *ACT* 2 (1). http://www.oalib.com/paper/2085371.

Toprac, Paul, and Mark Abdel-Meguid. 2010. "Causing Fear, Suspense, and Anxiety Using Sound Design in Computer Games." In *Game Sound Technology and Player Interaction: Concepts and Developments*, edited by Mark Grimshaw, 176–91. Hershey, PA: IGI Global.

Vreeland, Richard. 2012. "Philosophy of Music Design in Games." Presentation at the 2012 Game Audio Network Guild Summit. https://www.youtube.com/watch?v=Pl86ND_c5Og.

Weske, Jörg. 2002. "Digital Sound and Music in Computer Games." *3DAudio*. http://3daudio.info/gamesound/index.html.

Whalen, Zach. 2004. "Play Along – An Approach to Videogame Music." *Play Along – An Approach to Videogame Music* 4 (1). http://www.gamestudies.org/0401/whalen/.

Wilde, Martin D. 2004. *Audio Programming for Interactive Games*. Monograph. Oxford and Burlington, MA: Focal Press.

Wilhelmsson, Ulf, and Jacob Wallén. 2010. "A Combined Model for the Structuring of Computer Game Audio." In *Game Sound Technology and Player Interaction: Concepts and Developments*, edited by Mark Grimshaw, 98–130. Hershey, PA: IGI Global.

Wood, Simon, Graeme Harper, and Ruth Doughty. 2009. "Video Game Music – High Scores: Making Sense of Music and Video Games." In *Sound and Music in Film and Visual Media: An*

Overview, edited by Graeme Harper, Ruth Doughty, and Jochen Eisentraut, 129–48. New York and London: Continuum.

Wooller, Rene, Andrew R. Brown, Eduardo Miranda, Rodney Berry, and Joachim Diederich. 2005. "A Framework for Comparison of Processes in Algorithmic Music Systems." In *Generative Arts Practice*, 109–24. Sydney: Creativity and Cognition Studios Press.

Young, David M. 2012. "Adaptive Game Music: The Evolution and Future of Dynamic Music Systems in Games." Bachelor's Thesis, Ohio University.

2
GAME SCORING'S INTERACTIVE MULTIMEDIA CONTEXT

In this chapter, I begin to construct my own approach to game scoring analysis by considering its interactive multimedia context. As video games can be confused with interactive films, it is tempting to use tools and concepts derived from film scoring research, such as the concept of a "diegesis," to study game scores. In film scoring research, the "diegesis" refers to the narrative world of a film, and film score researchers often distinguish between "diegetic sound," or sound that emanates from within the narrative world of a film, and "non-diegetic sound," or sound that has a source outside of this world. While this concept might be appropriate for film scoring research, it does not map well onto game scoring analyses. I will first consider game "worlds" as different than those imagined for film, through a second, though shorter, case study of *FEZ*. Ironically, this will first necessitate an attempt to locate the "source" of game audio in the "diegesis" or world of *FEZ*, much like a film scoring researcher would, though my aim will be to de-construct the concept of a gaming diegesis by considering players' audial perspectives. Next, I consider what an interactive context means for game scoring research through a case study of music for *The Legend of Zelda* (1987). Again, game scoring's context, that is, its dependence on gameplay — non-musical performance — makes it necessarily an at least partially aleatoric mode of composition.[1] In other words, the subversion of the traditional roles of creator and consumer in video games extends to game scoring as well, because of its predominantly ludal context.[2] As Collins (2013: 5) argues, it is the very interactivity of gameplay that produces immersion, given the "back and forth" of feedback and control in the gameplay experience. This observation suggests the intriguing possibility that game scoring — as aleatoric composition — is inherently immersive rather than narrative in function. In the final part of this chapter, I offer three game scoring categories that further demonstrate the interactive context of gaming, and how game scorers can both accommodate and facilitate it with their music.

Spatial emulation, the gaming "diegesis," and game scoring

Can Mario hear the music of his world, the Mushroom Kingdom? This possibility is not exactly excluded by the (re)presentation of space in games, as it might be in a film. Here I

DOI: 10.4324/9781003045465-2

will discuss an example from *FEZ* (2012) that demonstrates some of the problems with categorizing any music or sound in a game score as "diegetic" or "non-diegetic." *FEZ* contains background music composed in relation to the specific "spatiality" or physical dimensions of the game world. In the score for *FEZ*, a spatial conception of music aided the composition process, though it also complicated the game's reception, due to the fact that aural space is conceived very differently from visual space.[3] In a review for *FEZ*, Adam Tuerff (2012: 5) mentions an example of aurally-represented space in the programmed score:

> [Vreeland] does an amazing job of scoring the game. To try and put it concretely I would say it's nostalgic, atmospheric, and wonderfully complements the pixellated [sic] beauty of the game itself. There's even a "low pass filter" effect that kicks in when you go behind something in-game just to make the music that much more a part of the gameplay experience.

A low-pass filter is a filter that allows signals with a frequency lower than a pre-determined cutoff frequency to pass, and attenuates signals with frequencies higher than this cutoff. In *FEZ*, this programmed filter makes it so that when players direct Gomez, the "protagonist" of *FEZ* behind an obstacle, only the low frequencies of whatever music is currently playing are audible, resulting in a "muffled" sound, as if Gomez (or the player) were hearing the music from behind a wall, for example, as pictured in Figure 2.1:

The specific effects of this technique on the gameplay experience are numerous, though it can be argued that its main purpose is to enhance immersion, as the experience of the player and that of Gomez, the avatar, are aurally linked. The sonic effect works seamlessly and subtly in *FEZ* despite its completely unconventional spatial logic. As Gomez

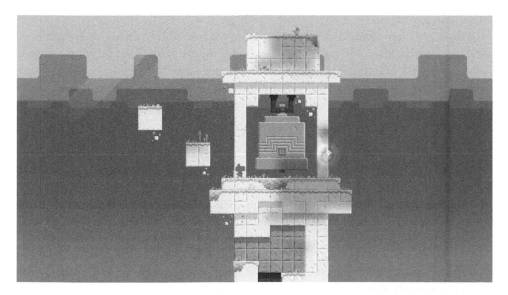

FIGURE 2.1 Gomez is behind a column in the "Bell Room," and so the low-pass filter would be triggered at this point in the score. Players can disable the low-pass filter by bringing Gomez to the foreground, by either directing him there or rotating the camera's perspective. The latter action is the main gameplay mechanic of *FEZ* (2012).

dips behind a structure, the music becomes obscured and muffled, suggesting that there is some link between him and the soundscape players hear. The sound source, then, can be attributed either to Gomez himself — if the music comes from Gomez, it would make sense for it to become obscured at the same moment he does — or to a source in front of the structures, Gomez and perhaps even the game environment. The latter suggests that Gomez is the listener; players hear what Gomez hears, and so naturally as Gomez dips behind a tree or building the sound becomes attenuated, because it is "blocked." However, in this scenario, the — imagined — sound source breaks the fourth wall in terms of its spatiality. It would have to exist in front of the visual field — the screen — and, moreover, face that field just as the player does.

In the score for *FEZ*, a spatial conception of music aided the composition process, though this conception can also complicate an analysis of its presentation. For example, it is unclear whether to conceptualize this music as "diegetic" or "non-diegetic." Its perceived location is less important than the fact that it changes according to a certain gameplay state, as this change serves to indicate that Gomez is obstructed from view. Thus, all that is necessary to *emulate* — a game's version of — reality is the presentation of elements that react with self-referential consistency, rather than adhere to real-world physics.

A comparison of gaming with animation is relevant to this discussion, as cartoons exhibit internally-formed "rules" that are consistently enforced, yet do not always adhere to real-world physics.[4] For example, when TNT powder unexpectedly explodes in close proximity to Wile E. Coyote in a *Looney Tunes* short, we can expect him to be singed, covered in black soot and ash, and most importantly, still "alive" when the smoke clears. This example doubles as an analogue to the concept of multiple "lives" in video games that are expended through "dying" as a result of unsuccessful gameplay. Just as Wile E. Coyote will surely attempt to capture the Roadrunner again, a recently-passed Mario, for example, will be resurrected and returned to the beginning of a level in *Super Mario Bros.*, to begin his own narrative again.

Games have their own rules that are based on avatar abilities, and both are inherently linked to gameplay design. In the next section I will explore gaming as a medium comprised of multiple media, and the implications of this circumstance for the study of game scores. Games introduce a third element besides sound and visuals: haptics. Haptics are basically impossible to study in isolation, nor can they be removed from analyses of the gaming experience. In fact, haptics serve as the main point of contact between player and game.

Interactivity: a new element

Gaming's interactivity presents significant complications to media analysts. The gamer actively *performs* the gaming experience, though their actions are orchestrated within a set of predetermined possibilities. One key element of interactivity is the idea (and reality) of control. Collins (2013: 4) argues that gamers "participate" in the audio events of a game:

> The player directly triggers some sound events through her input device, and her actions nearly always affect the overall soundscape of the game. Often she may have a gestural interaction with that sound [...] This self-produced sound distinguishes the game experience from that of most other media, which often disconnect the player from her physical self, and the sonic events do not respond to her physical actions.

Gaming involves a different kind of reception from the kind involved in non-interactive media. Both the operatic and cinematic experiences, for example, occur without direct interaction from audiences. Even if Richard Wagner's *The Ring*, for instance, varies in narrative every time it is told, then, each performance is rehearsed and performed *for* the audience, rather than enacted *by* a gamer. In recorded media such as film, this "non-interaction" becomes even more visible, due to the "fixed" nature of audiovisual connections.

Collins (2013: 4) notes that in gaming, "the player has a unique physical and gestural connection to the sound events." She (2013: 4) suggests that when we are responsible for sounds, we have a greater knowledge of their causes and effects, and so the "connection between the physical action and the sonic reaction is arguably much stronger." Collins uses this concept to discuss customizable soundtracks in modern video games, in which the player may import their own favourite tracks to be used as background music. However, there are many different ways in which players have control over game scores — whether direct or indirect — and these alter their connection to these sounds. To demonstrate how players' control over game sounds changes their relationship to the musical experience of gaming, in the next section I will conduct a case study of music from *The Legend of Zelda* (1987), with a focus on its large-scale gameplay and scoring structures.

Audial responsibility in the interactive multimedia text: a case study of the score for *The Legend of Zelda* (1987)

Game scorers must allow different gameplay choices to produce different scores, even within a single gaming session, and they must do this even while they work to produce a broader aesthetically coherent and unified "score." One example of a game score that meets this challenge is Koji Kondo's score for *The Legend of Zelda* (1987). In order to discuss game scoring's performative element, I shall first examine Kondo's score in terms of aesthetic coherence, through a comparative musical analysis of the "Game Over" and "Ending" themes. Then I will briefly discuss gameplay's bearing on the occurrence of these themes, and the subsequent bearing of player responsibility, on their musical effects.

Koji Kondo's composition of the "Ending Theme" for *Zelda* is linked to the overall structure of the game's score, since it is an elaboration on the "Game Over" theme. Average — novice, or first-time — *Zelda* players can expect to hear the "Game Over" theme many times, as it sounds every time Link, the game's protagonist (or the player's "avatar") loses all of his health and dies (Figure 2.2):

Strangely, the "Game Over" theme only uses one channel of the Nintendo Entertainment System's (NES) Audio Processing Unit (APU): one of its pulse wave channels.[6] In this case, the channel is used at its lowest "duty setting," that produces the thinnest timbre available, and so this theme sounds very sparse in content.[7] Figure 2.3 is the score for this theme:

The monophonic texture and thin, metallic (almost like tin) timbre of this theme make it sound very much like a theme played by a wind-up music box. This analog is useful for my purposes, since, as in a video game, the visual design of a music box is typically "set" by an accompanying score, and requires interaction to make it sound. Moreover, this interaction determines compositional parameters such as tempo, dynamics and length. The metaphor works well in this particular gameplay state, in that players must decide either to "wind up" the game to play again, or end their session and, thus, their score.

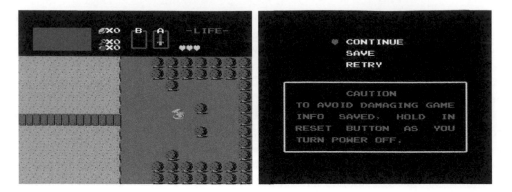

FIGURE 2.2 When Link loses all of his health, he spins around as the terrain's palette becomes entirely red (left) — an animation sequence that is accompanied by a descending "Death" jingle. Link then turns grey and disappears as the screen goes completely black (not pictured). The Game Over screen is then displayed (right), and the "Game Over" theme begins.[5]

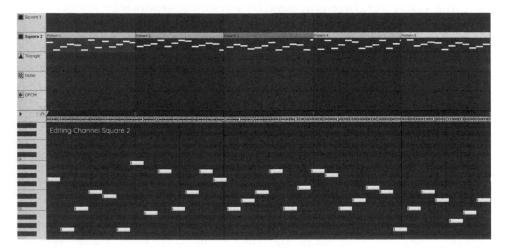

FIGURE 2.3 The "Game Over" theme that plays after its "introduction," the "Death" jingle. While rapidly descending figures serve to disorient the listener in the "Death" jingle, the regular rhythm and repeated pattern of the "Game Over" theme encourage reflection, and gently nudge the player to decide to "CONTINUE," "SAVE" or "RETRY." In a macabre twist, the player's limbo state is accompanied by a melody in C-major — a key that is decidedly happy in mood.[8]

In addition, the thin texture of the "Game Over" theme seems to convey the message that players did not "wind up" the music box enough in the first place. If player responsibility creates a greater investment in sounds from *Zelda*, the connection here is decidedly negative. Players of course neither want the "Death" jingle nor the "Game Over" theme to sound, because they are aural reflections of losing, and not winning. The effects of these connections — embarrassment — are even heightened by gameplay spectators (or perhaps listeners, if they are not watching). The "Game Over" theme conveys the fact that gamers tried to navigate the world of *Zelda*, but ultimately failed.

If players "wind up" the music box enough — that is, if they are successful at beating *Zelda* — they unlock an elaboration on the "Game Over" theme, namely, the "Ending" theme. Figure 2.4 shows this theme:

Patterns 1–5 of the "Ending" theme consist of the "Game Over" theme in full (rendering it a kind of introduction). These notes are sustained longer in the "Ending" theme, which subtly indicates contrast with the "Game Over" theme. Again, these varied sustains evoke the music box, where the more tightly it is wound, the stronger — in terms of both "attack" and "sustain" — each note is voiced.[9] Players who beat *Zelda* have arguably operated the game in the "proper" way, resulting in the fullest version of its score, similar to the music box. At the beginning of the third measure, the bass part is introduced by the triangle wave channel. The bass line is articulated entirely in *staccato*, which reminds the listener of the shorter sustains involved in the "Game Over" theme. This bass line also provides a stable beat for two events to occur at pattern six: (1) the introduction of a "counter-melody" in the pulse channels; and (2) the introduction of a percussion line, voiced by the noise channel. The "counter-melody" I refer to is not exactly a counter-melody, since it completely replaces the "Game Over" melody at the beginning of the piece, instead of accompanying it.[10] The bass part is therefore integral in linking these two musical ideas.

Similar to the "Game Over" theme, the counter-melody in the "Ending" theme is in the key of C-major. Kondo wrote the melody with different note lengths in order to accent the beat in different ways, as opposed to the "Game Over" theme, which is composed only of quarter notes. Many of the longer notes are part of a C-major chord, such as whole notes E and G at the beginning of pattern 20, or half-notes C and G at the beginning of pattern

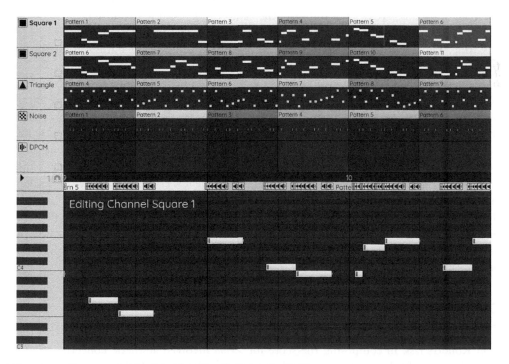

FIGURE 2.4 Patterns 6–11 of the "Ending" theme for *Zelda*.

43. These notes emphasize the tonic of the piece, effectively rewarding the listener with fully-resolved fanfares.

Yet, this piece does not even sound to players if they do not beat *Zelda*. Nor does the "Game Over" theme sound unless players direct Link to lose all of his health and die. Game scores produced by players of *Zelda* could include neither of these themes, only one, or both of them. For example, I may play *Zelda* for two hours, never experience a "Game Over," and beat the game. I would then hear the "Game Over" theme once, but only as an introduction to the "Ending" theme (the "Death" jingle would not sound at all in this case). The "Ending" theme would then seem to contain no reference to another part of the score. On the other hand, if my journey through *Zelda* was marked by death, I would be familiar with the "Game Over" theme, and the "Ending" theme would allow me to recall and (hopefully) come to terms with these fatal experiences. One more scenario would have to include veteran *Zelda* players who unlock the "Ending" theme without a problem, yet the introduction to this theme reminds them of past, less-successful playthroughs, effectively summoning a kind of nostalgia for the feeling of innocence and adventure involved in playing (and losing) the game for the first time.

Different gameplay experiences produce varying degrees of relationships with game scores. Activation — through "large-scale" gameplay patterns, no less — of the "Ending" theme automatically makes players "invest" more in its sounding, though this investment might also be heightened by past experiences of the "Game Over" leitmotif. This effect is compatible with gaming's goal of providing an immersive experience as both memory of, and *responsibility* for sounds, seem to enhance this.

How is this different from watching a film, and listening to its soundtrack? Game design surely involves visual editing techniques similar to film, though the timing and order of these edits are not "fixed." For instance, the "cut" to the "Game Over" screen in *Zelda* is dependent on the player directing Link to lose all of his hearts, which could happen at nearly any time. Thus, "editing," taken in the sense of demarcating visual lengths of time in film, happens in the gameplay or "presentation" stage of a game. Gameplay structures game scoring, and makes players have a greater investment in, and understanding of, this structure. It cuts up game scores into sections, and, taken on their own, these sections are simply phrases of sound material. However, when music analysts consider their relationship to gameplay, they become identifiable "units." Even gamers easily recognize sound splices because they occur as a result of their own gameplay. Thus, a "death jingle" is not just the name of the "Death" jingle in *Zelda*, but could serve as the name of a type of sound unit in game scores.

As with *The Ring*, the "story" of *Zelda* varies every time it is played. If narrative inconsistencies create an indeterminacy in patterns of signification, then game scores may also "lay bare" the way textual meaning is negotiated. In the case of the "Game Over" and "Ending" themes in *Zelda*, meaning is structured by gameplay because the affect of the "Ending" theme is in part dependent on the sounding of the "Game Over" theme. A musical relationship between the two both highlights, and is structured by, the specific experience of gameplay.

Case study conclusions: John Cage and game scoring as aleatoric composition

Koji Kondo's task in composing the score for *Zelda* involved aesthetic concerns different from those involved, for instance, in film scoring.[11] The main challenge that he faced in scoring *Zelda* is one that all game scorers face: to allow different gameplay choices to produce different scores, even while working to produce a broader aesthetically coherent and unified "score." The relationship between the "Game Over" and "Ending" themes indicates an aesthetically coherent "score," while gameplay's bearing on the occurrence and musical effect of these themes suggests the centrality of interactivity and indeterminacy in game scoring. Thus, Alistair Williams' (2001: 39) brief discussion of the work of aleatoric composer John Cage might be relevant to this type of scoring:[12]

> Cage's indeterminate scores are more obviously textual in their reduction of control over sounds, but do not always grant performers and listeners active roles as constructors of meaning. In this sense, his works are structuralist artefacts controlled by anonymous, steering mechanisms.

Taken in isolation, game scores certainly appear to be "structuralist artefacts controlled by anonymous, steering mechanisms." One can imagine a simple installation to illustrate this point: a gamer plays a game — such as *Zelda* — while a "listener" listens to the resultant sounds in isolation, without a sense of its visuals or gameplay. From this perspective, a game score would sound strange, though it would yield an experience similar to hearing a Cage piece, since it would be structured according to non-musical parameters (in this case gameplay). However, if the above discussion has shown anything, it is that game scores may not be analyzed in isolation. Game scoring's steering mechanisms are one part anonymous — software programming — and one part human. Gamers perform, listen and even take part in *composing* game scores. In this sense, they not only construct their own meaning, but construct their own "text" to be interpreted.

Paradoxically, the kind of experience that allows game scoring to meet the criteria of aleatoric composition is not musical. A gamer may become a musical performer by recognizing and utilizing instrumental aspects of the music system programmed into the game they are playing, in their own compositions.[13] However, this situation eliminates the chance element provided by gameplay in the ludic experience, thus making the "output" non-aleatoric. So, while it is true that *hearing* game scoring as aleatoric composition involves the subversion of the traditional roles of composer, performer and listener in narrative terms, this subversion does not change the fact that game scoring itself is dependent on gameplay. And furthermore, this experience does not imply that game scoring produces a musical composition that is unified in any way. Rather, to hear game scores as aleatoric composition means to interrogate any notion of their unity, and to give due consideration to their interactive multimedia context.

In the final sections of this chapter, I will introduce three game scoring categories, namely, Title Music, Source Music and Results Music, that demonstrate the interactive multimedia context involved in gaming, and how game scorers may accommodate and facilitate it.

Game scoring taxonomy: Title Music

At some early point in game operation, players will inevitably navigate to a title screen that showcases the game's title logo. *The Legend of Zelda* and *Super Mario* series of games have title screens for each of their games, though timing and player interaction with these screens have changed considerably over the course of gaming history, and with the ongoing evolution of gaming technology. The original Famicom Disk System version of *The Legend of Zelda*, for instance, was released in Japan in 1986 on a proprietary floppy disk known as a "Famicom Disk." "Side A" of this disk contained the title screen and introductory video, while "Side B" contained the save file screen and the entire gameplay adventure. (Gamers must always start with "Side A" to get to "Side B" when playing the disk version of *Zelda*, and so the title screen cannot be skipped.) While the Japanese disk version of *Zelda* required ejecting, flipping and re-inserting a disk to pass the title screen, the North American cartridge version of the game simply required pressing "START" on the NES controller (see Figure 2.5):

The two initial versions of *Zelda* also have slightly differing sound hardware to work with, as the Famicom Disk System added an extra frequency modulation (FM) synthesizer to the Famicom's (NES in North America) APU. Thus, the Title Music for the disk version is more robust in instrumentation, and contains bell-like tones provided by the FM synth, making it sound slightly more urgent, as well as more traditionally fantastical.[14]

The title screen (see Figure 2.7) for *The Legend of Zelda: Ocarina of Time* (1998), for N64, is very different in terms of interactivity. *Ocarina* begins with the "NINTENDO 64" logo, which fades away to a black screen. Then, a grassy hill fades into view as the sound of a horse galloping plays from the right speaker, and Link enters on his horse from a distance, at the right side of the screen.[15] After Link makes it to the left side of the screen, the

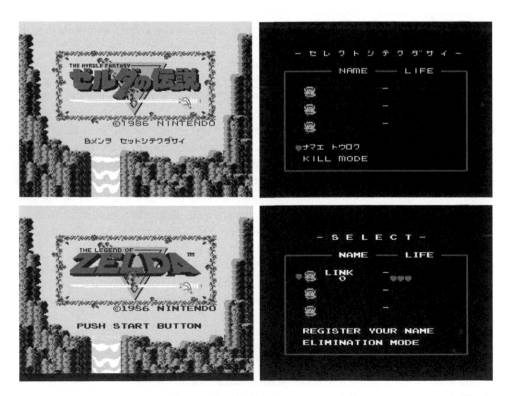

FIGURE 2.5 *Zelda no Densetsu: The Hyrule Fantasy* (1986) title and file screens (top); and *The Legend of Zelda* (1986) title and file screens (bottom).

Title Music starts, and it is mixed with the sound of the horse's hooves hitting the field. The video cuts to Link's perspective as the grass below him streams by, and the title logo for *Ocarina* fades into view in the centre of the screen. The rest of the introductory video involves Link riding his horse around the main area, "Hyrule Field," as the Title Music plays, and as the title logo stays on the screen. The game proceeds this way if gamers do not operate the controller after powering on the N64 with the *Zelda* cartridge inserted. Players can actually trigger the title logo earlier by pressing "START," which also triggers the Menu Sound Effect for the title logo — a bright ascending synthesizer jingle that sounds "low-resolution" enough that it could come from the NES APU. Since players may either allow the title logo to fade in automatically or trigger it manually, they may experience *Ocarina*'s title in either a cinematic or ludal fashion, respectively. However, regardless of the way players experience the title logo, pressing "START" once the logo is shown triggers the same sound effect, and takes gamers to the file screen.

In addition, since the Title Music is the same as the Introduction Music for *Ocarina*, gamers have slight control over when the music shifts from Introduction Music to Title Music, as they have slight control over the timing of the title logo. The Title Music for *Ocarina* actually quotes a Gameplay Sound Effect from the original *Zelda*: the warp "Flute" jingle (Figure 2.6). While players could trigger the warp "Flute" jingle at any time in normal gameplay of the original *Zelda* (once/if the player has obtained the flute item), which replaces whatever music is playing, this jingle forms part of the main theme for the *Ocarina* Title Music.

The nature of these types of quotations are reminiscent of Williams and Clement's (2001) analysis of Wagner's music. While the Flute leitmotif is related to the main theme of the Title Music for *Ocarina* from a purely musical standpoint, the melody functions differently according to its context in gameplay. In the original *Zelda*, the "Flute" jingle elucidates Link's act of instantly travelling great distances, or "warping." In *Ocarina*, Link must eventually find a mysterious weapon known as the Master Sword that allows him to travel seven years into the future, and so the melody in the Title Music may signify Link's ability to

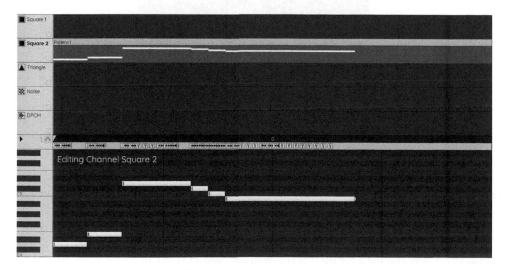

FIGURE 2.6 The warp "Flute" jingle from *The Legend of Zelda*.

FIGURE 2.7 The introductory video and title screen for *The Legend of Zelda: Ocarina of Time* (1998). The video shows players how fast time moves in the game; as Link and his horse move across the screen, the moon's movement is visible and the sky becomes lighter as dawn approaches (top row). The onscreen text items appear in a specific order (middle row): (1) title, (2) copyright and developer, and (3) "PRESS START," the latter of which repeatedly fades in and out of view (bottom).

travel across time in an instant. It may also convey a kind of longing nostalgia, as well as a break with simpler, two-dimensional gaming, as *Ocarina* is the first three-dimensional *Zelda* game, and its Title Music references the first game in the series. Of course, players will have a different type of reaction to this reference if they have heard it before. Notably, the "Flute" sound effect was also used for the "Warp Whistle" sound effect in *Super Mario Bros. 3*, and so if gamers have played any NES at all, it is likely they have heard it before. Interestingly, the "Adult" version of Link is old enough — in real life, and at the time of *Ocarina*'s release — to have experienced NES games, while the "Child" version of Link is not. Players of any age and experience might play *Ocarina*, and their musical knowledge of the *Zelda* series and early Nintendo video games affects their experience of the Title Music.

The introductory video for *Ocarina* is also slightly odd in that it presents Adult Link on a horse; the horse may only be obtained in the latter half of the game, when Young Link travels seven years into the future and becomes Adult Link. However, just as adults do not absolutely need a driver's license to proceed through life, players of *Ocarina* do not need a horse to beat the game — it is an entirely optional "sidequest." It also does not allow players to beat the game faster, as exemplified by current speed-running record-holders, who skip the sidequest completely, unless they are also attempting a "100% Completion" run.

While obtaining a horse in *Ocarina* is not necessary, it remains desirable — the introductory video certainly encourages players to seek out this sidequest, and the Warp Flute reference may symbolize its utility in reaching destinations faster. Many of the significations possible with the Title Music are therefore dependent on players' experience with both the *Zelda* series and *Ocarina* specifically.

The latest game in the *Zelda* series, *The Legend of Zelda: Breath of the Wild* (2017), exemplifies a new type of title screen interaction that modern first party Nintendo games make use of, and that feels more like an "interactive film." When players start *Breath of the Wild* for the first time, they are not greeted with a proper title screen. Instead, a black screen is displayed, and the title of the game fades into view in plain white text, unaccompanied by sound. The introductory cut-scene plays, and players gain control of Link after he has woken up from an induced coma in a strange-looking cavern. Leaving the cavern, which involves learning basic actions such as running and climbing, triggers the "real" title screen (see Figure 2.8).

Once players perform this action, the game takes control of Link and directs him to a lookout point, where he surveys the game's vast world. Notably, this instance is the only time during — potentially hundreds of hours of — normal gameplay where the game takes control of the player's avatar in this fashion. Thus, players learn basic mechanics in a dark cavern until they reach outside, where the possibilities for these mechanics open up. At the exact moment that *Zelda* players see the breadth of the game's world, they cannot control Link, and this intensifies their desire to explore.

The Title Music, which might be better called the Title Motif for its brevity, plays at this point. It is a section of the main theme for *Breath of the Wild* that players can expect to hear during narrative portions of the game, though it is typically played on string instruments, whereas here it is played on solo piano. Players can also expect to hear more solo piano in general, as it is used to perform much of the main gameplay background music of the "overworld."

The same "hybrid" cinematic-ludal situation is present in *Super Mario Odyssey*, where players direct Mario to wake up and jump up from the ground where he fell, after the introductory video. After doing that, players must ascend a tower, which involves learning the main gameplay mechanic of *Odyssey*: throwing Mario's hat onto enemies, which transforms Mario into those enemies and gives him their abilities. Whereas the Title Motif for *Breath of the Wild* is the first music players hear in the game, *Odyssey* players experience Cut-scene Music and Gameplay Music before the Title Motif. After players ascend the tower and face a mini-boss, they must throw their hat onto an electricity pole, in order to transform into

FIGURE 2.8 The "real" title screen for *Breath of the Wild* (2017), accessible after players direct Link out of a "tutorial" cavern.

electric current and travel to the next world. As "electric Mario" charges into the distance, the camera stays fixed, the *Super Mario Odyssey* title logo is displayed (see Figure 2.9), and the Title Motif plays.

This type of title design connects the perceived "beginning" of the game to a player's "readiness." In both *Breath of the Wild* and *Odyssey*, players must work their way through a tutorial section that requires they perform the main gameplay mechanics of each game. Thus, rather than presenting the title screen upon start-up, with little player interaction,

FIGURE 2.9 The title screen for *Super Mario Odyssey* (2017).

modern Nintendo games require playing part of the game to "unlock" the title screen. While the latter might seem similar to an "interactive film," it is actually a lot different from the cinematic experience in general. The title screen for a film, for instance, is not connected to audience interaction with the film; it will play at the same time every time the film is played, no matter who is watching. Moreover, a film's title screen is only thematically connected to actions that are contained within the film's narrative. In *Breath of the Wild*, *Odyssey* and many other modern video games, the title screens are both physically and thematically connected to gameplay mechanics because players must learn and enact such mechanics in order to even see and hear title screens and motifs. Thus, Title Motifs are more rewarding in nature than Title Music, and gameplay mechanics are more intimately connected with the game's *meaning* — that players ascertain as they progress — with a delayed title screen.

While delayed title screens and Title Motifs are a new development for *Zelda* and *Mario* games, they are not a new development for gaming in general, nor for another long-running video game series, *Final Fantasy*. In fact, the very first *Final Fantasy* (1990) features a delayed title screen with looping Title Music (see Figure 2.10):

Game scorers and designers sometimes refer to Title Motifs as "stingers," or short musical ideas that immediately punctuate the events that trigger them. Some games, such as those in the *Tomb Raider* series, feature many different stingers for many different gameplay events, though these are still distinguishable from a single, centrally-focused stinger — a Title Motif. Title Motifs, because of their function in uniting a multi-faceted work — a game — must be extremely memorable, and may take many attempts to compose. For example, Rich Vreeland estimates that he developed 100–150 piano sketches for the music for the trailer for *Hyper Light Drifter* (2016), of which one was selected by the game's lead developer, Alex Preston, to serve as the Title Motif.

FIGURE 2.10 The title screen for *Final Fantasy* (1990 in North America, 1987 in Japan).

Game scoring taxonomy: Source Music

Source Music is music that emanates from an *identifiable* physical object or marker in a game. In-game playable instruments are an example of Source Music, featured in many games in the *Zelda* series. Table 2.1 is a list of *Zelda* games featuring playable instruments, with descriptions of each:

There are also many examples of developers programming popular music as Source Music in their games, most notably in the three-dimensional installments in the *Grand Theft Auto* (GTA) series. Starting with *Grand Theft Auto III* (2001), *GTA* developers began scoring entire "radio stations" for their games that players may listen to whenever they direct their

TABLE 2.1 A list of playable instruments in games in *The Legend of Zelda* series

Game	Instrument(s)	Description
The Legend of Zelda (1986)	Recorder (Flute; Whistle)	Players assign the Recorder, also known as the "Flute" or the "Whistle," to the "B" button, and when they press "B" the "Warp" jingle plays, and Link warps to one of four locations in the overworld. Additionally, the only way for Link to defeat the boss in the fifth dungeon is to weaken it by playing the recorder (which is also found in the same dungeon).
Zelda II: The Adventure of Link (1988)	Flute	Obtained from the Ocean Palace, the fifth dungeon in the game. It is automatically assigned to the "B" button when Link is in the overworld, and its only use is to calm and avoid the River Devil, who blocks entrance to the southern portion of the map. The Flute has a different jingle than the Recorder in *Zelda 1*.
The Legend of Zelda: A Link to the Past (1992)	Flute (Ocarina in Japanese Version)	An optional item that Link may obtain after the fifth dungeon (including Hyrule Castle), and assign it to the "Y" button. It has sentimental value to a character in the game, though the character may not use it anymore, and so Link plays it for him one last time and keeps it. After this event, players may go to Kakariko village and play it again beside the weathervane. A duck will then pop out of it, which Link can use to warp to locations in the Light World. Mysteriously, whether Link has obtained it or not, the jingle plays after Link defeats the penultimate boss, and the duck appears, to fly him to the final boss.
The Legend of Zelda: Link's Awakening (1993)	Ocarina	Link may obtain the Ocarina from the Dream Shrine, and assign it to a button after completing the third dungeon. He may learn three "songs" on it that play as truncated jingles: the "Ballad of the Wind Fish," used at the end of the game to wake the Wind Fish; "Manbo's Mambo," used to warp to Manbo's Pond in the overworld, and back to the beginnings of dungeons in the underworld; and "Frog's Song of Soul," used to bring inanimate objects to life.

Game	Instrument(s)	Description
The Legend of Zelda: Ocarina of Time (1998)	Fairy Ocarina Ocarina of Time	Link obtains the Fairy Ocarina from his friend Saria after the first dungeon, and replaces it with the Ocarina of Time, from Princess Zelda, after the third dungeon. Link may learn up to twelve "songs," as well as compose one himself. The latter, as well as the "Sun's Song," used to change day to night and vice-versa, and "Epona's Song," used to milk cows and summon Epona, are optional. Six of the "songs" are "warp songs" that correspond to the six Adult Link dungeons. The other "songs" are mostly used for special narrative junctures. Players operate the Ocarina with five buttons on the N64 controller that are each assigned their own pitch: D, B, A, F and a lower octave D. They must actually memorize the themes to play them, and the sheet music is expressed in button presses.
The Legend of Zelda: Majora's Mask (2000)	Ocarina of Time (Deku Pipes, Goron Drums and Zora Guitar)	Link retrieves the Ocarina of Time as Deku Link near the beginning of the game, though the instrument changes to Deku Pipes. The game takes place in a three-day cycle system that can be reset by playing the "Song of Time" (players can also slow and fast-forward time with variations of this piece). Four "songs" are used for gaining entrance to dungeons, while a multi-location warp function is assigned to only the "Song of Soaring." The "Song of Healing" is used to "heal" suffering spirits in the game's narrative. The instrument changes according to Link's form: as Deku Link, it is the Deku Pipes; as Goron Link, it is the Goron Drums; and as Zora Link, it is the Zora Guitar. Players operate the instrument the same way as they did in Ocarina, and it has the same pitches.
The Legend of Zelda: The Wind Waker (2003)	Wind Waker	A conductor's baton that Link obtains before the first dungeon, and has central significance to the narrative. Players may find up to six "songs" in the game. The "Wind's Requiem" allows players to control the direction of the wind, and thus sail the ocean in any direction. The "warp song" is the "Ballad of Gales," and the "day-night song" is the "Song of Passing." The "Command Melody" allows Link to control certain characters with his mind, and two other "songs" grant him access to dungeons. The Wind Waker may be played in three different time signatures that each have two "songs:" 3/4, 4/4 and 6/4. It has a total of five notes sung by choir, though the timbre and tempo changes according to time signature.

(Continued)

Game	Instrument(s)	Description
The Legend of Zelda: Twilight Princess (2006)	Wolf Howl Hawk Grass Horse Grass or Horse Whistle	Throughout the game players can find "Howling Stones," stone obelisks with holes that filter the wind into a melodic sound. As Wolf Link, players may ascertain the melody through attempting to howl along with it, by operating the analog stick to up, centre or down. If they are successful, players are transported to a mysterious realm as a human, where a knight teaches them a new sword technique. As Link, players can find Hawk Grass to call hawks to aid them, and Horse Grass or the Horse Whistle to call Epona. The latter two instruments play assigned jingles.
The Legend of Zelda: A Link Between Worlds (2013)	Bell	The witch Irene befriends Link early in the game and gives him the Bell that players may use to call her and warp to weathervanes they have previously visited. It has an assigned sound effect/jingle that resembles both a real bird and the squeaking of a metal weathervane, encapsulating both its theme and function.

avatars to enter a vehicle. These virtual radio stations are composed to sound like real-life radio stations, though there are a number of obvious differences. First, each radio station is scored as one long, fixed and loopable audio track, meaning that the broadcast simply repeats in the same way after it ends, complete with voice acting for radio DJ's and commercials for fake products. Second, when players exit their vehicles, the in-car radio cannot be heard from the outside (likely due to technological restrictions), though it continues to stream, similarly to a real radio station, much to *GTA*'s credit. The ability to hear the in-car radio from outside the car was added in *GTA* games for later systems. Third, and finally, some instances of radio programming are tied to important narrative points. For example, in the first mission where players drive a car in *Grand Theft Auto: Vice City* (2002), Michael Jackson's iconic "Billie Jean" plays to evoke the 1980s setting (Figure 2.11):

Nevertheless, *GTA*'s incorporation of a somewhat realistically-programmed radio system enhanced the chaotic, "free-form" gameplay that depends mainly on vehicle theft. As players gain a "Wanted" level by performing various crimes, they depend on getaway after getaway from the police, and every time they steal a car — in either desperation or indifference — they are treated to the radio station that the original owner of the car was listening to. The audio programming thus "personalizes" every vehicle theft in the game, since there are multiple variables that are factored into what "getaway music" the player will encounter. First of all, certain vehicles and drivers will predominantly listen to certain radio stations, and so if players become familiar with these trends they may be able to predict what station will play in the next car they steal. However, players have no way of knowing what "point" in the station's broadcast loop the radio will start at, once they enter the car. It could be mid-advertisement, or at the climax of a record that perfectly sets the getaway, to name two contrasting examples.

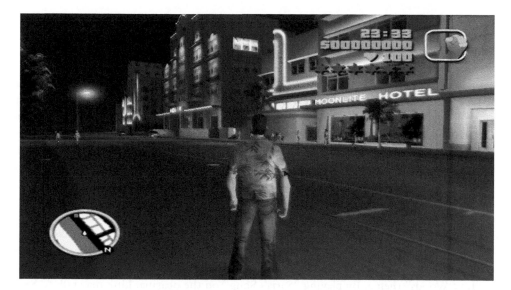

FIGURE 2.11 A gameplay screenshot from *GTA: Vice City* (2002, 2012).[16] The game's aesthetic and narrative elements are based on 1980s media set in Miami, such as the television series *Miami Vice* (1984–1990), and the film *Scarface* (1983).

Source Music requires an identifiable physical source, but does this source need to be visible? "Physical" only denotes that a source exists, and not necessarily that it can be seen by players. The source simply needs to be identified as physically present in the programming, and it can exist as an invisible marker. For example, the "Lost Woods" theme from *Ocarina* transforms into Source Music after players speak with Princess Zelda and learn "Zelda's Lullaby." Players receive hints to go visit Link's childhood friend Saria, who resides in the Lost Woods area, before attempting the second dungeon of the game. When players direct Link to the Lost Woods at this point in the narrative, they will notice that the music plays louder in some areas and quieter in others. Navigating a couple of four-sided "rooms" of the forest will lead players to Kaepora Gaebora, who gives Link a hint set by his exclusive Dialogue Music, detailed in the section on that component, in Chapter 4:

> Hey, over here, Hoo hoo! Link…Good to see you again! Listen to this! Hoot hoot…. After going through the Lost Woods, you will come upon the Sacred Forest Meadow. This is a sacred place where few people have ever walked. Shhhh… what's that? I can hear a mysterious tune… You should listen for that tune too… Hoo hoo ho! Do you want to hear what I said again? [Player selects 'No.'] If you are courageous you will make it through the forest just fine. Just follow your ears, and listen to the sounds coming from the forest! Hoot hoot!

Kaepora Gaebora instructs players to "follow [their] ears," which refers to the background music for the Lost Woods. If players follow their ears, they will successfully direct Link through the Lost Woods, as the music grows louder for making the right turn, and attenuates for making the wrong one. This programming is an ingenious trick because it appears as though the music is actually coming from the next "room," and players direct Link closer to this source. In reality, Link is the source of the audio being triggered; players effectively have control over a volume dial for the "Lost Woods" theme in this instance.

For first-time players, the volume of the "Lost Woods" theme becomes their reference point for navigating the Lost Woods at this point in *Ocarina*. The "Lost Woods" theme is therefore an example of Navigational or Navi-Source Music, or Source Music that aids navigation. While it may seem like a very niche game score component, there are, in fact, numerous examples of Navi-Source Music across gaming history. For example, in *Pokémon Black Version* and *White Version* (2010), players can find important non-player characters, or NPCs, by listening for an additional instrument to enter the mix in each town. The volume of this instrument increases as players grow closer to the designated NPC. Similarly, in *Crypt of the Necrodancer* (2015), players can find the shopkeeper in each level by listening for his singing along to the Area Music. Finally, in *Metal Gear Solid V: The Phantom Pain* (2015), players may find cassettes of Cold War-era popular music by listening for boom-boxes playing each tune in the game, such as Joy Division's 1980 hit single "Love Will Tear Us Apart."

If players successfully navigate through the Lost Woods, and then through the Sacred Forest Meadow to reach Saria, she will teach Link "Saria's Song," a solo ocarina version of the "Lost Woods" theme. By playing "Saria's Song" on the ocarina, Link may talk to Saria at any time in the game, making the piece a kind of communicative device. The transformation of the "Lost Woods" theme into a navigation tool, and then a memorized composition that players play themselves for communication purposes, seems to convey metaphorically the different levels of control players have over game scores. While this progression may seem as though players take ownership of the "Lost Woods" theme in the end, I would contend that they have more physical control over it at the moment where it is meant to serve a navigational function. Source Music always relates directly to player position in some way, but the notion that it comes from a narrative source at all is based purely on the conceptual reality that the game's narrative elements are meant to support.

Source Music case study: Kondo's "Lost Woods" vs. Vreeland's "Reflection"

On a related note, the "Lost Woods" theme mobilizes into Source Music because of progression, in both gameplay and narrative senses. Once players pass this point in the game — once Link learns "Saria's Song" — the theme returns to its "non-adaptive" or "static" form, and plays at a constant volume every time players return Link to the Lost Woods. Thus, "Lost Woods" is also an example of a progression-dependent music system change, as with the Hub Music for *Super Mario Galaxy* and *Yoshi's Island*, though instead of simply denoting game progress through orchestration, as with those examples, it becomes Navi-Source Music at a single point in *Ocarina*'s narrative, and then returns to non-adaptive Area Music. Music programming changes such as these are effective at highlighting a point in a narrative, such as Link's return to visit his friend in *Ocarina*.

In *FEZ*, Rich Vreeland (2016: "Reflection") uses a similar, though less ludal approach to "Reflection," the non-looping theme that plays as Gomez leaves his village for the first time:

> I wanted the moments after Gomez leaves his village to be reflective, so I continued with the Home idea, but stretched it out and tried to make it sound more solitary and inward. Ironically, this happens to be one of the longest songs in the game, but it only plays the first time you leave the village, and if you're not totally horrible at platform-ing, you can get to the next area of the game way before the song is over.

"Reflection" does not become Navi-Source Music, but it is still similar to the "Lost Woods" theme because it is programmed according to game progression. In both game scores, players "lose" music after progressing past specific points in each game, though in very different ways. In *Ocarina*, players may no longer depend on the "Lost Woods" theme to navigate the area after they have found Saria in the Sacred Forest Meadow; they must remember the path they originally took. In other words, players lose the navigational function of the "Lost Woods" theme after they use it the first time. In *FEZ*, players simply only have one chance to listen to "Reflection" in a given playthrough, and the length at which it plays is dependent on how long players take to reach the top of the tower in the room, up to the length of the piece. If the end of the piece plays, the music will not play again, and so "Reflection" is arguably more ephemeral than the "Lost Woods" theme, in the context of scores for each game. *FEZ* players may return to the tower room, though it is not necessary, as it is for *Ocarina* players to return to the Lost Woods. If they do return to the tower room, only ambient sounds will play. Arguably, then, the function of "Reflection" is to mark a narrative point in the game, and to encourage — rather than technically guide — specifically inexperienced players to reach the top of the tower. The navigational function of the "Lost Woods" theme is also progression-dependent, and so it too is composed specifically for inexperienced players.

A comparison between these two themes yields a potential problem for the definition of Source Music. While the above discussion of the "Lost Woods" theme shows that it is Source Music without a visible source, does this conclusion mean that *any* kind of source is acceptable for Source Music? For example, game progression itself, composed of fluctuating values for programmed categories, appears to be the only source for "Reflection." As Area Music, it is extremely ephemeral, and thus is not *as dependent* on area as it is on game progression. I can only conclude that if "Reflection" is also Source Music, this category is wholly different for game scores than it is for film scores. While Vreeland himself might not refer to "Reflection" as Source Music, the above discussion shows that game progression may also be a source, as it is the parameter he used for triggering "Reflection."

Can any parameter be a source for Source Music? In the broadest possible sense, any sound in a game has a programmed virtual "source" because any sound may be programmed to play according to any programmed value in the game's code. Game scoring is essentially software programming, after all. While this argument might make it seem as though game scorers face an overwhelming number of possibilities, this is only the case in theory. In reality, game scorers attempt to link musical ideas to game parameters in a meaningful way, and are limited by the specific design of each game they score. For example, Vreeland was aware that *FEZ* players would discover the tower room early in the game after learning basic gameplay mechanics, and that they are unlikely to return, and so he programmed "Reflection" to only play once, to set this transitional space. In *Ocarina*, Kondo was aware that players would return to the Lost Woods after their initial visit, and so the theme is left intact, though importantly, it serves a navigational function early in the game as adaptive music. When players return as Adult Link, they remember this navigational function specifically because it is not there — the theme is not adaptive — and are forced to either remember their way or navigate the Lost Woods through trial-and-error, a considerably more difficult task. Thus, game scorers may grant game progression more affect through progression-dependent music changes.

Game scoring taxonomy: Results Music

"Results Music" is any music or jingle meant to accompany the presentation of the "results" of gameplay. "Results" are an indication of successful or unsuccessful gameplay, and so the definition of Results Music is at least as broad as Rest Music, for example, though it is not subjective. The reason why Results Music may be objectively defined is that gameplay results rely on objective game design factors. For example, as I described in the case study above, if I direct Link to lose all of his hearts in the original *Zelda*, he will "die" and I will experience a "Game Over," thus making the "Death" jingle and "Game Over" themes Results Music. On the broadest possible scale, then, Credits Music is also Results Music, since it signifies that a player has successfully reached the ending of the game. On the narrowest possible scale, sound effects and jingles serve the same function as Results Music, because they are sounds that indicate success or failure for gamers performing very specific actions, such as collecting a coin in *Super Mario Bros.* Completing a level in the same game would trigger a mini-cut-scene, accompanied by the "Flagpole Fanfare" theme, another example of Results Music, which lies somewhere in the middle of the previous two examples in terms of the "scale" of gameplay results.

Mid-scale gameplay results are arguably the most important types of results in any game, since they break up gameplay into identifiable sections. The results of a single race in a racing game, for instance, constitute an example of mid-scale results. The results of a four-race tournament would constitute results on a larger scale. Sports games involve mid-scale results that originate from the sports themselves, such as the break between periods in a hockey game, where statistics are displayed in both real life and in the games meant to emulate it. Similarly, many *Zelda* games are broken up into a number of "dungeons," or levels that may take hours to complete.

Competitive local multiplayer games are an interesting context for Results Music, since games have to present results that cannot possibly satisfy every competitor. For example, losers of a particular round of competitive local multiplayer gameplay cannot possibly experience the "victorious" thematic content of the Results Music in the same way as the winners. Given the options to convey "bad" results to the losers, or to convey "good" results to the winner, game developers and scorers prefer the latter. Single-player game scorers do not have this concern, and are almost always tasked with writing music for negative results, such as *Zelda*'s "Death" and "Game Over" themes.

Tiered results in single-player games are another interesting context for Results Music. For example, the jet-ski racing game *Wave Race 64* (1996) has different themes for when players place first, second, third or fourth in a race, as well as for each of these places in a four-race tournament (see Figure 2.12):

Appropriately, the pieces increase in excitement with more impressive results: the music for fourth place involves the slowest tempo and the most laidback sound; while the music for first place involves a quicker tempo and more triumphant thematic content; and the music for the other two places are scored somewhere in between these, in terms of excitement.

Ending or Credits Music is an example of large-scale Results Music, and is typically the most "sought after" music in a single-player game. As I elucidated in Chapter 2 with the score for the original *Zelda*, Ending Music can reward players who have played and mastered a game, and sometimes even more so if they have failed many times. Ending Music is also Rest Music because ending scenes and credits typically do not involve interaction. It takes

FIGURE 2.12 As I cross the finish line of the first race of a tournament in *Wave Race 64*, the announcer exclaims "Oh! Nice try!" The music for "Fourth Place," a subdued, groove-based electronic keyboard melody begins as the game's "AI" takes over control of my jet-ski (top, right). I may watch the computer control my jet-ski for as long as I want, as my lap times are displayed. When I press any button, the screen cuts to the race results screen (bottom, left), and the announcer exclaims, "You finished fourth, and got one point. Keep trying!" The music continues until I navigate the results screens to the next race.

place in arguably the most exceptional context in gaming, and so much so that it could almost be called a non-gaming context. Players who have reached the definitive ending of a game typically have nothing left to accomplish. As with speed-runs, the "timer" on gameplay effectively stops just before the ending cut-scene and credits, at the final button press in the context of gameplay. Thus, Ending Music has a very different context than Area Music, for instance.

Accordingly, many game scores have Ending Music that, while in the same style and timbre as the rest of the music, has very different thematic content. With every other piece of music that sounds, gamers still have other tasks to perform, and video game narratives often elucidate this fact by presenting challenging situations, obstinate villains and an overall sense of hardship for their avatars. Thus, Gameplay Music has very different functions than Ending Music. The former must convey some sense of responsibility, while the latter must do the opposite: convey a sense of freedom from responsibility, and to encourage celebration of one's accomplishments.

Hirokazu Tanaka's "Ending" for the Famicom Disk System version of *Metroid* (1987) is an example of Ending Music that contrasts thematically with the other music in the game. The mood of *Metroid* is more similar to *Hyper Light Drifter* than *FEZ*, to name two modern reference points. That is, *Metroid* conveys an unsympathetic attitude towards players, with its claustrophobic and cold space cavern environments, and the horrifying threat of a deadly virus as the primary, impersonal villain. Players traverse the dark underworld caverns of a fictional planet in the style of a side-scrolling action-platformer, in order to find and destroy the "Mother Brain," the keeper of the stolen "Metroid" virus that threatens life in the game's universe. The Title Music for *Metroid* conveys the game's setting, mood and gameplay through an extremely simple one-note bass line that is punctuated by a "buzzing" FM synthesizer. These two parts define the texture of the piece, while the pulse channels of the NES APU accent it with sparse, dissonant notes that convey the isolation of the avatar, Samus, in her unforgiving environment (Figure 2.13):

Tanaka (2002: 8) explains why he chose to compose *Metroid*'s Title and Gameplay Music in this style:

> Then, sound designers in many studios started to compete with each other by creating upbeat melodies for game music [...]
>
> The industry was delighted, but on the contrary, I wasn't happy with the trend, because those melodies weren't necessarily matched with the tastes and atmospheres that the games originally had.

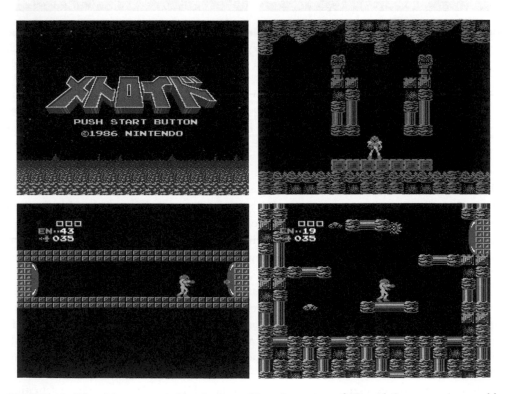

FIGURE 2.13 The title screen and beginning of Japan's version of *Metroid*. Samus explores cold, claustrophobic space caverns in an attempt to track down a deadly virus.

> The sound design for *Metroid* was, therefore, intended to be the antithesis [of] that trend. I had a concept that the music for *Metroid* should be created not as game music, but as music the players feel as if they were encountering a living creature. I wanted to create the sound without any distinctions between music and sound effects. The image I had was, 'Anything that comes out from the game is the sound that game makes.'

Tanaka (2002) notes that he wanted to create an original-sounding game score that sounded distinct from the melody-based music of other games in the 1980s. He also implies that game sound design should prioritize atmosphere over traditional musical goals, and, following this logic, he attempted to score *Metroid*'s music and sound effects as indistinguishable from each other. Finally, Tanaka (2002) conceptualized the game *Metroid* as perhaps a Metroid virus or the Mother Brain, and his sounds as the sounds from that "living creature." As the NES APU uses the same channels for both sound effects and music, the texture of each is already similar. Moreover, as I discussed above, with the introduction to the Title Music for *Metroid*, Tanaka opts for a more static, atmospheric sound than a melody-based score. Finally, with Tanaka's description of the game as a living creature, the bass line in the Title Music could arguably represent its breathing or movement.

With the "Ending" for *Metroid*, Tanaka (2002: 11) uses the very same "upbeat melodies" he denounces in the quote above:

> As you know, the melody in *Metroid* is only used at the ending after you killed the Mother Brain. That's because I wanted only a winner to have a catharsis at the maximum level. For [that] reason, I decided that melodies would be eliminated during the gameplay. By melody here I mean something that someone can sing or hum.

Figure 2.14 shows the score for the second, and "most sing-able," of three sections of the "Ending" for *Metroid*:

Patterns 16–20 represent the last part of the first section, a "build-up" where the triangle channel repeats a high-pitched, disjunct, primarily ascending arc phrase to provide tension. This technique of course leaves the sound devoid of bass until pattern 21, where the triangle channel resumes its normal role. In the build-up, the FM synthesizer channel descends to

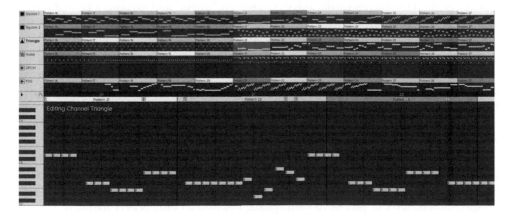

FIGURE 2.14 The middle section of the "Ending" theme to *Metroid*.

a whole note at D — supported by a whole note at F by square channel 2 — then ascends just before the start of the second section to indicate its "launch" into the sixteenth-note patterns in pattern 21. Square channel 1 harmonically and rhythmically supports the FM channel, while square channel 2 mimics the triangle channel, providing harmonic support to the bass line. The noise channel also picks up energy at pattern 21 by dropping a snare drum into its rhythm. At pattern 24, pulse channel 2 picks up the lively melody of the FM channel, which results in a pleasant change in timbre and retains the listener's interest. At pattern 24, the FM channel begins the melody that will lead the track to its conclusion. This melody almost sounds as though it could be sung, as it contains more sustained notes that contrast with the steady eighth and sixteenth notes of the other channels.

As with tiered Results Music, there may be multiple possible levels of success in completing a game. For example, games with alternative endings typically have what players refer to as "bad" or "fake," and "good" or "true" endings. The "bad" ending does not indicate failure, but gamers call it the "bad" ending simply because the "good" ending typically has more difficult conditions to unlock, and typically offers a greater reward.[17] For example, *Sonic the Hedgehog* games for Sega Genesis have one ending for destroying the final boss, and one for doing that and collecting all the "chaos emeralds." The latter requires deep exploration of the main stages and completion of several mini-games, and so it is a higher achievement for *Sonic* players. Narratively, moreover, "good" endings typically consist of more satisfying conclusions, and game scorers accordingly set these with "good" ending music.

Similarly, *Gimmick!* contains both "good" and "bad" endings that each have their own unique cut-scene and music. The "bad" ending requires the player to progress through each level and destroy the final boss, while the "good" ending— as with the "good" ending for *Sonic* — requires the player to defeat an additional, more difficult "final boss" that is only unlocked by finding and collecting special gems in each level. While I do not have the space to discuss it in-depth here, it is worth noting that these endings vary in terms of narrative outcome, and that the "best" one may only be experienced through advanced gameplay. It is also worth noting that the music for the "bad" ending, "Siesta," is less energetic and climactic, and involves less tension — and thus less resolution — than the music for the "good" ending in *Gimmick!*, "Good Night (Take 2)." Much of the music for *Gimmick!* is based on classic television series themes, such as the one written for *Cheers*. Appropriately, "Siesta" sounds similar to the credits for each episode of a series, while "Good Night (Take 2)" could arguably be used for a series finale, as it elaborates on "Siesta" and involves a greater musical climax.

Finally, some games have *modular* endings. Modular endings involve a number of components that vary according to how the player played the game, and what conditions they have met. For example, the classic board game *Clue* (1949) contains modular endings with three variables that relate to a murder mystery, which players must correctly identify to win: (i) the location of the murder, (ii) the weapon used in the murder, and (iii) the identity of the murderer. So, one possible ending to the game is: (iii) Colonel Mustard murdered the victim with (ii) the candlestick in (i) the parlor room.

Unlike *Clue*, modular endings in video games also exist along a spectrum from "bad" to "good," with the "best" ending being the one most difficult to unlock. However, they do not necessarily need to have rankings. Modular endings might not reflect the difficulty or accomplishment level of players in their quests, but instead only reflect narrative elements that change with each ending. Nevertheless, players have only to engage games *as games* to rank these endings in terms of difficulty anyway, as it is simple to quantify the actions required to unlock each ending. While composing Ending Music, scorers need to be aware of both narrative and ludal significance of each ending in games, because they need to elucidate both the players' sense of accomplishment and the story's particular sense of closure — both of which may vary considerably with modular endings.

Chapter conclusions

In this chapter, I have introduced some of the complications that arise in analyses of interactive media and audio, such as those that incorporate tools and concepts from film scoring research. I attempted to use the latter to analyze the spatiality of sound in *FEZ*, and found it quite difficult to say whether even background or Area Music in games is meant to be diegetic or non-diegetic. I concluded that since games include their own physics and spatiality, that react in a consistent, yet not necessarily realistic manner, to player and protagonist interaction, our own aural sense of space might not necessarily apply to games. This conclusion highlights the consistency of interactivity in games, such as the presentation of the "Game Over" screen every time players direct Link to lose all of his hearts in *The Legend of Zelda*. I conducted a case study of the music for that screen, as well as the "Ending" theme for *Zelda* to elucidate Koji Kondo's attempt at unity in his score, as well as how players' experiences of the two themes change according to their gameplay patterns. Finally, I offered the first three categories of my game scoring taxonomy, Title, Source and Results Music, as case studies of interactivity in game scores, from a large-scale perspective on gameplay.

In the next chapter, I consider gaming technology's "structuring" of game scoring activity, and specifically how game sound hardware determines the musical framework for game scorers to compose. While game scorers compose music that must remain malleable to the contours of gameplay patterns, they are also limited by the technologies they compose that music for.

Notes

1 Aleatoric music is music in which some element of the composition is left to chance, and/or some degree of freedom is afforded its performer. For more on this, see Antokoletz (2014).
2 Collins (2013).
3 See Enns (2014, 2015).
4 Ward (2002).
5 Screenshots of NES games are taken by the author, using the *FCEUX* emulator for Microsoft Windows.
6 This composition is strange because the NES APU has a total of five channels, so four are left dormant in this case. The NES APU has two pulse wave channels, typically used for melody and accompaniment; one triangle wave channel, typically used for bass; one noise channel, typically used for percussion; and one delta-modulation (sample) channel, most commonly used for sound effects or additional percussion. I analyze the NES APU in more depth in the next Chapter.
7 "Duty" refers to the amount of time a waveform remains active — the part that we can hear — in relation to its inactive state. The NES APU can produce pulse waves at 12.5%, 25% and 50% — or a standard square wave — duty settings, each with a respective increase in "thickness" of timbre.
8 This theme was much shorter, much less "happy" in thematic content, and much less linked to the "Ending" theme in the prototype version of *Zelda*. We can deduce from this fact that Kondo's re-working of the tune was probably an attempt at greater thematic unity.

9 A sound's volume envelope is related to its "ADSR." As White (1987: 7) notes:

> [ADSR is short for] 'Attack decay sustain release,' time constants associated with signals gen-erated by electronic music synthesizers. The attack time is the time it takes the signal level to rise from zero to its maximum value. The decay time is the time required for the level to fall to the sustain value, and the sustain time is the time it remains at this value. The release time is the time it takes for the level to fall to zero after the sustain time is elapsed [...] The ADSR actually defines the envelope of the generated signal.

10 The NES APU does not have enough voices to produce a proper counter-melody here.

11 Ludo-musicological research that focuses on aesthetics in game scoring includes: Bridgett (2013); Cheng (2013); Cheng (2014); Collins (2006, 2007, 2008); DeCastro (2007); Herzfeld (2013); Hug (2011); Lendino (1998); Nacke and Grimshaw (2010); Summers (2012, 2016); Sweeney (2011, 2014, 2015, 2016); and Youngdahl (2010), among others.

12 A few ludo-musicologists have explored game scoring as a form of aleatoric composition, includ-ing: Enns (2014, 2015); Havryliv and Vergara-Richards (2006); Kamp (2009); Phillips (2014); Rayman (2014); and Sweeney (2011, 2014).

13 Kamp (2009). Some other examples of game scoring research that focuses on games as "instru-ments" include, but are not limited to: Austin (2016); Dolphin (2014); Herber (2008); Kayali, Pichlmair, and Kotik (2008); Lind (2016); Medina-Gray (2014); Miller (2013); Moseley and Saiki (2014); and Moseley (2011).

14 Next to the "Overworld" theme for *Super Mario Bros.*, the "Title" theme — also used as the "Overworld" theme, though without an introduction section — for *The Legend of Zelda* is likely the most famous piece of music in video game history. It is significant that while the programmed game scores for the North American and Japanese versions of *Super Mario Bros.* were identical, the scores for the North American and Japanese versions of *Zelda* were different, at least in terms of instrumentation. Thus, North American and Japanese gamers were musically introduced to *Zelda* in slightly different ways, while the gameplay adventure remained the same. *Zelda* is also strange because it is a Japanese game with a Western Medieval fantasy setting, so a comparison of (the reception of) these two versions would surely be an interesting case study for future research on regional differences in gaming and game scoring.

15 This sound plays from the right speaker only in "Stereo" and "Surround Sound" audio modes for the game. In "Mono" mode, the horse gallops play from both speakers. Virtual audio spatializa-tion technologies enhance the way audio space is represented. That said, a mono *Ocarina* player is not missing out on any of the music in the game, nor any crucial game scoring gesture. I must also note that I examine all games in this book in "Stereo" mode, unless only mono is available, as with the NES APU. And while "Surround Sound" mode exercises the full capabilities of modern game scores, it remains the case that the vast majority of gamers play in stereo, due to its accessi-bility and affordability.

16 This screenshot is from the PC version of the game, and features slightly updated visuals. It was originally released for PlayStation 2.

17 Some games even withhold the credits for the less impressive ending, only showing them when players unlock the "true" ending.

References

Antokoletz, Elliott. 2014. *A History of Twentieth-Century Music in a Theoretic-Analytical Context.* Taylor & Francis. https://books.google.ca/books?id=qrkTAwAAQBAJ.

Austin, Michael, ed. 2016. *Music Video Games: Performance, Politics, and Play.* London: Bloomsbury.

Bridgett, Rob. 2013. "Contextualizing Game Audio Aesthetics." In *The Oxford Handbook of New Audiovisual Aesthetics*, edited by John Richardson, Claudia Gorbman, and Carol Vernal-lis. Oxford Handbooks Online. http://www.oxfordhandbooks.com/view/10.1093/oxfordhb/9780199733866.001.0001/oxfordhb-9780199733866.

Cheng, William. 2013. "Monstrous Noise: Silent Hill and the Aesthetic Economies of Fear." In *The Oxford Handbook of Sound and Image in Digital Media*, edited by Carol Vernallis, Amy Herzog, and John Richardson. Oxford: Oxford UP.

———. 2014. "Acoustemologies of the Closet." In *The Oxford Handbook of Virtuality*, edited by Mark Grimshaw, 337–48. Oxford: Oxford UP.

Collins, Karen. 2006. "Loops and Bloops: Music on the Commodore 64." *Soundscape: Journal of Media Culture* 8 (1). http://www.icce.rug.nl/~soundscapes/VOLUME08/Loops_and_bloops.shtml.

———. 2007. "Video Games Killed the Cinema Star." *Music, Sound and the Moving Image* 1 (1): 15–20.

———., ed. 2008. *From Pac-Man to Pop Music: Interactive Audio in Games and New Media*. Aldershot and Burlington, VT: Ashgate.

———. 2013. "Implications of Interactivity: What Does It Mean for Sound to Be 'Interactive'?" In *The Oxford Handbook of New Audiovisual Aesthetics*. Oxford Handbooks Online. http://www.oxford-handbooks.com/view/10.1093/oxfordhb/9780199733866.001.0001/oxfordhb-9780199733866.

DeCastro, Daniel. 2007. "Quality Video Game Music Scores, Considering the Standards Set, and Personal Reflections." Master's thesis, New York University.

Dolphin, Andrew. 2014. "Defining Sound Toys: Play as Composition." In *The Oxford Handbook of Interactive Audio*, edited by Karen Collins, Bill Kapralos, and Holly Tessler, 45–61. Oxford: Oxford UP.

Enns, Mack. 2014. "Game Scoring: FEZ, Video Game Music and Interactive Composition." In *Post Conference Proceedings*, edited by R. Hepworth-Sawyer, J. Hodgson, R. Toulson & J. L. Paterson. 2013 Innovation in Music Conference. York.

———. 2015. "Game Scoring: Towards a Broader Theory." Master's thesis, University of Western Ontario,. http://ir.lib.uwo.ca/etd/2852.

Havryliv, Mark, and Emiliano Vergara-Richards. 2006. "From Battle Metris to Symbiotic Symphony: A New Model for Musical Games." University of Wollongong Research Online.

Herber, Norbert. 2008. "The Composition-Instrument: Emergence, Improvisation and Interaction in Games and New Media." In *From Pac-Man to Pop Music: Interactive Audio in Games and New Media*, edited by Karen Collins. Aldershot and Burlington, VT: Ashgate.

Herzfeld, Gregor. 2013. "Atmospheres at Play: Aesthetical Considerations of Game Music." In *Music and Game: Perspectives on a Popular Alliance*, edited by Peter Moormann, 147–57. Berlin: Springer.

Hug, Daniel. 2011. "New Wine in New Skins: Sketching the Future of Game Sound Design." In *Game Sound Technology and Player Interaction: Concepts and Developments*, edited by Mark Grimshaw, 384–415. Hershey, PA: IGI Global.

Kamp, Michiel. 2009. "Ludic Music in Video Games." Master's Thesis, Utrecht University.

Kayali, Fares, Martin Pichlmair, and Petr Kotik. 2008. "Mobile Tangible Interfaces as Gestural Instruments." 5th International Music Workshop. Vienna, Austria.

Lendino, James. 1998. "Scoring for the Modern Computer Game." In *Proceedings of the International Computer Music Conference*. San Francisco, CA: International Computer Music Association.

Lind, Stephanie. 2016. "Active Interfaces and Thematic Events in The Legend of Zelda: Ocarina of Time." In *Music Video Games: Performance, Politics, and Play*, edited by Michael Austin, 83–106. London: Bloomsbury.

Medina-Gray, Elizabeth. 2014. "Meaningful Modular Combinations: Simultaneous Harp and Environmental Music in Two Legend of Zelda Games." In *Music in Video Games: Studying Play*, edited by Kevin J. Donnelly, William Gibbons, and Neil Lerner, 104–21. New York: Routledge.

Miller, Kiri. 2013. "Virtual and Visceral Experience in Music-Oriented Video Games." In *The Oxford Handbook of Sound and Image in Digital Media*, edited by Carol Vernallis, Amy Herzog, and John Richardson, 517–33. Oxford: Oxford UP.

Moseley, Roger. 2011. "Playing Games with Music, and Vice Versa: Performance and Recreation in Guitar Hero and Rock Band." In *New Perspective on Performance Studies: Music Across the Disciplines*, edited by Nicholas Cook. Ann Arbor: University of Michigan Press.

Moseley, Roger, and Aya Saiki. 2014. "Nintendo's Art of Musical Play." In *Music in Video Games: Studying Play*, edited by Kevin J. Donnelly, William Gibbons, and Neil Lerner, 51–76. New York: Routledge.

Nacke, Lennart, and Mark Grimshaw. 2010. "Player-Game Interaction through Affective Sound." In *Game Sound Technology and Player Interaction: Concepts and Developments*, edited by Mark Grimshaw, 264–85. Hershey, PA: IGI Global.

Phillips, Winifred. 2014. *A Composer's Guide to Game Music*. Cambridge, MA and London: MIT Press.

Rayman, Joshua. 2014. "Experimental Approaches to the Composition of Interactive Video Game Music." Master's Thesis, University of East Anglia.

Reale, Steven. 2014. "Transcribing Musical Worlds; or, Is L.A. Noire a Music Game?" In *Music in Video Games: Studying Play*, edited by Kevin J. Donnelly, William Gibbons, and Neil Lerner, 77–103. New York: Routledge.

Summers, Tim. 2012. "Video Game Music: History, Form and Genre." PhD Dissertation, University of Bristol.

———. 2016. *Understanding Video Game Music*. Cambridge: Cambridge UP.

Sweeney, Mark. 2011. "Analysing Crysis." Master's Thesis, University of Oxford.

———. 2014. "The Aesthetics of Videogame Music." PhD Dissertation, University of Oxford.

———. 2015. "Aesthetics and Social Interactions in Mmos: The Gamification of Music in Lord of the Rings Online and Star Wars: Galaxies." *The Soundtrack* 8 (1: 25–40)

———. 2016. "Isaac's Silence: Purposive Aesthetics in Dead Space." In *Ludomusicology: Approaches to Video Game Music*, edited by Michiel Kamp, Tim Summers, and Mark Sweeney 172–97. Sheffield and Bristol, CT: Equinox.

Tanaka, Hirokazu. 2002. "Shooting from the Hip: An Interview with Hip Tanaka." Gamasutra. https://www.gamasutra.com/view/feature/131356/shooting_from_the_hip_an_.php.

Tuerff, Adam. 2012. "What's in a Hat? — Fez Review." Gaming Trend. http://gamingtrend.com/game_reviews/whats-in-a-hat-fez-review/.

Vreeland, Richard. 2016. "Reflection." Disasterpeace. https://music.disasterpeace.com/track/reflection.

Ward, Paul. 2002. "Videogames as Remediated Animation." In *Screenplay: Cinema/Videogames/Interfaces*, edited by Geoff King, Tanya Krzywinska, and Geoff Siegel, 122–35. London and New York: Wallflower.

Youngdahl, Erik. 2010. "Playing the Past: History and Nostalgia in Video Games." Undergraduate Thesis, Westleyan University.

3
GAME SCORING AND GAMING TECHNOLOGY

Game scoring is distinct from other types of scoring, because it is structured entirely by gaming technology. Video game music exists within, and as a part of, a much larger medium.[1] As such, a host of priorities, values and concerns specific to that medium inhere in the game scoring process that do not inhere in other compositional activities.

Video game developers have historically exhibited a visual bias in resource allocation during game development, for instance. This "ocularcentrism" has had perhaps the most profound influence on game scoring.[2] Music is routinely subordinated to graphics when games are produced, even if players have cited music as a crucial facet of the gaming experience since the advent of home gaming consoles.[3] This situation means that the compositional process is fundamentally structured for game scorers in a peculiar way: musical ideas must be "programmable," as it were, even as the hardware and software resources earmarked for musical programming are chronically scarce. Koji Kondo (2010: 16) speaks to the game scorer's unique predicament:

> Due to the differing capabilities of game systems, the way I make music has changed. The Famicom could only produce 3 tones and didn't have a large variety of sounds, so I had to do a lot of scheming. There wasn't a lot of memory, either, so I had songs where I couldn't fit everything in, and I made songs with a limited number of sounds. When the Super Famicom came along, it had 8 tracks to work with.[4]

Kondo suggests that different gaming consoles present different possibilities for scoring, and that composers must adjust their scoring strategies accordingly. Each console provides a particular set of rules and limitations that fundamentally structures the game scorer's compositional ideation and practice in unique ways. If there is no means to program a musical idea, the game scorer must consider other options, and technology is likely to structure and restrain the game scorer's compositional process for as long as it is required to actualize a game score.[5] Kondo (2010: 18, emphasis added) continues:

DOI: 10.4324/9781003045465-3

Even now I compose with the amount of memory in mind. So I can't say the process is entirely without limitations. On *Mario Galaxy*, for example, I didn't use a live orchestra, I made the music to match up with the game, so by synchronizing with the on-screen action the songs changed interactively. For the boss battles, you power up and become stronger when you take damage, right? At that point, the orchestra grows fuller, the chorus comes in... that's game music for *you*.[6]

How specifically does gaming technology structure game scoring? Which particular technological limitations — restraints on the compositional process — do game scorers navigate when they work? To answer this question, I will provide a detailed case study of game scoring for the Nintendo Entertainment System (NES), surveying how that technology structures the compositional process for NES games in particular. This discussion requires examination of that console's sound hardware configuration, with an eye to uncovering the musical possibilities and limitations it presents to composers. As part of this examination, I survey well known moments when game scorers have, to borrow Kondo's term, "schemed" *within* the NES' sound hardware configuration to produce their celebrated game scores, consciously compromising and adjusting certain aesthetic concepts to better suit the NES hardware. I focus in particular on the way game scorers have "schemed", or navigated, the crucial first step of the scoring process, namely, the so-called "orchestration" (i.e., selection of musical instruments or timbres for different musical ends). In fact, orchestration in game scoring is radically different from orchestration in other genres, and it is game scoring's fundamental structuring by gaming technology that specifically accounts for this difference.

After my case study of the NES APU, I offer three more game scoring categories, namely, Logo Jingles, Loading Music, and Voice Acting and Vocals. The music and sounds in these categories are especially susceptible to changes in gaming technology, and so they will also illustrate how game scoring is structured by gaming technology.

Case study — the Nintendo Entertainment System's sound hardware configuration

Here I will consider the Audio Processing Unit (APU) of the NES from a specifically compositional point-of-view. By considering the musical nature of each of the NES APU's five available channels for scoring, I will discuss game scoring's general technological structure. That is, by demonstrating that all aesthetic possibilities in game scoring for the NES are in the first instance determined by the NES' sound hardware configuration, and that composers are free only insofar as they may assemble and superimpose only those musical terms that the NES APU can generate, I will concomitantly demonstrate that, in general, all compositional ideation in game scoring must occur within a broader hierarchy of technologically structured possibilities — a hierarchy that ultimately begins and ends with an idea's "programmability."[7] If musical ideas cannot be programmed, they simply cannot exist; and whether or not a musical idea can exist in game scoring is determined by the sound hardware configuration used to actualize it.

The NES sound hardware configuration is known as the APU, which is a processing unit implemented in the NES' Central Processing Unit (CPU).[8] The APU comprises five discrete channels: two pulse wave generators (PWC), a triangle wave generator (TWC), a noise generator (NGC) and a delta modulation channel (DMC) that triggers low-resolution (i.e., shorter bit-depth) audio samples. According to the official NES development Wiki ("NES-Dev Wiki", 2019):

> Each channel has a variable-rate timer clocking a waveform generator, and various modulators driven by low-frequency clocks from the frame counter. The DMC plays samples while the other channels play waveforms.

The APU's operation depends, most fundamentally, on processing units called "timers," that are "clocked" by an overarching "word-clock" count from the CPU.[9] Timers are responsible for clocking the actual waveform generators in each sound channel, and they provide modulation (i.e., sound processing) parameters for each available channel in the APU.[10] The main difference between the APU's waveform channels, and its DMC, is that the former generate their own sounds in "realtime," via analogue monophonic synthesizers, while the latter stores, recalls and triggers digital audio samples from memory. I will consider each individual channel in the APU in greater detail, in turn, in the following section.

Channel overview: pulse wave channels

The NES APU contains two identical pulse wave channels. These channels have a "bright" and "sharp" timbre, which is to say, they oscillate frequencies falling in the midrange and upper-midrange of human hearing (i.e., roughly 700 Hz to 12 kHz). As such, composers tend to use these channels to convey the primary melodies of their game scores. Moreover, since they have two *identical* PWCs at their disposal, scorers will often orchestrate their melodies as a unison, shared between both PWCs. When composers see fit to use other channels to convey their melodies, they typically use the PWCs in tandem to generate rudimentary chordal accompaniment.[11]

A total of 16 dynamic settings, ranging from silence to "full-scale," or maximum volume, and three different "volume envelope shapes," are available in the NES APU.[12] These envelope shapes include: (i) constant; (ii) linear decreasing; and (iii) looping linear decreasing, or, "sawtooth" (see Figure 3.1). However, game scorers seldom use a "constant" envelope shape *per se* ((i) in Figure 3.1). This envelope shape is deployed so that, later on, a more sophisticated envelope generator can be used to modulate it, producing a more complex shape. The "linear decreasing" shape ((ii) in Figure 3.1), on the other hand, is typically deployed to emulate the decay and release of acoustic instruments, that is, to simulate the manner in which acoustic instruments fade to silence.[13] Finally, the "sawtooth" envelope shape ((iii) in Figure 3.1) is used to produce a variety of results such as, to name a celebrated example, the electric guitar timbre heard in Takashi Tateishi's "Opening" theme for *Mega Man II*.[14]

Aside from these envelope shapes, the NES APU's two PWCs have three distinct timbres available, due to a feature known as "variable duty cycles:"

> Duty cycle is the fraction of time that a system is in an "active" state. The duty cycle of a square wave is 0.5, or 50%. Some music synthesizers, including square channels of 2A03[15] and VRC6,[16] can vary the duty cycle of their audio-frequency oscillators to obtain a subtle effect on the tone colors.[17]

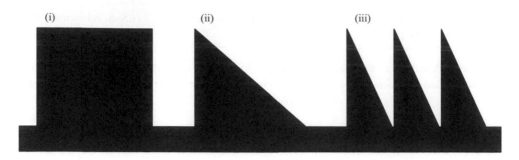

FIGURE 3.1 The three envelope shapes generated by the PWCs in the NES APU. These are (i) "constant;" (ii) "linear decreasing;" and (iii) "sawtooth."

The "system" in this definition simply refers to a sound wave, while "active state" refers to the state of a waveform above the horizontal axis. Changes in duty cycle alter the timbre of any given sound. Game scorers have four variable duty cycles available to them through the NES APU's PWCs: 12.5%, 25%, 50% and 75%. Figure 3.2 shows these duty cycles as they appear after a single pulse wave.

A lower duty cycle produces a thinner, "sharper" timbre, while a higher cycle produces a fuller, "smoother" timbre. A 50% duty cycle thus produces the fullest and smoothest sound available through the PWCs, a 12.5% duty cycle produces its thinnest and sharpest sound, and a 25% duty cycle falls directly between these timbral extremes.[19] NES game scorers are not strictly limited to using only one or another duty cycle, however. Composers can

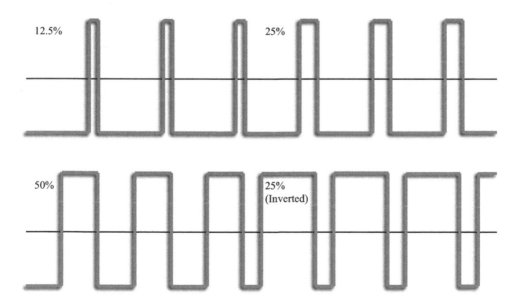

FIGURE 3.2 The duty cycles available to the NES APU pulse wave channels. The 75% duty cycle is instead offered as an inverted 25% duty cycle to illustrate that it has a nearly identical (in fact, indistinguishable to the human ear) timbral quality to a normal 25% duty cycle. Thus, the NES, for musical purposes, only has three distinguishable duty cycles for its two pulse wave channels.[18]

program the APU to produce variations in duty cycle at any given moment, even when one of the PWCs is in the midst of oscillating a particular frequency ("mid-note," as it were), which increases the score's timbral potential exponentially. More often, though, as Schartmann (2013) explains, duty cycles are switched to demarcate different musical sections, to change instrument, and to generate simple textural variety. He (2013: 44) cites an excellent example:

> The introduction to "Wood Man's Theme" in *Mega Man 2* (1989) …begins with a low-percentage duty cycle, only shifting to 50% — a much "rounder" sound — when the theme begins in earnest. Thus the music's introductory measures are played by a different "instrument" than the principal theme.

Finally, pitch-bending is available through the PWCs, thanks to the APU's "sweep unit." The "sweep unit" increases or decreases a PWC's "period," that is, its rate of oscillation, that in turn determines the frequency or "pitch" of the sound the PWC produces (higher periods of oscillation produce higher frequencies, while lower periods produce lower frequencies). Pitch-bending is most often used by NES game scorers to create a "vibrato" effect, as can be heard in Koji Kondo's "Flute" melody for *The Legend of Zelda* (1986).[20]

Channel overview: triangle wave channel

The triangle wave channel (TWC) has only a limited range of musical capabilities. This channel is most often used by game scorers to generate low frequencies, i.e., frequencies below 450 Hz, typically to set bass parts in a score. Though square waves are generally considered an ideal synthesized bass timbre, given their constant amplitude and harmonic structure, triangle waves are better-suited for this task than any other waveform available in the NES APU.[21] A triangle wave generally sounds much "smoother" and "rounder" than a pulse wave, for instance, because it alone features a regularly cyclical envelope shape and, consequently, it outputs a preponderance of odd-ordered harmonics. Moreover, the triangle wave features a less intense harmonic structure, and a longer period of decay, than do pulse waves, meaning that the TWC alone generates fundamental frequencies below 450Hz without concomitantly outputting loud harmonic content above about 7 kHz.[22]

As noted, game scorers frequently use the TWC to produce a reliably "smooth" and "round" bass line. However, the channel can also be used to generate frequencies above 450 Hz, resulting in a timbre most closely resembling that of a flute (this flute sound is featured prominently in the "Title" theme from *The Legend of Zelda*). The TWC can also generate a sound like a tom-tom drum, when used to oscillate a rapidly descending glissando. This sound is heard in various themes throughout the *Mega Man II* soundtrack, most notably in the "Get a Weapon," "Bubbleman," "Crashman," "Heatman," and "Dr. Wily Stage 1" themes.[23]

The TWC can generate higher frequencies than the PWC generates, because of its special timer. That said, we shall see that these frequencies are typically used to produce a "glitch" effect. The highest frequency that the NES PWC can generate is approximately 12.4 kHz.[24] Humans are only capable of hearing frequencies from 20 Hz to 20 kHz, and even then most hearing capable humans older than 18 do not hear very well above 16 kHz. This fact means that the PWCs are not capable of servicing the upper expanses of human hearing (i.e., 12–20 kHz). The TWC, on the other hand, can generate supersonic frequencies (i.e., frequencies over 20 kHz), because its timer is clocked by the CPU rather than the APU.[25]

Oscillating supersonic frequencies comprises a compositional technique for silencing the triangle channel, without sacrificing valuable CPU cycles from the 2A03[26] for a "silence" request.[27] When game scorers experimented with this technique, however, they found that an oddly percussive sonic artifact — i.e., a "popping" noise — sounded whenever the TWC returned to oscillating in the audible range. The supersonic frequency is initially generated when scorers write a timer value of zero that, according to the programming equation $f_{tri} = f_{CPU}/(32*(t + 1))$ (where "f_{tri}" is the resultant frequency of the triangle wave, "f_{CPU}" is the base frequency of the CPU and "t" is the timer value), generates the channel's highest available frequency. This frequency is so high, however, that the mixer receives an irregular and abrupt sequencer value, for which it cannot compensate. The latter results in "artefacting," that is, audible distortion, most closely resembling a "popping" noise. This "popping" can be heard in the score for *Mega Man II*, most notably in the "Crash Man" theme.

The TWC has a rhythmic advantage over the other APU channels, because of the accuracy of its timer. Developers of the NES APU felt it necessary to imbue only the TWC with the clocking accuracy required to achieve "pinpoint" rhythmic precision, that is, developers deemed it necessary to devote a crucial portion of only the TWC's CPU-load to achieving rhythmic rather than textural precision. This additional feature thus technologically structures — it provides the only technical means for achieving — the TWC's primary compositional function, namely, setting bass parts.

As noted, the NES APU's two PWCs are more likely to be used to set tracks with sustained pitches and upper-midrange frequency content, which is to say, for setting melody and rhythm section parts. The bass sections in NES game scores, however, are often very repetitive and melodically simple, and require rhythmic accuracy over and above anything else. That said, I should quickly note that this requirement does not mean that composers can only use the TWC to provide bass support for upper-register melodies. Some composers have even gone so far as to use a TWC bass line for the primary melody. This inversion of compositional convention can most notably be heard in the "Underworld" theme from Kondo's score for *Super Mario Bros.* (1985).

Channel overview: noise channel

The NES APU noise generator channel (NGC) oscillates "noise," i.e., sound featuring an irregular or "random" waveform. Actually, the NGC outputs two different kinds of noise: "white noise" and "periodic noise."[28] Most commonly, however, the NGC is set to "white noise mode" and used to set the percussive elements of a game score. In fact, scores most often use the NGC to orchestrate the components of a typical "trap" drum set: kick drum, snare drum, hi-hat, etc. The sound of a snare drum ((i) in Figure 3.3), for instance, emerges when scorers set the NGC to "white noise" mode, and shape its dynamic envelope so it features a rapid "attack" and gradual "decay" and "release" contours. An open hi-hat ((ii) in Figure 3.3), on the other hand, emerges when scorers filter the NGC's "white noise" through an envelope featuring gradual "attack" *and* "release" phases, while the sound of a closed hi-hat ((iii) in Figure 3.3) emerges from exactly the same envelope contour, but with a rapid "release" replacing the open hi-hat's gradual contour.

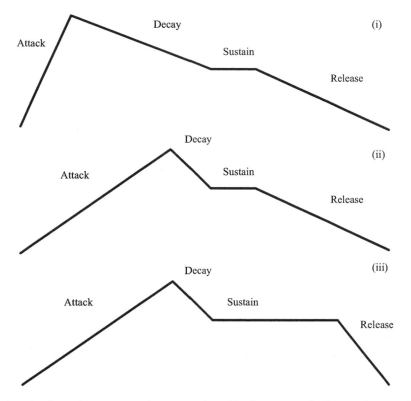

FIGURE 3.3 The three dynamic envelopes mentioned in the paragraph above. They are (i) a snare drum, (ii) an open hi-hat, and (iii) a closed hi-hat.

The NGC's "periodic noise" mode is less frequently evoked by game scorers, and it is seldom used to orchestrate the percussion elements of a score because of its generally harsher, more metallic texture. Periodic noise is a sound with an irregular waveform generated by a series of frequencies that repeat — which results in a more "structured" sound than white noise, for instance, and that may even sound melodic. In fact, scorers occasionally even use the mode to set a score's melody. NES game scorers simply prefer the NGC's "white noise" mode for setting percussive elements because it has less pitched content and, thus, sounds more like acoustic percussion instruments. That said, braver NES game scorers have occasionally experimented with using the NGC's "periodic" mode to produce unprecedented effects. A good example can be heard in the "Quick Man" theme from *Mega Man II*. In this case, the NGC switches rapidly back and forth between "white noise" and "periodic noise" modes, to produce a complex rhythmic pattern. The music thus underscores and heightens the intensity of the gameplay, even as Tateishi incrementally increases the tempo all the while.

Channel overview: delta modulation channel

The delta modulation channel (DMC) is unique amongst all the channels comprising the NES APU, in that it triggers rather than oscillates, that is, it is used to sequence audio samples stored in its memory. Though the NES' sampling abilities are primitive by modern standards, the very fact that the NES featured a DMC for triggering samples when the NES was first released, in 1985, was extraordinary for any home video game console of its time.[29] Moreover, the DMC expanded the breadth of sounds a game scorer could produce exponentially.

Through the technology of the DMC, NES game scorers support their compositions using any (sampled) sounds they want, albeit in compromised "quality."[30] Game scorers most often use the DMC to produce sound effects, vocal "bites" and percussion.[31] Koji Kondo, for instance, used the DMC extensively in his score for *Super Mario Bros. 3* (1988 in Japan, 1990 in North America), mainly to sample the percussion instruments (i.e., bongos, timpani and tom-toms) heard in the eight different "World Map" themes players access sequentially as they progress through the game. The DMC allowed Kondo to produce increasingly exotic orchestrations and rhythmic arrangements for each map theme.

NES game scoring techniques

Now that I have surveyed some of the capacities of each of the five channels that comprise the NES APU, whose sonic capacities in turn comprise the entire sonic palette available to NES game scorers, I turn my attention to exploring some of the more conventional compositional uses game scorers devise for these channels. In so doing, I will elucidate "the sound" of game scoring's technological structure. I examine, in turn, so-called: (i) "2-channel echo;" (ii) "1-channel echo;" (iii) "arpeggios;" (iv) "triangle kick drums;" and (v) "melodic samples."[32] After I have examined these compositional uses, I will briefly demonstrate how game scorers draw all of these disparate musical terms together, into a cohesive sonic unity, using the NES APU's mixer.

To be clear, many of the game scoring techniques detailed below would ramify in traditional musicological analyses as "sound effects" or post-production editing devices. At present, we are accustomed to the ability to apply effects such as "echo" or "reverb" with the click of a button in a modern digital audio workstation (DAW) such as Apple's Logic Pro. At least in the case of the NES APU, game scorers do not have such a luxury. Furthermore, in the case of all game scoring, the ability to generate such effects depends entirely on the capacities of the gaming technology at hand.

This phenomenon is not entirely new, though, as echo effects appear in many programmatic orchestral works. Baroque scores from the seventeenth and eighteenth Centuries, such as Arcangelo Corelli's *Christmas Concerto* (1714), often contained echoes as imitative devices, whereby a musical motto was played by an orchestra and then repeated immediately afterwards much more quietly. Similarly, game scorers do not simply sample and replicate echoes but, rather, create echo effects through musical means. Sound effects, in game scoring, then, are musical devices, rather than mere ornamentation.

NES game scoring techniques: 2-channel echo

One of the most common game scoring techniques for the NES APU is so-called "2-channel echo." As an acoustic phenomenon, echo is difficult to produce for NES game scores because few channels are available to orchestrate it.[33] In fact, the only channels composers can use to create a 2-channel echo are the PWCs, since the phenomenon requires identical sounds to be played at decreasing volumes and ever lengthening delay rates. And the same is true, of course, for reverberation effects.[34]

Scorers can generate a reverberation or echo effect by setting a melody between both PWCs, each successive iteration played in alternating channels at successively lower amplitudes and ever lengthening delay rates. The "African Mines" theme, composed by Hiroshige Tonomura for *Ducktales* (1989), provides a clear example of this effect in game scoring, in this case deployed to evoke the reverberant acoustics of an underground mine.[35] Neil Baldwin likewise uses the effect in his "Puzzle Room" theme for *Magician* (1990), the effect here evoking the cramped, dark and confusing landscapes of each puzzle level. As its name suggests, however, 2-channel echo requires a significant amount of the NES APU's available resources, monopolizing two of only five available channels (Table 3.1). Game scorers thus developed a technique for creating echo and reverberation effect using only one voice very early on in the NES' development. I explain this technique next.

NES game scoring techniques: single-channel echo

Using various methods, each developed by individual scorers to conserve APU resources, NES game scorers create "echo-like" sounds using only one channel (Table 3.2). Geoff Follin, for instance, achieves this effect by combining dramatic dynamic leaps with pitch bends (downward glissandi). The effect can be heard clearly in Follin's score for *Wolverine* (1991), a licensed action video game based on the Marvel Comics superhero of the same name. Follin's theme for "Level 1" includes descending melodic accents from one of the PWCs. Follin adjusts the volume envelope of each accent to decay rapidly at first, but release slowly, and he deploys downward pitch-bends to emphasize the lengthened release time. This technique results in an eerie pulse wave, accompanied by what sounds like an echo, thereby audifying *Wolverine*'s dystopic surroundings.

Tim Follin, Geoff Follin's brother, provides another good example of single-channel echo, and the highly individuated nature of its compositional production in game scoring. In this case, the effect appears in Follin's score for the feature film-licensed game, *Indiana Jones and the Last Crusade* (1991, Taito).[36] Instead of using repeating and diminishing dynamic leaps combined with pitch bends to create the effect, however, as his brother did in the score for *Wolverine*, Tim Follin here exploited the psychoacoustic phenomenon known as "subjective loudness," whereby lower register pitches have less subjective loudness than

TABLE 3.1 A few NES tracks that prominently feature 2-channel echo

Composer	Track	Game (year)
Nobuyuki Hara Shinichi Seya Naoki Kodaka	"Title"	*Journey to Silius* (1990)
Nobuyuki Hara Shinichi Seya Naoki Kodaka	"Stage 1 ~ Stage 5"	*Journey to Silius* (1990)
Hiroshige Tonomura	"African Mines"	*Ducktales* (1989)
Neil Baldwin	"Puzzle Room"	*Magician* (1990)
Takashi Tateishi	"Flash Man"	*Mega Man II* (1988)
Hiroyuki Masuno	"Main Theme"	*Déjà Vu* (1990)
Koji Kondo	"Title"	*The Legend of Zelda* (1986)

TABLE 3.2 A few NES tracks that prominently feature single-channel echo

Composer(s)	Track	Game (year)
Iku Mizutani Kouichi Yamanishi	"Prologue"	Shadow of the Ninja (1991)
Iku Mizutani Kouichi Yamanishi	"Stage 2: Underground Sewers"	Shadow of the Ninja (1991)
Tsukasa Tawada	"Stage 1: Evil Forest"	Moon Crystal (1992)
Geoff Follin	"Level 1"	Wolverine (1991)
Tim Follin	"Tank – Cutscene"	Indiana Jones and the Last Crusade (1991)
Tim Follin Geoff Follin	"Title Screen"	Silver Surfer (1990)
David Warhol George Sanger David Hayes	"Wendy's Theme"	Maniac Mansion (1990)

higher pitches.[37] In the "Tank – Cutscene" theme, for instance, Follins sets repeating downward pitch bends in one PWC to create a single-channel echo. Each pitch of the theme thus sounds as though its volume swells, even though each pitch features a slow, constant fade throughout. This technique, combined with the downward pitch bends, creates a reverberant effect using only a single PWC.

Neil Baldwin developed yet another method for producing single-channel echo in his score for *Hero Quest*, an unreleased NES game developed in 1991. While the above examples involve single-channel echoes applied to sustaining pitches, Baldwin wanted to apply echo to a pattern of changing eighth notes for the "Final Track" theme of *Hero Quest* (1991). This goal required a different technique. Baldwin thus decided to compose quieter duplicates of each note of the melody, delayed by roughly an eighth note. This operation produces a much larger sense of space in the "Final Track" than elsewhere in the score, an effect further reinforced by the deployment of strong "transient" instrumentation, such as percussion.

NES game scoring techniques: arpeggio and psychoacoustic block chords

An arpeggio is sometimes referred to as a "broken chord," since its component pitches are articulated sequentially rather than simultaneously. Arpeggios are extremely important in NES game scoring but difficult to produce, again because of the limited number of channels available in the NES APU. Triadic chords are simply impossible to produce via the NES APU, in fact, because only two of its channels, namely, the PWCs, are capable of producing identical timbres simultaneously. Game scorers thus face yet another technical dilemma: triadic chords are fundamental to the music they compose, yet they lack the technical means to produce them. To solve this dilemma, NES game scorers produce triadic block chords psychoacoustically, as it were. That is, rather than sounding all three pitches of a triadic chord simultaneously, game scorers arpeggiate the pitches so quickly that the human ear is incapable of distinguishing one waveform from another. Consequently, the ear "sums" the component waveforms into a single triadic unity.

As a musical figure, these "psychoacoustic triads" are more typically associated by historians with Commodore 64 game scores and its MOS Technology Sound Interface Device (SID).[38] However, facing similar technical limitations, NES game scorers —

TABLE 3.3 NES tracks that feature arpeggio and psychoacoustic block chords prominently

Composer(s)	Track	Game (year)
Yoshinori Sasaki	"Rising"	*Castlevania III* (1990)
Jun Funahashi		
Yukie Morimoto		
Tim Follin	"BGM 1"	*Silver Surfer* (1990)
Geoff Follin		
Neil Baldwin	"Level 2"	*James Bond Jr.* (1991)
Alberto Gonzalez	"Title Screen"	*Asterix* (1993)
Ron Hubbard	"Level 1: The Streets"	*Skate or Die 2* (1990)
Alberto Gonzalez	"Act 6: The Mountains"	*The Smurfs* (1994)
Charles Deenan	"Title Screen"	*M.C. Kids* (1992)

particularly those working in Europe, where the SID remains popular — have adopted "psychoacoustic" arpeggiated chords. The technique can be heard in, among other scores, *Silver Surfer* (Tim and Geoff Follin, 1990), *Magician* (Neil Baldwin, 1990), *Skate or Die 2* (Ron Hubbard, 1990), *Solstice* (Tim Follin, 1990), *Darkman* (Jonathan Dunn, 1991), *M.C. Kids* (Charles Deenan, 1992) and *Asterix* (Alberto González, 1993) (Table 3.3).

NES game scoring techniques: TWC kick drum sounds

As noted, percussion in NES game scores is typically set using the NGC and the DMC. Game scorers wanting to give their kick drums extra "punch," for instance, pair noise from the NGC with audio samples of a kick drum triggered in the DMC. However, the latter may require simply too much storage memory to be a feasible component of a game score, and so composers must resort to other means to produce the effect. One such means involves oscillating a triangle wave bass part in the TWC, but rapidly bending its pitches downwards, that is, by orchestrating extremely fast downward glissandi in a bass line produced by the TWC. These glissandi, when filtered through an extremely short sustain and release envelope, produce a sound more like a kick drum than a low frequency triangle wave. Like the "psychoacoustic block chord" technique elucidated in the section immediately above, this "kick drum" technique is also especially popular in European game scores for the NES, and can be heard in scores for *Hero Quest*, *Silver Surfer* and *Robocop 3* (Jeroen Tel, 1993) (Table 3.4).[39]

NES game scoring techniques: melodic samples

NES game scorers use the DMC mostly to trigger audio samples of vocals, percussion and sound effects. It is simpler to use the DMC to produce these sounds, because they rely less on pitch than timbre and timing to produce their musical effects. Using the DMC melodically is much more complicated than using the NES APU's other four channels, because the DMC has specific limitations with regard to "re-pitching" samples:

1. samples may only be lowered in pitch;
2. lowering a sample's pitch results in a slower playback speed;

TABLE 3.4 NES tracks that prominently feature the TWC kick drum technique

Composer(s)	Track	Game (year)
Neil Baldwin	"Unused Music 1"	*Hero Quest* (1991, unreleased)
Neil Baldwin	"Unused Music 2"	*Hero Quest* (1991, unreleased)
Tim Follin	"BGM 1"	*Silver Surfer* (1990
Geoff Follin		
Jeroen Tel	"Title Theme"	*Robocop 3* (1992)
Alberto Gonzalez	"Act 6: The Mountains"	*The Smurfs* (1994)
Mari Yamaguchi	"Charge Man"	*Mega Man V* (1992)
Mari Yamaguchi	"Get a Weapon"	*Mega Man V* (1992)

3. sixteen pitches are available, including the original sample's pitch, though these are not arranged chromatically; and
4. some notes output slightly sharp or flat.[40]

Because of these limitations, each of the highest DMC pitches in an NES game score require their own samples. Lowering the pitch of these samples causes them to sound at a slower rate, producing distortion and significant "tonal artefacting" (i.e., detuning). A full chromatic scale is difficult to obtain through re-pitching, because the 15 other set pitches are not arranged chromatically, even when starting with a tonic of C4. *Retro Game Audio* (2012: "NES Audio: Sunsoft Bass and Melodic Samples") outlines the resultant pitches with a starting sample at a pitch of C in the fourth octave:

C4 G3 E3 C3 A2 G2 F2 D2
C2 B1 A1 G1 F1 E1 D1 C1

Yet even these notes are not exactly correct, as some notes output sharp or flat. Table 3.5 is the pitch table for the DMC from NES-Dev.

The "period hex values" correspond to information read by the DMC memory reader as waveform period lengths. In the table above, these periods are converted to frequencies in Hz and finally notes with deviation given in cents, where one cent is 1/100 of a semitone. NES game scorers may play their desired samples at only these frequencies.

The games created by Sunsoft during the latter half of the NES' shelf life contained some of the few scores to use DMC samples melodically. *Batman: Return of the Joker* (1991), *Hebereke* (1991), *Journey to Silius* (1990), *Gremlins 2* (1990), *Gimmick!* (1992) and *Super Spy Hunter* (1992) all use DPCM samples primarily to add definition to the bass sections of their scores (Table 3.6). In these scores, a real electric bass guitar was sampled by Sunsoft composer Naoki Kodaka and played back through DPCM. These samples accompany a triangle wave bass, and the combination of these two channels results in a sound with the smooth and round timbre of a triangle wave but bearing the characteristic textural markers of an electric bass guitar.

In order to create this sound, however, a chromatic scale was necessary for the sampled bass section. Kodaka responded to the strange pitch table of the NES DMC by sampling the bass at five different notes:

A# B C C# D

TABLE 3.5 The DMC channel pitch table from NES-Dev

#	Period hex value	Frequency	Note
1	$1AC	4181.71 Hz	C-8 -1.78c
2	$17C	4709.93 Hz	D-8 +4.16c
3	$154	5264.04 Hz	E-8 -3.29c
4	$140	5593.04 Hz	F-8 +1.67c
5	$11E	6257.95 Hz	G-8 -3.86c
6	$0FE	7046.35 Hz	A-8 +1.56c
7	$0E2	7919.35 Hz	B-8 +3.77c
8	$0D6	8363.42 Hz	C-9 -1.78c
9	$0BE	9419.86 Hz	D-9 +4.16c
10	$0A0	11186.1 Hz	F-9 +1.67c
11	$08E	12604.0 Hz	G-9 +8.29c
12	$080	13982.6 Hz	A-9 -12.0c
13	$06A	16884.6 Hz	C-10 +14.5c
14	$054	21306.8 Hz	E-10 +17.2c
15	$048	24858.0 Hz	G-10 -15.9c
16	$036	33143.9 Hz	C-11 -17.9c

From these five notes he could then use the re-pitch function of the DMC to lower these samples, resulting in something close to a full chromatic scale. Since these samples mimic the notes of the TWC, the discrepancies in pitch and timing — as stated, lowering pitch is not an exact process and causes slower playback — created by the DMC are less noticeable to the listener. In fact, these discrepancies are more likely to be interpreted as musically interesting, rather than inaccurate, if they are noticed by the listener (Table 3.6).

TABLE 3.6 A few NES tracks that feature melodic samples

Composer(s)	Track	Game (year)
Masashi Kageyama Naohisa Morota	"Strange Memories of Death"	*Gimmick!* (1992)
Nobuyuki Hara Shinichi Seya Naoki Kodaka	"Stage 3"	*Journey to Silius* (1990)
Nobuyuki Hara Shinichi Seya Naoki Kodaka	"Hebe Adventure"	*Hebereke* (1991)
Nobuyuki Hara Shinichi Seya Naoki Kodaka	"Stages 2 & 6: Desert of Doom / Weapons Factory"	*Super Spy Hunter* (1992)
Naoki Kodaka	"Title Screen / Ending"	*Fester's Quest* (1989)
Hidenori Maezawa	"Stage 1 — Lightning and Grenades"	*Super C* (1990)
Ryuichi Nitta	"World 1: Ice Rock Island"	*Fire 'n Ice* (1993)

Putting it all together: the APU mixer

Exact calculation of the resultant amplitude of all the channels in the NES is almost impossible, due to the APU's non-linear mixing scheme. Each channel contains its own digital-to-analog converter, or DAC, to convert digital information to an analog audio signal. These DACs are implemented in such a way that non-linear interactions between channels are produced. For example, a high value in the DMC output unit will reduce the volume of the TWC and NGC, while a high TWC output has no effect on the volume of the DMC.

Koji Kondo used this peculiarity of the NES APU to his advantage in the score he produced for *Super Mario Bros.* (1985). Kondo re-set the dynamic output of the DMC simply to limit the TWC's dynamic output. In fact, Kondo did not even use the DMC to trigger samples, as is its intended function. Rather, he used it as a limiter.[41] This example is not meant to be taken as a unique case, though, as the non-linear nature of the NES APU mixer affects every decision the NES game scorer makes. Since the manipulation of one channel will likely affect another's output, the entire arrangement changes with, say, a duty cycle change on the PWC. NES game scorers must know not only how their orchestrations will affect the output of a single channel, but also how that output influences the output of every other channel as well.

Case study summary

As a case study of the NES APU, and the way it structures game scoring for the NES, this case study is by no means exhaustive. It is not meant to be. Neither is it meant to stand alone as a work dedicated to increasing knowledge about NES hardware. It should be taken simply as an elucidation of the technical structure of game scoring in general, concretized through a case study of the NES APU.

Other sound hardware configurations across gaming history have different musical capabilities, and so case studies of these would surely yield different game scoring strategies. Even sound hardware configurations released alongside the NES APU had significantly different capabilities. I chose to analyze the NES APU in this chapter because it comes from an era in game scoring when hardware-based limitations were more "visible" than they are in modern game scoring. In fact, due to the rise of the Sony PlayStation and optical game storage, hardware-based limitations became less visible in game scoring around the time that Belinkie (1999) penned his seminal study on video game music.[42] The increase in storage space for video games offered by optical storage meant that software developers could store music files in their games alongside, say, texture graphics image files. Thus, hardware developers no longer designed dedicated synthesizers and noise generators, to name two examples, for particular sound hardware configurations. Similarly, game scorers no longer "programmed" analogue synthesizers, as all sound operations could now be performed in software, or at some layer of removal from actual instruments. This is not to say that hardware limitations no longer had any bearing on game scoring ideation, but that they began to exert more indirect control over how games were designed and programmed. For example, larger games (re-)introduced the need for load times in games, thus ensuring that every gameplay experience past cartridge technology is broken up into pre-loaded "chunks" or "sandboxes." This example is only one of many, of how modern gaming technology structures the experience of modern gaming, and thus game scoring.

It bears mentioning here that software programmers perform the main work of bridging the gap between game designers, game scorers and video game hardware. Even in the NES era, game developers had to program their own music systems for games to produce sound — the "development" packages sent by Nintendo to developers never included a sound driver, and even Koji Kondo himself famously had to write his own. Developers often re-used sound drivers in subsequent games because of the complexity in programming them, thus resulting in a signature audio profile such as the "Sunsoft sound," to name one example I covered in this case study.

In the next section of this chapter, I offer three more game scoring categories, namely, Logo Jingles, Loading Music, and Voice Acting and Vocals, and describe them via examples that further illustrate the structural relationship between gaming technology and game scoring activity.

Game scoring taxonomy: Logo Jingles

Logo Jingles are short sections of music meant to accompany static or animated logo visuals for video game production and development companies. Gamers typically hear these before any other audio in a given game score. These jingles are similar to film production and distribution company logo jingles that appear "before" a film begins, such as the infamous synthesizer slide that ascends and crescendos alongside the "THX" surround sound logo, recorded for films that use that technology. However, unlike film logo jingles, many Logo Jingles in games may be skipped at a player's press of a button. Gamers typically start and restart games many times over the course of playing through them, and so this function is typically a relief to them.

As with their position in film scores, it is difficult to say whether Logo Jingles occupy a meaningful place within a game score. Technically, developers program these sections of music as part of the limited memory space of games. However, as part of the aural experience of playing a game, Logo Jingles seem to exist "outside" gameplay and game scores — even more than Menu Music, for example. Their function is not to increase immersion, but to signify the efforts (and/or financial investment) of game development and production companies.

Nevertheless, as players hear the same Logo Jingles every time they start the same game, these jingles may become routine signifiers of anticipatory excitement, and, as with other sounds in a game score, they may leave an impression on players. For example, the vocal jingle for the "SEGA" logo for games in the *Sonic the Hedgehog* series is probably the most recognizable Logo Jingle in gaming history, though it was scored only because of a unique development situation that involved severe time constraints and a surplus of cartridge read-only memory, or ROM storage space. *Sonic* creator Yuji Naka (2005: 5) explains that the development team was working on an animated "Sound Test" screen to round out the game, but they did not have time to complete it:[43]

> But the biggest thing I remember we had that we didn't use in *Sonic 1* was the break-dancing. We had this idea for the sound test. The composer for the game was one of the members of Dreams Come True, a famous Japanese band, so we wanted to do something special for the game's music. See, we wanted to have a separate sound-test screen with an animation of Sonic break-dancing while a "Sonic Band" played

the game music. We were working on the images, and had enough space left on the cartridge memory for it, but once again time constraints prevented us from putting it in the program.

As I explained in my breakdown of the NES APU, vocal samples take much more memory to sound as though a human voice is voicing them, than it takes for synthesizers to play tones, in older programmable sound generator (PSG)-based sound hardware configurations. "Samples" are made up of actual audio files, while PSG synthesizers only require programmed instructions to perform (much like a player-piano). Accordingly, Naka (2005: 5) did not consider incorporating vocal samples into *Sonic* until the development team was forced to scrap the "break-dancing" sequence:

> So what should we do with that leftover space? I suddenly had an epiphany! It said to me… "SE-GA!" It came from our TV commercials, and that became the game's startup sound. I thought it made a good impression when you heard it, right? Though to fit it in, we had to delete all the break-dancing picture data we had made up to that point. [Naoto] Oshima was heartbroken, since we didn't need his pictures anymore. But seriously, that sound alone took up 1/8 of the 4-megabit ROM!

The "SEGA" jingle was originally written for a Japanese television commercial for an early Sega console, the SG-1000, which was released exclusively in Japan in 1983. As a prelude to *Sonic the Hedgehog* — a game that was designed to compete with Nintendo's successful *Super Mario* series — the jingle, along with the Sega Genesis, a 16-bit successor console to the Sega Master System that was designed to compete with the NES, helped introduce the company to North America. In this historical context, human voices in game scores were both rare and novel for gamers, and so the "SEGA" jingle made a strong impression on them.

The "SEGA" jingle is also the first sound players hear upon booting *Sonic*, and thus, in the context of a *Sonic* game score, has no music that precedes it. The two chords of the jingle, an Eb-Major chord followed by a C-Major chord, performed by male choir vocals and a bass synthesizer, are a minor third interval apart, which, in certain musical contexts, evokes tragedy and sadness. However, an isolated musical context does not allow for a minor third to evoke these emotions, since there are no other intervals to compare it to. Actually, the minor third interval is also a common interval for the two notes of a standard doorbell sound — another isolated musical context. Thus, there are many factors that contribute to the "attention-grabbing" effect of the "SEGA" Logo Jingle: First, the jingle includes sung human vocals, which was both a rarity and novelty for this time in gaming history; second, the gaming context of the jingle allows for it to communicate in isolation; and third, the interval is the same used in another "attention-grabbing" sound, and so the effect is reinforced by the usual reaction to a doorbell.

In 2017, the "SEGA" Logo Jingle was re-used in *Sonic Mania* (2017), an homage to the two-dimensional *Sonic* games of the 1990s (see Figure 3.4):

Sonic Mania was released for multiple modern platforms, though its developers aimed to re-capture the *Sonic* experience of the 16-bit era by incorporating level design, graphics and music from the original Genesis *Sonic* games. In fact, the composer, Tee Lopes, incorporated the "SEGA" logo jingle in its original, "16-bit quality" format, instead of updating it to a more polished, or modern sound.[45] Thus, the original Genesis vocal-reproduction quality was more desirable for the score, as it represented the "sound" of *Sonic* in the 16-bit gaming era.

FIGURE 3.4 The logo and title screen for *Sonic Mania Plus* (2017) one of the Nintendo Switch versions of the game. Note the pixellated, rough edges on the "SEGA" logo that could be easily smoothed out in a modern high-definition game. The "white" background used for the logo screen is off-white to represent the presentation of whites on earlier cathode ray tube (CRT) television sets.[44]

Game scoring taxonomy: Loading Music

Once players navigate a game's menu and decide to "start" gameplay, they may be greeted with a loading screen, particularly if it is a modern game. The issue of loading times for games has persisted from the advent of disk- and especially disc-based games to the present, mainly due to the speeds at which data is read from a storage medium such as a hard drive or CD-ROM, for instance.[46] Essentially, these speeds have not increased at the same rate that Graphics Processing Units (GPUs) and CPUs have increased in performance, meaning that more impressive visuals or "graphics" can be rendered — that take up more space — but they still load at the same speed.[47] Online multiplayer games involve synchronizing each player's connection to the game, which can take even longer.

Loading screens are (typically) definitive breaks from game operation, and many gamers treat them like television commercials, using the opportunity to prepare a snack or some other task while they wait, and so their level of investment in what is happening on-screen is much lower. As with television commercials, the changes in audio for loading screens can signify to gamers that they need to return their attention to the screen. That said, modern loading screens do not typically feature Loading Music, and so the change in audio is usually a fade to silence when loading begins, and, when the loading is complete, a fade into gameplay audio. Thus, loading screens for modern games also yield long "rests" in their scores, and do not encourage engagement or immersion.

From an aleatoric composer's perspective, silent loading screens are successors to John Cage's famous "4'33" composition. As with Cage's piece, the only musical parameter involved in a silent loading screen is the length that it "plays" for. As with Cage's fixed duration for his piece, load times for games are generally stable, and so players become accustomed to specific rest lengths in their scores. The difference between "4'33" and silent loading screens is that Cage arbitrarily determined the duration of his piece, while load times for games are dependent on many gaming technology and design factors. Nevertheless, these technologically-determined durations are somewhat arbitrary in a *musical* sense, and game scorers have the burden of accommodating them in their scores.

Cassette tape-based games for the Commodore 64 have loading screens due to the rate at which the data is processed from tape. The "Ocean Loaders" for Ocean-developed games are famous examples of loading screens with music scored specifically for them. Table 3.7 is a list of Ocean Loaders that were each used in multiple Commodore games:

In the first generation of CD-ROM-based games, such as those for the Sega Saturn and the Sony PlayStation, some developers seemed to want to mitigate the breaks in continuity caused by load times, since there exist more examples of *interactive* loading screens in this era. Interactive loading screens include some form of interactivity, such as a mini-game or a manipulable animation that is accessible while the main game loads. For example, the original *Ridge Racer* (1993) developed by Namco for PlayStation, contains *Galaxian* (1979), a much earlier Namco arcade game, in its loading screen before the main game. If players defeat all the enemies on this loading screen, they unlock access to all the cars available in *Ridge Racer* once it loads.

Unfortunately, many developers have been discouraged from developing Interactive Loading Screens, due to a successful patent application by Namco that was active from 1995 to 2015. The abstract for Namco's patent on Interactive Loading Screens runs as follows:

> A recording medium, a method of loading games program code, and a games machine is provided. The recording medium has a program code relating to an auxiliary game and a program code relating to a main game [...] Unnecessary wastage of time can be prevented by first loading the smaller, auxiliary game program code into the games machine, before the main-game program code is loaded, then loading the main-game program code while the auxiliary game is running.[48]

The patent is carefully worded to avoid considering interactive loading screens as a creative choice for game designers. Rather, they are figured as a special type of coding that involves a game loading an "auxiliary program" while the "main program" loads. Namco was successful in their patent application because they referred to this feature as a *mechanism* made possible by software programming. Their patent therefore raises a crucial question for the study of games, and hence game scores: are video games (copyright-able) cultural artifacts

TABLE 3.7 Loading Music for popular Commodore 64 Ocean loading screens

Title	Composer	First appearance	Description
"Ocean Loader 1" (3m31s)	Martin Galway	*Hyper Sports* (1985)	First loader music to become popular, and used in multiple games.
"Ocean Loader 2" (4m23s)	Martin Galway	*Comic Bakery* (1985)	A slower remix of "Ocean Loader 1," and the most used of all the Ocean Loaders.
"Ocean Loader 3" (2m47s)	Peter Clarke	*Slap Fight* (1987)	A composition that begins the same as the first and second Ocean Loaders, and then changes to a different, more upbeat tune.
"Ocean Loader 4" (3m10s)	Jonathan Dunn	*Target Renegade* (1988)	A completely new composition that relies on a driving bass line.
"Ocean Loader 5" (3m10s)	Jonathan Dunn	*Operation Wolf* (1988)	A remix of "Ocean Loader 4," with different melodic accents over the same bass line.

or (patent-able) programmed "systems?" Normally it is difficult to apply for a patent on creative practice with success, but in this case it is less clear if the mechanism constitutes that or a special programming technique. As I have shown with the score for *FEZ*, above, special programming techniques constitute much of the creative work involved in game scoring, and so in that example it is clear that creative practice and software programming are one and the same.

Namco's patent was damaging to creative practice in game development because it prevented other companies from developing interactive loading screens. While the patent did not prevent companies from employing Loading Music, it did prevent them from developing auxiliary mini-games for loading screens. So, if Loading Music is present at all in games from 1995 to 2015, it is typically non-interactive, though the length at which it plays for is determined by the loading time, and that is dependent on both design and gameplay factors.

Game scoring taxonomy: voice acting and vocals

As I have explained in the section on Logo Jingles, and elsewhere in this chapter, human voices are a desirable component of game scores, though they tend to use a large amount of valuable memory. The first generation of CD-based games expanded the amount of memory available to designers, which resulted in a major increase in voice acting and vocals for game scores. While it is now the norm for major games to have voice acting for main characters and cut-scenes, the era that introduced the CD-ROM still included games released on cartridge, most famously for the Nintendo 64. As a result, cartridge games such as those for N64 typically have very different scores from original PlayStation games, for instance, that are filled with vocals. *Ocarina*, for example, only contains various grunts and yelps for Link, and the entire story is in text. In fact, Link has only spoken real words in very rare instances in the entire *Zelda* series, even as audio memory limits increased for each game's platform. This situation is more of an anomaly than the norm, as most major games include spoken dialogue for their avatars.[49]

Voice acting is most common in cut-scenes for games that involve narrative-advancing dialogue. For example, *Metal Gear Solid* utilizes voice acting for all its cut-scenes, in order to develop a paranoid, tension-filled espionage-driven world and story. The game's drama is supported by characters who feel instantly real, thanks to human voice acting.

Arcades that feature many arcade game machines contain sound textures rivalling Phil Spector's "Wall of Sound," thus making it difficult for games to stand out in the soundscape, though arcade game developers can use vocal sound effects to accomplish this feat. For example, the vocal sound effects of *Street Fighter II* distinguish the game's score from, for instance, the drone of the "Chomp" sound effect in *Pac-Man* (1980). Each character in *SF2* has a special attack that, when performed by players, triggers an accompanying vocal sound effect. The most famous and recognizable of these effects is the one scored for Ryu and Ken's "*hadouken*" or "wave motion fist" attack, in which the performer thrusts their palms forward and sends a "surge" or ball of energy towards their opponent (see Figure 3.5):

Since long-distance attacks are an alternate strategy in *SF2*, players may wish to dodge their opponents, keep at a safe distance and frequently use the "*hadouken*" attack to wear them down. This strategy will result in many instances of the "*Hadouken!*" vocal sound effect, which is the same for both Ryu and Ken, in all regions of the game's release. Thus, in Western gaming markets at least, the Japanese vocal effect stood out amongst otherwise

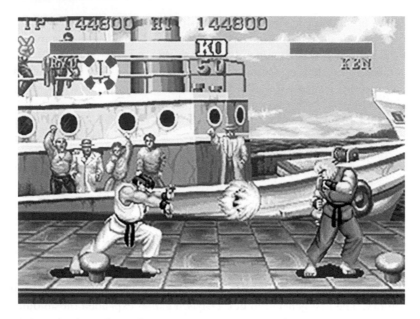

FIGURE 3.5 A screenshot of Ryu from *SF2* performing a *"hadouken."*

English vocal effects for other arcade machines, not to mention games that did not feature vocal effects at all. Though *"hadouken"* translates to "wave motion fist," it is safe to say that it refers to a specific *Street Fighter* attack for most gamers. A *"hadouken"* attack does not have a dedicated button, but requires a button combination, or "combo," as with many other attacks in *Street Fighter* games and fighting games in general. The vocal effect therefore indicates that players performed the button combo successfully, and that a ball of energy will surge towards their opponents.

Chapter conclusions

I hope I have demonstrated in this chapter that, when they compose, game scorers think musically in relation to a particular sound configuration hardware, which limits the possibilities they can imagine for composition in very particular ways. Indeed, musical ideation is structured by the technology — the sound hardware configuration — for which game scorers compose. This is not to say that musical ideation and creativity in game scoring is technologically determined. Rather, it is simply to say that musical ideation and creativity is *structured* in game scoring by particular sound hardware configurations. In this chapter I have sought to elucidate this structure using the NES APU as a case study, paying particularly close attention to some of the better known musical possibilities that game scorers have gleaned — or, to borrow Kondo's phrase, "schemed" — from that particular sound configuration hardware. I then offered three more game scoring categories, namely, Logo Jingles, Loading Music, and Voice Acting and Vocals, to further demonstrate the gaming technology's structural influence on game scoring activity.

In the next chapter, I explore the various contexts for video game sound and music in game programming, by continuing my game scoring "taxonomy" of categories. While in this chapter my focus was mainly on a particular sound hardware configuration, and how it structures game scoring, in the next section I focus on game design's bearing on the scoring process. However, it should be clear from the above discussion that gaming hardware also determines what game design ideas are programmable, just as it determines what game scoring ideas are programmable. It is impossible to discuss game design without some discussion of gaming hardware limitations, and so both this chapter and the next include this. I will attempt to focus on how creative decisions within that field of limitations, otherwise known as game design, structure game scoring *as* software programming.

Notes

1 This book focuses exclusively on game scoring. For more on gaming culture *per se* consult: Schott and Horrell (2000); Carr (2005); Jansz, Avis, and Vosmeer (2010); Kontour (2012); Condis (2014); Chen (2014); Williams, Hendricks, and Winkler (2006); Kirkpatrick (2012); Schleiner (2001); Bryce and Rutter (2002); Morris (2004); Natale (2002); Steinkuehler (2005); Holbert and Wilensky (2010); Taylor (2003); Maguire et al. (2002); Schleiner (1999); Kücklich (2005); Wirman (2014); Deuze, Martin, and Allen (2007); Gros (2007); Örnebring (2007); Kennedy (2002); Sich (2006); Nieborg (2005); Salen (2007); Daniels and Lalone (2012); Cover (2006); Lin (2008); Murray (2006); Corneliussen and Rettberg (2008); and Jakobsson (2011), among many others.

2 For more on ocularcentrism and acoustic space see, for instance, Hodgson (2006).

3 Game scores — such as the soundtracks for, to name some better known examples, *Super Mario Bros.* (Koji Kondo, 1985), *The Legend of Zelda* (Koji Kondo, 1986), *Metroid* (Hirokazu Tanaka, 1986), *Final Fantasy* (Nobuo Uematsu, 1987), *Mega Man II* (Takashi Tateishi, 1988), *Sonic the Hedgehog* (Masato Nakamura, 1991) and *Donkey Kong Country* (David Wise, 1994) — have been celebrated on their own merits since their release. For more on this, see: Murphy (2012); Campbell (2013); and Hannigan (2014), among many others.

4 The Nintendo Family Computer, or "Famicom," is a video game console released in Japan in 1983. Its North American counterpart, the Nintendo Entertainment System, or NES, was released in 1985. The Super Famicom is a video game console intended to succeed the Famicom, released in Japan in 1990. Its North American counterpart, the Super NES, or SNES, was released in 1991.

5 This restraint is further exacerbated by the ocularcentrism inherent in gaming culture, as resources are allocated to visual ends.

6 The citation refers to *Super Mario Galaxy*, a 3D platform game developed and released by Nintendo in 2007, whose score Kondo composed with Mahito Yokota.

7 Hodgson (2006).

8 The CPU for the NTSC (North America and Japan) Famicom and NES was the Ricoh 2A03, or RP2A03, and for the PAL (Europe and Australia) NES, the Ricoh 2A07, or RP2A07. Further technological specifications will always be for the NTSC NES, except where noted. Purely technical information is taken from the official NES development Wiki.

9 This term refers to frequency, where "clock speed" would indicate the frequency at which a CPU is running, for instance. "Clocking" another processing unit such as a timer would then refer to providing information at regular intervals, at some fraction of the frequency which the CPU is running at.

10 According to Truax (1999: "MODULATION"): "Whenever a parameter of a sound or audio signal [...] is varied systematically, the signal is said to be modulated."

11 For example, see Koji Kondo's "Dungeon Theme" for *The Legend of Zelda* (1986), which uses the triangle wave for its main melody to frightening effect.

12 An "envelope shape" is the shape generated by a graph of one parameter of sound, such as volume, versus time.

13 This said, the volume envelope of acoustic instruments seldom decrease in a linear fashion. The NES is, of course, incapable of emulating such sounds in a verité manner.

14 Tateishi is credited by the alias "Ogeretsu Kun" in the game's credits, for some reason unbeknownst to the author.

15 The NES' CPU, developed by Ricoh, also referred to as the "RP2A03."

16 The VRC6 (Virtual Rom Controller, revision 6) is a memory management controller developed by Konami primarily for *Castlevania III: Dracula's Curse* (originally released as *Akumajō Densetsu* in Japan, 1989), released for the NES in 1990. Memory management controllers comprise many kinds of special chips designed by video game developers and implemented in NES and Famicom game cartridges, to extend the abilities of the stock NES and Famicom consoles. The Japanese Famicom, unlike the North American NES, had the ability to generate extra sound channels with these chips. For example, Konami's VRC6 added the ability to generate two extra square waves and one sawtooth wave for the score of *Akumajō Densetsu*. The scores for *Castlevania III* and *Akumajō Densetsu* are markedly different due to different scoring structures provided by different technological configurations — which pertain to musical capabilities in particular — while the games retain nearly identical visuals and gameplay.

17 *NES-Dev*: "Duty Cycle."

18 Ibid.

19 A "pulse wave" with a 50% duty cycle is more commonly referred to as a "square wave," since its active and inactive states are of equal length.

20 Sound effect or music? Do sound effects count as game scoring? I address these broader questions in Chapter 3.

21 According to White (1987: "Overtones"): "[overtones] are tones produced by a musical instrument which are higher in frequency than the fundamental [...] All musical instruments produce complex sound waveforms which repeat at their fundamental [or lowest] frequency."

22 To be clear, the TWC produces fundamental frequencies up to, and beyond, the supersonic limit of human hearing (20kHz). I am talking exclusively about harmonic content in this statement, that is, the harmonics comprising a (fundamental) frequency's overtone content.

23 This list of possible uses for the TWC is not exhaustive. At this point, being interested in primarily surveying the manner by which the NES APU structures game scoring for it, I am interested only in surveying the TWC's most common uses in relation to its technological capacities.

24 Determined by the equation $f_{pulse} = f_{CPU}/(16*(t+1))$ where "f_{pulse}" is the resultant frequency of the pulse wave, f_{CPU} is the base frequency of the CPU (1.78977267 MHz for a North American NES) and t is the timer value.

25 "Clocking" simply refers to the process of providing information at regular intervals, in this case at some fraction of the frequency which the NES CPU is running at. The TWC's maximum frequency on a North American NES is actually 55.9 kHz. This value is determined by the equation $f_{tri} = f_{CPU}/(32*(t + 1))$ where "f_{tri}" is the resultant frequency of the triangle wave, "f_{CPU}" is the base frequency of the CPU and "t" is the timer value.

26 The 2A03, also referred to as the "RP2A03," is the name of the NES' CPU developed by Ricoh.

27 Perhaps more than any other technique I examine, this technique encapsulates game scoring. To compose a tacit section for a particular instrument, the scorer must actually compose frequencies above the human audible threshold, that is, supersonic frequencies.

28 According to Kaernbach (2000: 1): "Noise is a sound with an irregular, random waveform. Unlike a musical or speech sound, it contains a lot of different frequencies. It is called "white noise" if all audible sound frequencies are represented with the same strength. This designation is in analogy to vision: white light contains all visible frequencies of light." Similarly, periodic noise is a sound with many different frequencies, though these frequencies eventually repeat, unlike with white noise. The NES NGC is not capable of producing "true" white noise, as its frequency pattern does repeat after 32,767 steps. This pattern, however, is too long for the human ear to notice its regularity, and it ends up sounding like white noise anyway. The NGC generates periodic noise through a frequency pattern either 93 or 31 steps long, depending on where it is in the 32,767-step sequence when it is triggered.

29 For more on the history of sound technology in gaming, see Belinkie (1999) and Grimshaw (2010).

30 I would contend that 1-bit samples also have their own aesthetic, so "compromised quality" is used here only to denote the radical simplification of audio information performed by the DMC, and the fact that a 1-bit sample features a significantly lower "figurative" resolution than, say, a 24-bit sample.

31 A vocal "bite" is simply a brief sample of a vocal phrase, whether musical or not.

32 By now, these NES game scoring techniques are well-known to NES game scoring enthusiasts, and they are detailed in video format by *Retro Game Audio* (2012), a web site dedicated to the

elucidation of such techniques. I present my own description of these techniques here, as part of an extended analysis of NES game scoring technology.

33 Echo is a reflection of sound which arrives at the listener at least 25 milliseconds after the direct sound.

34 According to Izhaki (2008, qtd. in Hodgson [2010: 171]), "reverb" is: "the collective name given to the sound created by bounced reflections from room boundaries … In modern times, we use reverb emulators, either hardware or software plug-ins, to simulate this natural phenomenon."

35 Developed by Capcom, the company that also develops the *Mega Man* series. Key personnel from that series were tasked with developing *Ducktales* for the NES and the Game Boy, and handheld video game console developed and released by Nintendo in 1989. The Game Boy version utilizes the Game Boy sound hardware, similar to the NES APU, in order to create the same effect with two pulse waves.

36 The "Follin Bros." have collaborated on game scores and are collectively known as such in gaming culture. They are celebrated by chip music enthusiasts for developing techniques such as single-channel echo.

37 The ear is not equally sensitive to all frequencies, particularly in the higher and lower ranges. In 1933, Fletcher and Munson charted the response to frequencies across the entire audio range, as a set of curves showing the sound levels of tones perceived as equally loud. These curves are called "equal loudness contours" or "Fletcher-Munson curves." According to White (1987: "Fletcher-Munson Effect"): "The most sensitive range of human hearing is between 3kHz and 4kHz; the sensitivity falls off rapidly at lower frequencies and somewhat more slowly at higher frequencies. In other words, sounds must be more powerful at lower and higher frequencies than 3 to 4kHz in order to be heard at the lowest audible levels."

38 For a history of video game music up until 1999, see Belinkie (1999).

39 This technique is most commonly used for kick drums, to be sure. However, it is possible to use it to create other drum sounds, such as a woodblock, by incorporating the same technique at higher frequencies.

40 Retro Game Audio (2012: "NES Audio: Sunsoft Bass and Melodic Samples").

41 According to White (1987), a "limiter" is a special type of compressor which prevents the signal from exceeding a predetermined level. White (1987) also notes that a "compressor" is an audio device that reduces the dynamic range of a signal.

42 I refer to personal computer and home console-based games here. Handheld and mobile games still relied on older game scoring hardware technologies, such as the Nintendo Game Boy Color, which relied on a similar configuration to the NES APU until it was discontinued in 2003.

43 A "Sound Test" is a program or mode typically embedded in a game's options menu that allows players to listen to all or most of the sounds on the score.

44 Screenshots of Nintendo Switch games are taken by the author, using original hardware.

45 Actually, the Genesis sound hardware may only output samples in 8-bit quality. Since it is from the 16-bit generation of consoles, though, the 8-bit sample playback can be said to be part of the "16-bit sound."

46 "Disk" usually refers to magnetic storage such as mechanical hard drives and floppy disks, while "disc" usually refers to optical storage such as compact discs (CDs) or digital versatile discs (DVDs). Both carry data that is read a "chunk" at a time, unlike game cartridges such as those for NES, SNES, Sega Genesis or N64, which read the entire game's data-set at console boot. The latter technology is called a read-only memory cartridge, or ROM cartridge, and is not to be confused with flash memory cartridges such as SD cards, or games for Sony PSP Vita, Nintendo 3DS or Switch, for example. Flash memory cartridges are arguably faster than discs, but their data is still read a "chunk" at a time.

47 For more on this see Nathan Grayson's (2017) article "Why Games Still Have Bad Loading Times" for the Kotaku site.

48 Hayashi (1995).

49 While *The Legend of Zelda: Skyward Sword* (2011) was the first *Zelda* game to include voice acting for dialogue, it consisted only of human voices and no real words. *Breath of the Wild* (2017) is the first *Zelda* game to include voice acting of actual words in dialogue scenes, and also happens to be the first *Zelda* game where players may not name their own character, and instead have to play as "Link." Thus, while previous *Zelda* games allow more player participation in forming Link's identity, *Breath of the Wild*'s "Link" seems more like a fully-formed character, due to the simple fact that he already has a name.

References

Belinkie, Matthew. 1999. "Video Game Music: Not Just Kid Stuff." *VGMusic*. December 15. http://www.vgmusic.com/vgpaper.shtml.

Bryce, Jo, and Jason Rutter. 2002. "Killing Like a Girl: Gendered Gaming and Girl Gamers' Visibility." *Proceedings of the Computer Games and Digital Culture Conference*, 243–56. University Press.

Campbell, Andy. 2013. "Video Game Music Is Making Symphony Orchestra Awesome Again, Thanks To 'Zelda' And 'rePLAY." *Huffington Post*. http://www.huffingtonpost.com/2013/11/01/zelda-replay-symphony-video-game-music_n_4182915.html.

Carr, Diane. 2005. "Contexts, Gaming Pleasures, and Gendered Preferences." *Simulation & Gaming* 36 (4): 464–82. doi:10.1177/1046878105282160.

Chen, Lai Chi. 2014. "What's the Cultural Difference between the West and the East? The Consumption of Popular 'Cute' Games in the Taiwanese Market." *New Media & Society* 16 (6): 1018–33. doi:10.1177/1461444813497555.

Condis, Megan. 2014. "No Homosexuals in Star Wars? Bioware, 'Gamer' Identity, and the Politics of Privilege in a Convergence Culture." *Convergence: The International Journal of Research into New Media Technologies*, April. doi:10.1177/1354856514527205.

Corneliussen, Hilde, and Jill W. Rettberg. 2008. *Digital Culture, Play, and Identity: A World of Warcraft Reader*. Cambridge, MA: MIT Press.

Cover, Rob. 2006. "Gaming (Ad) Diction: Discourse, Identity, Time and Play in the Production of the Gamer Addiction Myth." *Game Studies* 6 (1). http://gamestudies.org/0601/articles/cover.

Daniels, Jessie, and Nick Lalone. 2012. "Racism in Video Gaming: Connecting Extremist and Mainstream Expressions of White Supremacy." In *Social Exclusion, Power and Video Game Play*, edited by David G. Embrick, J. Talmadge Wright, and Andras Lukacs, 83–97. Lanham, MD: Lexington Books/Rowman and Littlefield.

Deuze, Mark, Chase B. Martin, and Christian Allen. 2007. "The Professional Identity of Gameworkers." *Convergence: The International Journal of Research into New Media Technologies* 13 (4): 335–53. doi:10.1177/1354856507081947.

Grayson, Nathan. 2017. "Why Games Still Have Bad Loading Times." Kotaku. https://kotaku.com/why-games-still-have-bad-loading-times-1795548921.

Grimshaw, Mark, ed. 2010. *Game Sound Technology and Player Interaction: Concepts and Developments*. Hershey, PA: IGI Global.

Gros, Begoña. 2007. "Digital Games in Education." *Journal of Research on Technology in Education* 40 (1): 23–38. doi:10.1080/15391523.2007.10782494.

Hannigan, James. 2014. "Is Video Game Music Art? Part 2: The Orchestra." *Classic FM*. http://www.classicfm.com/discover/video-game-music/hannigan-art-orchestra/.

Hayashi, Yoichi. 1995. "Recording Medium, Method of Loading Games Program Code Means, and Games Machine." Google Patents. https://patents.google.com/patent/US5718632.

Hodgson, Jay. 2006. "Navigating the Network of Recording Practice: Towards an Ecology of the Record Medium." PhD Dissertation, University of Alberta.

———. 2010. *Understanding Records: A Field Guide to Recording Practice*. London: Bloomsbury Academic.

Holbert, Nathan R., and Uri Wilensky. 2010. "*FormulaT Racing*: Combining Gaming Culture and Intuitive Sense of Mechanism for Video Game Design." In *Proceedings of the 9th International Conference of the Learning Sciences - Volume 2*, 268–69. ICLS '10. Chicago, IL: International Society of the Learning Sciences. http://dl.acm.org/citation.cfm?id=1854509.1854651.

Jakobsson, Mikael. 2011. "The Achievement Machine: Understanding Xbox 360 Achievements in Gaming Practices." *Game Studies* 11 (1): 1–22.

Jansz, Jeroen, Corinne Avis, and Mirjam Vosmeer. 2010. "Playing *The Sims 2*: An Exploration of Gender Differences in Players' Motivations and Patterns of Play." *New Media & Society* 12 (2): 235–51. doi:10.1177/1461444809342267.

Kaernbach, Christian. 2000. "Periodic Noise FAQ." *Christian-Albrechts-Universitat Zu Kiel*. http://www.uni-kiel.de/psychologie/emotion/team/kaernbach/pn/faq.htm.

Kennedy, Helen W. 2002. "Lara Croft: Feminist Icon or Cyberbimbo? On the Limits of Textual Analysis." *Game Studies: International Journal of Computer Games Research* 2 (2). http://www.game-studies.org/0202/kennedy/

Kirkpatrick, Graeme. 2012. "Constitutive Tensions of Gaming's Field: UK Gaming Magazines and the Formation of Gaming Culture 1981–1995." *The International Journal of Computer Game Research* 12 (1). http://gamestudies.org/1201/articles/kirkpatrick.

Kondo, Koji. 2010. Interview by Shinobu Amayake. http://www.glitterberri.com/ocarina-of-time/special-interview-koji-kondo/.

Kontour, Kyle. 2012. "The Governmentality of *Battlefield* Space: Efficiency, Proficiency, and Masculine Performativity." *Bulletin of Science, Technology & Society* 32 (5): 353–60. doi:10.1177/0270467612469067.

Kücklich, Julian. 2005. "Precarious Playbour: Modders and the Digital Games Industry." *Fibreculture* (5). https://five.fibreculturejournal.org/fcj-025-precarious-playbour-modders-and-the-digital-games-industry/

Lin, Holin. 2008. "Body, Space and Gendered Gaming Experiences: A Cultural Geography of Homes, Cybercafes and Dormitories." In *Beyond Barbie and Mortal Kombat: New Perspectives on Gender and Gaming,* edited by Yasmin B. Kafai, Carrie Heeter, Jill Denner, and Jennifer Y. Sun, 67–82. Cambridge, MA and London: The MIT Press.

Maguire, Flack, Michael van Lent, Marc Prensky, and Ron W. Tarr. 2002. "Defense Combat SIM Olympics-Methodologies Incorporating the 'Cyber Gaming Culture." The Interservice/Industry Training, Simulation & Education Conference (I/ITSEC).

Morris, Sue. 2004. "Shoot First, Ask Questions Later: Ethnographic Research in an Online Computer Gaming Community." *Media International Australia* 110: 31–41.

Murphy, Conor. 2012. "Orchestras That Play Video Game Music." *Big Fish Games.* http://www.bigfishgames.com/blog/orchestras-that-play-video-game-music/.

Murray, Janet H. 2006. "Toward a Cultural Theory of Gaming: Digital Games and the Co-Evolution of Media, Mind, and Culture." *Popular Communication* 4 (3): 185–202.

Naka, Yuji. 2005. Sega's Yuji Naka Talks! Interview by Heidi Kemps. http://xbox.gamespy.com/articles/654/654750p1.html.

Natale, Marc J. 2002. "The Effect of a Male-Oriented Computer Gaming Culture on Careers in the Computer Industry." *SIGCAS Computers and Society* 32 (2): 24–31. doi:10.1145/566522.566526.

"NES Audio: Sunsoft Bass and Melodic Samples." 2012. *Retro Game Audio.* http://retrogameaudio.tumblr.com/post/19576086117/nes-audio-sunsoft-bass-and-melodic-samples.

"NES-Dev Wiki." 2009. *NES-Dev.* http://wiki.nesdev.com/w/index.php/Nesdev_Wiki.

Nieborg, David. 2005. "Am I Mod or Not? – An Analysis of First Person Shooter Modification Culture." Creative Gamers Seminar – Exploring Participatory Culture in Gaming. Finland: University of Tampere.

Örnebring, Henrik. 2007. "Alternate Reality Gaming and Convergence Culture: The Case of *Alias.*" *International Journal of Cultural Studies* 10 (4): 445–62.

Salen, Katie. 2007. "Toward an Ecology of Gaming." In *The Ecology of Games: Connecting Youth, Games, and Learning,* edited by Katie Salen, 1–17. Cambridge, MA and London: The MIT Press.

Schartmann, Andrew. 2013. *Maestro Mario: How Nintendo Transformed Video Game Music into an Art.* New York: Thought Catalog.

Schleiner, Anne-Marie. 1999. "Parasitic Interventions: Game Patches and Hacker Art." *Disponibile Online.* http://www.opensorcery.net/patchnew.html.

———. 2001. "Does Lara Croft Wear Fake Polygons? Gender and Gender-Role Subversion in Computer Adventure Games." *Leonardo* 34 (3): 221–26. doi:10.1162/002409401750286976.

Schott, Gareth R., and Kirsty R. Horrell. 2000. "Girl Gamers and Their Relationship with the Gaming Culture." *Convergence: The International Journal of Research into New Media Technologies* 6 (4): 36–53. doi:10.1177/135485650000600404.

Sich, Christy. 2006. "From Game Studies to Bibliographic Gaming: Libraries Tap into the Video Game Culture." *Bulletin of the American Society for Information Science and Technology* 32 (4): 24–26.

Steinkuehler, Constance A. 2005. "The New Third Place: Massively Multiplayer Online Gaming in American Youth Culture." *Tidskrift Journal of Research in Teacher Education* 3 (3): 17–32.

Taylor, T. L. 2003. "Multiple Pleasures: Women and Online Gaming." *Convergence: The International Journal of Research into New Media Technologies* 9 (1): 21–46. doi:10.1177/135485650300900103.

White, Glenn D. 1987. *The Audio Dictionary.* Seattle, WA: University of Washington Press.

Williams, J. Patrick, Sean Q. Hendricks, and W. Keith Winkler. 2006. *Gaming as Culture: Essays on Reality, Identity and Experience in Fantasy Games.* Jefferson, NC: McFarland, Incorporated. http://books.google.ca/books?id=i7UBWz6LBK4C.

Wirman, Hanna. 2014. "Playing by Doing and Players' Localization of *The Sims 2.*" *Television & New Media* 15 (1): 58–67. doi:10.1177/1527476413505001.

4

GAME DESIGN AND GAME SCORING AS SOFTWARE PROGRAMMING

In this chapter, I continue my own "break-down" of the common components of game scores, in an attempt to demonstrate how game design structures game scoring as software programming. These components derive from specific gaming contexts. For example, many racing games offer original music for the "Results" screen that appears after a race, and so I deem this "Results Music." However, I aim to determine game score components that appear in all, or at least most, gaming genres, rather than analyze categories that apply to only a single genre or subset of games. Thus, "Results Music" is music that accompanies any kind of results screen in any game, such as the — untitled — distorted ambient drone that sets the digital watch-styled display of the multiplayer mode results screen of *GoldenEye 007* (1997) for N64, for example. An analysis of common game scoring categories will allow me to begin explaining how game design structures game scoring as software programming.

I should note that while game designers and game analysts might use similar frameworks for categorizing game audio, these categories are wholly derived from my own experience of playing games, and noting the various boundaries for each category, with a focus on categories that exist across most or all gaming genres. So, while this taxonomy might be useful for game designers and game scoring analysts alike, it should be read as descriptive of the player's experience of hearing as well as generating music and sound through gameplay.

Game scoring taxonomy: Introduction Music

"Introduction Music" is music that is composed to set an "introductory video" to a game. Introductory videos to games often look very different from actual gameplay. In fact, they feature cinematography and editing similar to film trailers because they are meant to showcase animation graphics and gameplay features in an efficient and entertaining format. Thus, game scorers typically compose Introduction Music to tie together snippets of disparate visual information — which often appear very quickly — in order to create a continuous "trailer" or "music video" for a game. For example, *Super Mario RPG* (1996), scored by Yoko Shimomura, begins with an introductory video of Bowser kidnapping

DOI: 10.4324/9781003045465-4

Princess Peach — a staple narrative of the *Super Mario* series of games.[1] This visual is accompanied by "In the Flower Garden," a short theme that begins with a peaceful wind instrument melody that is quickly overtaken by an ominous section played on horns and strings. After Peach is kidnapped, Mario enters the frame, a short, militant drum pattern plays and elucidates his sense of duty, and he performs a signature leap into his new adventure. After Mario leaps, the second and main part of the Introduction Music, "Happy Adventure, Delightful Adventure," begins. This theme features an upbeat drum pattern punctuated by whistles and wood blocks; a bright main theme performed on xylophone; and a prominent bass line. These elements combine to evoke excitement, playfulness and adventurousness, and Shimomura creates musical continuity as the visuals change, by repeating and developing the xylophone theme throughout the piece. Figure 4.1 shows some screenshots of the introductory video:

Games released on platforms beyond the 16-bit generation often contain introductory videos that appear even more similar to music videos, because they often use compiled popular music as Introduction Music. For example, *Gran Turismo 3: A-Spec* (2001) features popular music for its introductory video. In fact, for each of the Japanese, European and North American versions of *GT3*, a different track is used to set the introductory video. While all versions of the game contain original menu music composed by Isamu Ohira, each contains a different compiled score, and so each introductory video serves as a music video for its respective version. While a comparison of these is not possible in the space I have here, it is worth noting that the introductory video to a game must leave a positive first impression and build excitement in gamers, and that each version of *GT3* has a different compiled score to accomplish this in its respective region.

FIGURE 4.1 The introductory video to *Super Mario RPG* (1996). Scenes of Mario running around in the "overworld" are edited together with battle gameplay footage, cutscenes and various mini-games. In addition, zooming circle edits draw the viewer's focus to each character as they are introduced by text, by blacking out areas around each avatar.[2]

Game scoring taxonomy: Demo Music

Demo Music is music that accompanies programmed demonstrations of gameplay, or gameplay "demos." Gameplay demos are didactic; they teach gamers how to play a game via a pre-programmed sequence of actions, or a pre-recorded video of gameplay. Gamers commonly access gameplay demos through one of three means: (i) Allowing the game to run from start-up without controller operation, as with the title sequence to *SMB3*; (ii) navigating to a demo or "tutorial" mode through a game's menu system; or (iii) starting a new game, where the beginning of the game offers a recorded demo before, or in the midst of early gameplay.[3]

As with the title sequence to *SMB3*, gameplay demos often do not contain music. This fact alone elucidates video game music's lack of importance in learning and mastering most types of gameplay.[4] In the majority of games, familiarity with music is not necessary to play, even if it is a gamer's first time playing a game. As a result, many gameplay demos feature unaccompanied Gameplay Sound Effects. Gameplay Sound Effects pronounce specific gaming actions, such as attacking or defending in a fighting game, for instance. Unlike most background music for games, they react directly and succinctly to specific controller operations and on-screen movement. Thus, in the context of actual gameplay, background music preserves the continuity of the action, as it is more consistent and less directly reactive to controller operations than sound effects. Since gameplay demonstrations do not involve human gameplay, but a pre-programmed sequence, background music is not necessary to preserve continuity, especially as the sequence will be performed the same way every time by the game platform's CPU.

In addition, watching a gameplay demo is not as interactive or immersive as playing a game, nor is it meant to be. Thus, if there is Demo Music present in a game, it may either be an attenuated version of gameplay background music, or music composed specifically for the demo at hand. If it is the former, gamers may hear a preview of gameplay background music they can expect to hear while playing, though it is attenuated. If they decide to start the game proper, they will be met with the full volume version of this music, thus rewarding them for making it through the demo sequence, and enhancing the excitement of performing newly-learned mechanics. Thus, game scorers typically compose Demo Music to encourage *engagement* with a game, rather than *immersion*. Players must engage with a game *as a game* in order to learn its rules in a demo sequence, and so that they can perform actions in a state of immersion during actual gameplay.

Original Demo Music is typically more groove-based than melody-centred. For example, "How to Play," composed by Hirokazu Ando for the first *Super Smash Bros.* (1999) (*SSB*), features a prominent bass line that provides a steady groove, as an acoustic guitar and a toy piano accent the beat.[5] The bass line holds players' attention as they watch the "How to Play" gameplay demo video that begins if they wait long enough at the *SSB* title screen (without operating their controllers). The gameplay demo consists of Mario fighting his brother Luigi, interrupted by freeze-frames and textual instructions — along with button icons — for performing each fighting move. See Figure 4.2 for screenshots of this demo:[6]

Since gameplay demos do not involve player interaction, there are no "stakes" involved for gamers watching them. In other words, demo videos are not meant to be as intense as actual gameplay, because this might intimidate novice players. Thus, the music for the *SSB* gameplay demo does not evoke the excitement or intensity that its fighting stage music does.

FIGURE 4.2 The "How to Play" demo for *SSB* (1999) that explains the controls and gameplay mechanics of the game. While simultaneous four-player gameplay is possible in this game, the demo showcases a one-on-one match between the Mario brothers, in order to be more instructive, familiar and easy to follow.

The toy piano accents evoke playfulness, while the bass line provides stability in "How to Play," and so players might also gain a sense of the gameplay or ludal rhythm in *SSB* by watching the demo. The toy piano accents the beat at different points each time, and so players can imagine performing gameplay actions such as attacking and defending at different points in the music.

In actual gameplay, there are usually quantitatively different outcomes for players, such as winning or losing a fight, as they directly interact with the game at hand. This competitive situation both requires a different mood for the music, as well as opens up different avenues for music to interact with gameplay, as I will show in the section on Gameplay Music, below. As for Demo Music, the only interaction that is typically possible for gamers is to stop the gameplay demo by pressing a button, and thus end the Demo Music at any point. Gamers may return to gameplay demos multiple times, and Demo Music may play for various lengths as they wait for the part of the gameplay demo that they need, in order to remind themselves how to perform a specific action, for instance.

Game scoring taxonomy: Gameplay Music

"Gameplay Music" is music that accompanies the main gameplay aspects of a game. For several reasons, this category is what most people refer to as "video game music." First, Gameplay Music sets the most important, and hopefully the most enjoyable, parts of a game. Unlike Menu Music, for instance, Gameplay Music accompanies activities that are designed to immerse gamers. Interestingly, this pairing makes Gameplay Music less noticeable, as gamers are more invested in performing successful gameplay than recognizing musical content in immersive activities. This idea has even more fascinating implications when considered in relation to music–gameplay synchronization, which I explore in the next chapter. While Gameplay Music is less noticeable because of gameplay, this fact does not stop gamers from recognizing their own gameplay synchronizing with the music, whether through their own efforts, because of programmed score operations, the result of chance, or a combination of two or more of these.

The three different ways that music synchronizes with gameplay may each be compared to the real-life act of dancing. If gameplay synchronizes with music in a game because of a player's own deliberate efforts, it is more like dance because it involves adapting physical movement to musical elements. If it synchronizes with music because of the programmed score — in an adaptive manner — gameplay is more akin to goal-oriented activity that is not dance, but is nevertheless musically set as if it were occurring on a stage, and as a dance. If gameplay synchronizes with music because of chance, it is more like activity that has its own rhythm, which happens to line up with music that has its own, different rhythm. This last scenario is, in fact, arguably the least immersive because it draws attention to the synchronization as an unintended but valuable musical benefit to the gaming experience. Since the last scenario is so enjoyable, but not directly intended by gamers, immersion becomes either less important or more overt or "presentational" in form.

Second, most people designate Gameplay Music — instead of other categories — as video game music simply because it plays and repeats for longer in the context of an average game score. While gamers' playtime is also divided into operating menus, waiting for loading screens, watching cut-scenes and entering dialogue, to name a few examples, the main gameplay likely takes up the majority of it. So, while players may notice less musical aspects or experience them less consciously in Gameplay Music, it still plays and repeats for longer than any other game scoring component.

Third, from a gaming spectator's point of view, Gameplay Music accompanies the most exciting portions of a game. The main gameplay sections of games contain their most impressive — and resource-intensive — visuals, and gameplay spectators may imagine themselves watching a computer-generated film. However, unlike the narrative to a film, for example, the outcome and direction of gameplay is dictated by players in games. The interactivity involved in games therefore affects not only gamers' experiences, but also gaming spectators' experiences. Unlike in a film-going experience, a gameplay-viewing experience is affected by the spectator's knowledge of the rules of a game, as well as the success or failure of the gamer.[7] There are many different outcomes to gameplay, and gameplay spectators can enjoy the thrill of witnessing both degrees of performer freedom and chance operations involved in gaming activity. In addition, since they are not immersed in the same way that gamers are — they do not operate a controller, and do not carry the burden of performing successful gameplay (especially for spectation) — they can enjoy and focus on particular aspects of the game, such as its Gameplay Music.

I should note that "focusing on the music" in this scenario is not analogous to listening to records, or any other fixed audio media. Gaming spectators enjoy Gameplay Music as a kind of real-time commentary on gameplay, because it reacts and resonates according to the patterns of this activity. For example, I may direct Link to lose all of his hearts and experience a death in *The Legend of Zelda*, while spectators anticipate and enjoy the "Death Sound," followed by the "Game Over" melody. On the other hand, due to the same aspects of performer freedom and chance, spectators cannot *fully* anticipate Gameplay Music, even with comprehensive knowledge of the game at hand. Again, this experience is different from a film-going experience. For example, film-goers may attend a screening of a classic film they have seen before, and will thus be able to predict when events happen, including musical ones. Conversely, gameplay spectators who watch classic games they have both, played and watched before cannot predict with total accuracy when musical events will occur. Allowing the score to unfold with gameplay is an enjoyable activity in its own right, and so Gameplay Music serves an important purpose in gaming spectatorship and culture.

The category of Gameplay Music is, admittedly, a large one that encompasses many musical scenarios. I shall therefore attempt to divide it into smaller categories while sustaining my focus on the different contexts for game scoring. However, I must be careful not to approach these categories as specific to any single genre of games. I have chosen these categories because they can and do exist in every gaming genre, in an attempt to preserve breadth in my research. Nevertheless, some categories are more common in certain genres, and I will attempt to note whenever this is the case.

Gameplay Music: Hub Music

"Hub Music" is music that plays when players direct a game to a "hub" or level selection area. Hub worlds are an evolution of world map screens, or level selection screens organized into a traversable map. World map screens differ from hub worlds in that they are programmed differently from the levels of a game, usually offering limited interaction in a top-down map setting. They also differ from in-level or in-game maps that do not function as hubs, and are meant for navigation purposes only.[8] One of the first known uses of a traversable world map screen is in *Super Mario Bros. 3 (SMB3)*, where players can navigate to levels and secret areas. *SMB3* contains eight themed "worlds" that each have their own music on the world map screen, which I covered in some detail in my case study of the Nintendo Entertainment System Audio Processing Unit (NES APU), in the previous chapter.

The next home console game in the *Super Mario* series, *Super Mario World* (*SMW*) (1991) for the Super Nintendo Entertainment System (SNES), has seven "normally-accessed" worlds and two secret ones that do not need to be accessed to complete the game.[9] The map configuration in *SMW* changed from *SMB3* to allow back-tracking to previous worlds at any point, and players could direct Mario back to levels they did not fully complete, for instance. The different worlds are scored with different music, as in *SMB3*, but with one change: beyond the first world, "Yoshi's Island," if Mario is not in an enclosed section such as "Vanilla Dome" (World 3) or the "Forest of Illusion," (World 5) for instance, the "Map Overworld" theme plays. This music programming means that all even-numbered (non-enclosed) worlds — "Donut Plains" (World 2), "Twin Bridges" (World 4) and "Chocolate Island" (World 6) — share the same music, while all odd-numbered worlds have unique music. Thus, the "continuous" feeling of *SMW*'s world is owed not only to the ability to back-track to previous worlds, but also to the coherence of the music in the world map. Each "sub-world" retains its own uniqueness as in *SMB3*, but, unlike that game, the repetition of the "Map Overworld" theme suggests that *SMW*'s entire world is connected and unified.

Though no longer the norm in many genres in modern gaming, there are still many games that are made up of only levels, or their world map screens are broken up as in *SMB3*. In fact, while the *Super Mario* series pursued an evolution of the world map screen into a hub world in later games, the most recent games in the series suggest a return to older world-level frameworks. For example, *Super Mario 3D World*'s worlds are arranged in a fashion similar to the worlds of *SMB3*, with unique music for each, though back-tracking is also included. *Super Mario Odyssey* simply uses a spinning globe of Earth with dots for the location of each world, though it operates more like a traditional level selection menu screen. Players may only move the cursor left and right, and there is only one looping, unchanging theme scored for the menu.

The sequel to *SMW*, and the first *Yoshi* platformer game, *Super Mario World 2: Yoshi's Island* (1995) for SNES, uses a simpler form of world-level organization, where worlds and levels are organized into a menu. Players can see Yoshi moving to different parts of a map as they navigate to different worlds in the menu, and this animation represents him travelling large distances. Figure 4.3 is a screenshot of this menu screen:

While the map menu screen always looks generally the same, an instrument is added to the Menu Music each time players progress to the next world, thus adding a sense of variety, continuity and progression for *Yoshi's Island* players. By the time they progress to the last world, players hear the "Map" theme in its "fullest" version. By contrast, the official soundtrack version of this theme is not broken up into different tracks for each instrument, as they were programmed, but slowly adds instruments throughout a single track. This feat is impossible in the actual game, since the "Map" music preserves the amount of instruments according to game progression, and not navigation.

The next game in the *Super Mario* series, *Super Mario 64* (*SM64*) (1996), incorporates a fully-explorable hub-world, with the same gameplay mechanics as its actual worlds or "levels." *SM64* was the first three-dimensional game in the series, and was highly anticipated as such. The audio used in the first parts of a new game of *SM64* slowly eases players back into the world of the Mushroom Kingdom, in its new, more "realistic" setting. Below,

FIGURE 4.3 The map menu screen for *Yoshi's Island* (1995). Each time players advance to a new world, numbered by dividers at the top of the screen, they unlock another instrument in the mix of the "Map" theme.

I will describe the experience of starting a new game of *SM64* with a focus on its music, in order to elucidate how Hub Music functions in a new three-dimensional environment, also amidst the other sounds of a game.

When *SM64* players select a new file, the "Start Game" Menu Sound Effect — a two-note ascending slide played on synthesizer and cymbal brush — plays, the screen fades to white, and Princess "Peach" Toadstool fades into view with a blue sky as her backdrop. Peach has voice acting for a message of invitation to Mario that is accompanied by the "Peach's Message" Cut-Scene Music, a short synthesizer variation on "Inside the Castle Walls," the Hub Music for the game. After inviting Mario to the castle, Peach fades into the blue sky, and Lakitu, the "cameraman" for the game, slides into view as the frame pedestals downward.[10] The game introduces Lakitu because players have control over the camera in *SM64*, an important feature for 3D platforming games and 3D games in general.[11] As Lakitu descends to the ground, the "Opening" theme plays — another variation on "Inside the Castle Walls," but this time as a longer, lusher string arrangement that sets Lakitu's (and the camera's) smooth flying motion. When Lakitu reaches a green pipe that pops out of the ground (accompanied by the familiar "Pipe" sound from previous *Mario* games), a camera "click" sounds as the perspective switches from facing Lakitu, to that of Lakitu himself, as he officially "becomes the cameraman."[12] Mario suddenly leaps out of the pipe with a "Yahoo! Haha!" vocal effect, and the camera moves from in front of, to behind Mario, the avatar — the "third person" gameplay perspective for many 3D games. A dialogue box pops up in the top left corner of the screen with brief tutorial instructions for movement and interaction with signs and non-player characters.

After players navigate through the dialogue, they gain control of Mario for the first time in the game, accompanied by only environmental sounds, such as birds chirping. Notably, this instance is the first time in a *Mario* game that players have control of Mario without Gameplay Music, and it happens the first time players gain control of him in a 3D setting. In order to convey the new sense of space, the *SM64* developers opted to exclude music from setting the initial control of "3D Mario." When players begin to move Mario, they are greeted with realistic-sounding footsteps that change according to terrain. Whenever players press "A" to make Mario jump, he will make some sort of vocal exclamation, such as "Ya!" or "Wahaaa!" These sound effects will be triggered and heard by players for the rest of the game, and so the lack of music also helps players become accustomed to Mario's voice as they direct him.

Outside Peach's Castle, players soon find there is not much to do besides run around and jump, and so once they are familiar with the game's controls they should direct Mario to the castle entrance. When Mario reaches the moat bridge, Lakitu swings around in front of him to teach the player camera controls. This dialogue begins automatically and has a dialogue jingle that is re-used for dialogue with other characters that the player initiates.[13] After talking to Lakitu, players may continue inside the castle. Entering the castle prompts another dialogue, this time from Bowser, the game's villain, and different Dialogue Music plays. Bowser communicates unseen, and informs Mario that "No one's home! Scram!" A demonic-sounding synthesizer jingle and Bowser's laugh can be heard as the audio transitions to "Inside the Castle Walls," the Hub Music for the game.

"Inside the Castle Walls" is meant to sound "royal," since it is used to set the Princess' castle. Lush strings play, repeat and elaborate a bright, ascending motif that is organized in a rigid, on-beat rhythm punctuated by frequent rests. Plucked ascending strings respond to this motif each time it is played, and in a much smoother rhythm. The next musical idea is a response to the ascending contour of the first part, as it remains harmonically related, but has a descending contour and is played on a much lower register. As with much looping video game music, the loop point occurs when the dominant chord is reached, and so that the return to the tonic at the beginning of the loop sounds natural.

The castle in *Super Mario 64* is unusually empty, as everyone — including Princess Peach — is supposedly stuck inside the castle walls (see Figure 4.4):

"Inside the Castle Walls" conveys this fact via the first ascending section, where separated chords and plucked notes evoke the isolation and sterility of the abandoned castle. The second section, which follows a descending contour, is played in a *portamento* style, where notes and chords overlap. The lower register strings add a warmth that could represent the possible return of a more populated and "homey" atmosphere to the castle, though the length and complexity of this section seems to indicate that it will be a long (and challenging) time until that happens.

FIGURE 4.4 Gameplay screenshots from the beginning of *Super Mario 64* (1996). The castle, or hub-world, has few inhabitants, as they are trapped in the walls. Mario accesses different worlds or levels by jumping into paintings on the walls (top, right). Players may select a mission on a menu screen (bottom, left) once they direct Mario to jump into a painting, and their selection will trigger a fade into the level itself, and Mario will fall to the ground (bottom, right).

Gameplay Music: Area Music

As exemplified by adventure games such as *Ocarina of Time*, the line between Hub and Area or Level Music can be blurred, as the hub seamlessly blends in and transitions smoothly with the other environments, and contains similar gameplay. Other games simply have level or stage select screens that lead to the main gameplay portions, such as *Yoshi's Island*, as I discussed in the previous section. The map-level configuration for any game is up to game developers, and their decisions are based on gaming genre, hardware resources and program design.

Nevertheless, Area Music always accompanies the main gameplay activities of a game, regardless of the game's genre. In my general definition of a game "area," I do not require specific spatial dimensions, since these vary greatly between games and especially genres. Instead, I define game areas as main gameplay venues, as they are designed to accommodate specific gameplay activities. For example, the game area for *Tetris* (1984, Soviet Union, Electronika 60) is a two-dimensional vertically-oriented rectangular space. This area is occupied by "Tetris blocks," each made up of four "squares," that drop from the top of the screen, one by one, in one of five configurations.[14] The playfield itself is ten squares wide and twenty squares high, and players are tasked with arranging each block in an attempt to form horizontal lines of squares. When players complete a full line of squares across the playfield, it disappears and opens up more space. As with many other arcade games, *Tetris* does not have an ending, but instead features a "high score" system. Players that continue on find the blocks descending faster and faster, until eventually they cannot accommodate any more in the playfield, and the game is over. Thus, the area for *Tetris* does not vary, but is designed according to crucial gameplay parameters, and, conversely, structures gameplay itself.

In the next section, I will analyze music for two similarly-designed game areas that nonetheless come from two different gaming genres: (1) puzzle games and (2) rhythm games. I will first compare the two games in terms of one of Roger Caillois' (1958) categories of play, mimicry, to determine why video games contain music in the first place. As it turns out, game scores form an important part of gaming as a mimetic technology.

Area Music case study: game scoring as mimetic music technology in *Tetris* (1984) and *Guitar Hero* (2005)

In many puzzle games like *Tetris*, players constitute the "protagonist," if such a role exists in this genre. *Tetris* players control blocks one at a time as they fall from the top of the playfield, rather than controlling an avatar such as Sonic the Hedgehog, for example. In other words, puzzle games do not encourage "roleplaying" or mimicry aspects of gaming, and instead feature competitive and chance aspects. It is strange, then, that *Tetris* — designed in 1984 by Alexei Pajitnov — features a similar playfield to rhythm games such as *Guitar Hero* (2005, Sony PlayStation 2). The latter, according to Michiel Kamp (2009: 2), introduce a new, "performative" dimension to game scoring. Figure 4.5 contains screenshots of these two games' areas:

Kamp (2009) attributes this new dimension to the fact that *Guitar Hero* players emulate a real guitarist, by operating a guitar-shaped controller according to coloured "pads" that descend down a "track" to the rhythm of the music. Since the gameplay is based on musical

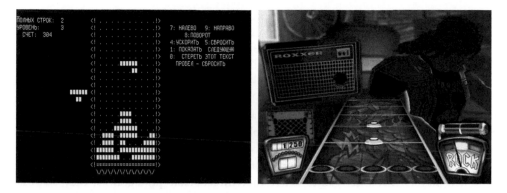

FIGURE 4.5 Gameplay screenshots of the original Soviet Union version of *Tetris* (1984, left) for the Electronika 60 computer and *Guitar Hero* (2005, right) for Sony's PlayStation 2 console.

rhythm, players may imagine themselves as a "guitar hero," a position that Kamp (2009) notes involves both ironic detachment *and* virtuosity.

Alternatively, Alexei Pajitnov did not base *Tetris'* gameplay on any musical parameter, nor did he design it to be played with a controller shaped like a musical instrument. Moreover, he did not afford *Tetris* players any clear narrative "role" to play, let alone a story. The closest role they can liken themselves to is a bricklayer who constantly has to deal with bricks of one of five distinct shapes that fall from the sky at faster and faster rates. Similarly, *Guitar Hero* features five different-coloured tracks for pads to travel down towards the player, and the number and speed of the pads increases with each difficulty setting. However, "guitar heroes" may complete each "stage" or track perfectly if they hit every pad on time; pads come in the same configuration every time if the same track is played on the same difficulty. The designers of the game therefore programmed it to allow for players to memorize gameplay patterns for each musical track.

Tetris, on the other hand, does not allow for memorization of specific patterns of blocks, because there is no pattern. Players instead develop strategies to deal with different block-building scenarios — created by both themselves and the random order of blocks — and the five different tetromino shapes, and must hone these strategies so that they become quicker at building lines to accommodate regular increases in gameplay speed. Finally, unlike *Guitar Hero* players, *Tetris* players cannot "win" a game of *Tetris* (if they are not playing against another player or CPU). They will always — if they do not quit and the game does not crash — eventually "lose" or "die" in the face of ever-increasing gameplay speed, whereas *Guitar Hero* players have the opportunity to become true masters of the game and "beat" every level "perfectly." *Tetris* gameplay simply continues until players can no longer accommodate the next block in the game area.

A comparison between *Tetris* and *Guitar Hero* yields a number of observations on gaming, game scoring and Area Music. To begin, both games have competitive aspects, but require different strategies to master. While *Tetris* encourages (systematized) improvisation in its gameplay through the random selection of different blocks (a chance operation), *Guitar Hero* encourages memorization by keeping its configuration static and centering its gameplay around rote operations and a compiled score. And while *Guitar Hero* encourages players to role-play as "guitar heroes," *Tetris* affords little narrative role-playing aspects. There is no avatar for a player to imagine themselves as in *Tetris*, for instance.

However, does mimicry require an avatar? In other words, does "role-playing" require a "role" in a strictly narrative sense? Sometimes the presence of a protagonist makes it difficult to write about gameplay on a semantic level — do players "direct" protagonists or do they "embody" them? In *Tetris*, it appears at first glance that players solely direct blocks, and that they obviously do not imagine themselves "as blocks" while playing. *Tetris* players do not role-play, due to the "object" nature of the blocks, as opposed to more "human" protagonists in other games. Players also find it difficult to relate to the blocks because they do not control one block, but many, and the order of these blocks is out of their control.

When players encounter games where they direct stable protagonists, they can easily role-play as their avatars in a narrative manner. Players of these games both direct and follow characters through narratives written into the games, and may relate to their character progression alongside game progression. However, mimicry or role-playing activity exists in a far different form in gaming, than in fixed narrative media such as novels or film. Most crucially, gaming itself is a mimetic technology. It involves mimicry in a *technical* sense that precedes any possible mimicry imagined by gamers or storywriters in a narrative sense. For example, if *Zelda* players explore the world of Hyrule and come across a secret cave, they may find a "Molblin," a character who is normally an enemy, who gives them rupees (the game's currency) and notes "IT'S A SECRET TO EVERYBODY." Shigeru Miyamoto (2016: 5), the creator of *The Legend of Zelda* and *Super Mario Bros.* series, explains that he wrote this line to appeal to both "Link," the character, and *Zelda* players themselves:

> That phrase has several meanings. It's a secret to be kept from friends and family that you can get rupees there. But for an enemy like a Molblin to bless you with Rupees [sic] means he has betrayed his comrades, so it's a secret to keep from them as well.

Miyamoto's comments clarify how players may identify with games as both players and protagonists, with the avatar serving as a "link" between these identifications. Players must operate controllers to "play" a game. Their controller operations are read by specific gaming hardware and relayed to the particular code of the game at hand. The code translates controller operations and instructs the hardware to produce video and audio effects. The video and audio may take any form that the gaming hardware and software may produce, including an avatar for Sonic the Hedgehog, or a tetronimo, to name two contrasting examples. In other words, in gaming, software programming automatically performs mimicry in a technical sense. Players, moreover, are akin to directors rather than actors, to continue the ongoing analogy to cinema. In some games, players have control over "casting," as they select or create their own avatar from scratch. Still other games, such as *Tetris*, involve no cast at all.

It is necessary for players to "direct" a game in some fashion, but not mandatory to "role-play" as any particular in-game character. Film direction, as with gameplay, involves discovering and developing actors' strengths and weaknesses. In games, protagonists have strengths and weaknesses to be discovered, though these are pre-programmed, unlike the traits of various film actors. Still, film directors typically begin with a pre-written story to convey through cinematic means, just as gamers begin with a pre-programmed story to unlock through ludal means (given there is a narrative).

One of the best ways to explain how films and games are different is to focus on the issue of protagonist/avatar pain and suffering. Directors expect characters in their film to "feel" pain in some form, at pre-determined points in a narrative. It is also safe to assume that this pain will be expressed in a dramatic form, and perhaps "drawn out" by actors, in order to maximize the visceral effect for the audience. Successful gameplay, on the other hand, demands that players detach themselves emotionally from their avatar's suffering, in order to move on from it *literally*. So, not only is narrative role-playing unnecessary in games, it always exists in a diminished form in competitive games. This fact explains why speed-runs are the most celebrated form of single-player gaming, and why massive tournaments are the most celebrated form of multiplayer gaming, in gaming culture. "Pain" for in-game characters indicates unsuccessful gameplay, on the level of a poorly-placed tetronimo. "Creativity" in competitive gaming involves engaging the game as a game, the most "detached" state possible in terms of role-playing and narrative. In other words, for competitive players, the desire to do well at a game takes over narrative concerns at every turn. Moreover, in single-player games, the programmed narrative only progresses through successful gameplay anyway.

What do the incompatibilities between competition and role-playing mean for video game music and game scoring? To begin, players create, through ludal means and goals programmed into a game, scenarios to be quickly and emotionally elucidated. Game scores cannot anticipate all avenues of player direction, and so composers program game music systems to react to gameplay states in various, often less immediate ways. This reactive process means that video game music is largely useless to highly competitive gamers, who are capable of anticipating their own missteps faster than programmed music systems. Nevertheless, music and sound provide players a "closeness" to their games that could not be achieved without it. While emotional detachment to protagonist suffering aids successful gameplay, the sounds that gamers conduct through their gameplay give immediate "experiential" feedback. To this point, Gameplay Music simultaneously elucidates the emotions of both the "main character" or avatar and the "director" or gamer, in gameplay. In games without clearly defined narratives such as *Tetris*, these roles are folded into each other.

Game scoring is a crucial part of gaming as a mimetic technology, insofar as music and sound events react to gameplay. However, since sound is non-essential to most gameplay, it can only react to it, in most cases. This scenario is not as creatively limiting for game scorers as it sounds. In fact, video game music composers have some of the most exciting scenarios to score, because gaming environments are largely consistent, yet players' actions are not. Game scores may therefore occupy a middle-ground between consistency and inconsistency, though they more often lean towards the former. An example of the latter might be a game where each level has a certain number of musical tracks that could play as background music, which is selected randomly. Though it is a very simple example, this scoring strategy could be extended to any game scoring category, to allow for more creative musical space.

Gameplay Music: Area Music (cont.)

While technical mimicry takes place before any other type of mimicry in games, game scores communicate more than just their own programming. Music may set one or more of three elements in games: gameplay, environment and/or narrative. In the following sections I intend to split Area Music into sub-categories that relate more to gameplay and narrative, and so in this section I will discuss Area Music specifically in relation to game environments. However, I should note that gaming environments host both gameplay and narrative, and ultimately it is impossible to separate these elements conceptually. In other words, environment impacts both gameplay and narrative in games, and vice versa. Game scorers thus have the difficult task of setting environments in terms of both gameplay and narrative simultaneously, in games that include a narrative.

For example, Rich Vreeland used aleatoric techniques to compose "Fear" and convey the feeling of exploring a cemetery in a thunderstorm, in *FEZ*. Vreeland wrote a progression of loud, bombastic chords, and programmed them to sound at completely random points within pre-defined measure ranges during gameplay. These chords coincide with the flashes of lightning and sounds of thunder from the storm. A high-pitched twinkling synthesizer drone resides in the back of the mix to represent the continuous downpour of rain. This drone seems to suspend the tension provided by each chord, while players feel the literal uncertainty of not knowing when the next chord will play, and thus when the music will progress. Figure 4.6 is a screenshot of one of the cemetery rooms in *FEZ*:

Similarly, Koji Kondo composed the "Hyrule Field" theme for *Ocarina* in an aleatoric manner, in order to provide musical variety for an area that players must return to many times over the course of the game. Kondo (2001: n.p.) explains his scoring process in an interview for *Game Maestro Vol. 3*, from 2001:[15]

> The field music is divided into short 8 bar blocks, but those blocks are played randomly to keep things fresh. Also, when Link stands still and rests, the music flows more peacefully, and when an enemy appears, the melody shifts to a more heroic theme. I made those with the idea of smooth transitions in mind… whether anyone noticed, I can't say (laughs). But I didn't want to interrupt the rhythm or flow of the music with a brand new song every time.

FIGURE 4.6 One of the cemetery rooms in *FEZ* (2012).

Kondo (2001) refers to three groupings of music he composed for *Ocarina*: (1) the Area Music for Hyrule Field that includes both (2) the Rest Music that plays when Link is standing still and (3) the Battle Music when enemies are in Link's proximity. Each of these groupings has a number of "8 bar blocks" or sections of music that can transition easily between each other, including across groupings. The Area Music comprises 13 different sections, while the Rest and Battle Music are each comprised of four different sections. Appropriately, the Area Music evokes adventure and exploration through the use of "triumphant" melodies played predominantly on brass instruments; the Rest Music suggests a meditative space through a lower volume, a thinner texture, soothing reed instruments and gently-plucked strings; and the Battle Music elucidates the tension of sword combat through added volume, a fuller texture, and dissonant, urgent piano phrases. Kondo (2014: 32) explains in a later interview for *IGN* that the relationship between musical rhythm and gameplay is crucial to the experience of playing *Ocarina*:

> [The] way the gameplay and the music were tied together through tempo was something we really took a lot of time adjusting and making just right in the original.
>
> I was worried that when they were doing the 3DS version, with the increased processing power, that the game might play a bit differently, and we didn't want the music to be sped up even slightly, or slowed down even slightly, based on the technology they were using. All I asked was that they paid a lot of attention to how the music interacted with the game, and that the tempo had the same balance. We didn't want to lose the way that worked in the original game. I just asked that they stayed true to that. For instance, the transition between music and sound effects.
>
> As you know, a lot of times music is about not just what's playing, but when it's not playing, and how that silence impacts the time when there is sound. That's just one area where, again, the tempo had a huge role in how the game felt when being played.[16]

While it is clear that Kondo (2014) is talking about tempo "tying together" the relationship between gameplay and music, it is somewhat unclear how this process plays out in the gaming experience, how gaming technology plays an important role in this relationship, and how "silence impacts the time when there is sound" in *Ocarina*. Kondo's (2014) response is to the following question from *IGN*:

> I read in an interview that for *Ocarina of Time 3D*, you had requested for the development team to stay faithful to the original N64 sound. Why did you think that was important? Why not remaster the music, similar to the way a game company would remaster graphics?

First of all, Kondo (2014) expresses concern over the game "playing a bit differently" as a result of being re-programmed for a newer gaming technology. While there are many differences between *Ocarina* and *Ocarina 3D*, perhaps the most important one for Kondo has to do with framerate, or the rate that animation frames are "drawn" and displayed by gaming software and hardware. While *Ocarina 3D* and most other modern games play at 60 frames per second, the original version of *Ocarina* played at a custom-set 19 frames per second. The human eye is fast enough to notice frame changes at below 30 frames per second, and so the original *Ocarina* seems slightly "choppy" or "slow" to modern gamers, while *Ocarina 3D* plays very smoothly. For Kondo, this discrepancy meant that the "tempo" of the original *Ocarina* gameplay was in danger of changing, as the developers of the remake had to program Link to move and animate at the same speed with the new framerate — a feat that requires more than simple ratio mathematics, and even then, the smoothness of *Ocarina 3D* only resembles the gameplay rhythm of the original. The need to tie music to gameplay in game scoring, as with the "Hyrule Field" music, presents another challenge to be faithful to the original, because it involves a kind of "re-synchronization" in programming.

Kondo is also concerned about the "transition between music and sound effects" in *Ocarina 3D*. It is difficult to say how these transitions would change, though it could have to do with how sound effects and music are mixed by the sound hardware.

Finally, Kondo is concerned about disturbing the effect of silence in his original score for *Ocarina*. To discover what he means by this concern, one only has to look for silence in the game's score. Silence occurs most frequently during "area transitions" in *Ocarina*, a common operation for Area Music. For example, when players direct Link to "Lon Lon Ranch" in *Ocarina*, the "Hyrule Field" theme fades out and the "Lon Lon Ranch" theme fades in — mimicking the visual fades for the "scene change." Kondo composed "Lon Lon Ranch" to elucidate a much slower way of life, primarily with a down-tempo country waltz harmonica melody that forms the centrepiece of the theme, supported by gentle banjo-plucking in the rhythm. I can only guess that Kondo was concerned about load times that do not quite line up with the N64's "processor tempo," and that the lengths of silence between Area Music would be disturbed by the 3DS' "processor tempo." Kondo's concerns reveal that game scoring is structured by gaming technology, all the way down to processor speed and framerate, as these largely dictate the rhythm of gameplay in *Ocarina*.

Area Music that changes to other Area Music when players move to a new area is *not* an example of what ludo-musicologists call "adaptive music," even though the music is technically "adapting" to an area transition. The term "adaptive music" is reserved for alterations to an existing musical theme, rather than changes between themes. These changes are prompted by numerous factors within the same Area, such as, for example, collecting a power-up, or running low on time in *Super Mario Bros*. Environmental or terrain changes within the same area might also prompt the need or desire for adaptive music. For example, games that require players to direct avatars both on land and underwater often employ adaptive scoring techniques to elucidate this environmental change. The "underwater versions" of much Area Music in games are simply low-pass filtered versions of the same music, for example. This effect creates a "submerged" quality to the sound that elucidates the players' physical surroundings. For example, all of the Area Music for *Banjo-Kazooie* (1998) transitions to an "aquatic" version, a harp arrangement, whenever players direct Banjo underwater.

In *Super Mario 64*, the water level music, "Dire Dire Docks," behaves differently for each of the two water levels it sets in the game. In the level "Jolly Roger Bay," the theme plays on electric piano while Mario is on the beach, and adds violins to the mix when he goes in the water. If players find a secret cavern hidden underwater, and direct Mario back on land (in the cavern), the music will also add percussion. In the level "Dire, Dire Docks," Mario falls into water when he enters the level, and so the theme plays with violins. Unlike Jolly Roger Bay, where players may return to the beach to hear the solo electric piano version of the water theme, this version is not available in Dire, Dire Docks. Instead, players always hear the percussive "cavern" version of the theme whenever Mario is on dry land. Thus, while this music programming is an archetypal example of adaptive Area Music for underwater states, it is also an example of a variable music system. Kondo opted to have the music adapt in slightly different ways when he scored each of these two levels, thereby musically distinguishing them from one another. Arguably, this distinction helps players think of them as two separate levels, rather than pair them together as the "water levels." The third water level in the game, "Wet-Dry World," supports this fact, as it uses the "Cave Dungeon" theme instead of "Dire, Dire Docks."

Gameplay Music: Time System Jingles

Time System Jingles are special pieces of music that are triggered by some interaction with a game's time system — whether it is internal or based on real time. These jingles signify a time "milestone" in a more overt fashion than time system–dependent background music changes, such as the music for *FEZ*, for example. Whereas "Day" background music might transition to "Night" music without *FEZ* players realizing, Time System Jingles are composed to highlight such a change. In *Ocarina*, for example, a wolf howl indicates that day has changed to night, while a rooster call indicates morning has come. In the morning, the rooster call is followed by a musical introduction to the day's Area Music, consisting of a bright ascending woodwind melody that is followed by a short phrase played by much fuller sounding strings. Unlike nightfall, indicated by only a sound effect, morning in *Ocarina* is set by both a sound effect and a musical phrase, likely because background music does not play at night, whereas it does during the day, and thus requires a musical introduction. Therefore, the "function" of the morning Time System Jingle is both ludal and narrative. The rooster call indicates the change in time, while the musical introduction evokes a bright and happy start to the day.

It is up to game designers and developers how they program and customize their games' time systems. In *Ocarina*, for example, time only moves forward in "Overworld" areas such as Hyrule Field and outside "Hyrule Castle," and not in towns or dungeons, for instance. In *FEZ*, on the other hand, the time system is almost always active.[17] Thus, if *Ocarina* had an uninterrupted time system akin to the one programmed for *FEZ*, the time system jingles of the rooster call and wolf howl would always sound at regular intervals. Instead, the timing of these sounds are dependent on both a degree of performer freedom and chance operations. Of course, players are not attempting to "time up" rooster calls and wolf howls for musical effect; in this case, and in most game scores, "performer freedom" amounts to gameplay decisions that are unrelated to musical goals, though music may still prompt action and vice versa. For example, a wolf howl in *Ocarina* indicates night has fallen. Nighttime is a much more dangerous time in Hyrule Field since skeleton creatures called Stalfos constantly rise up out of the ground to attack Link. Thus, the wolf howl may prompt players to direct Link to the nearest town or village for refuge. If players do not seek refuge in one of the game's villages, they can expect to hear the Battle Music for *Ocarina* as they traverse the enemy-ridden Hyrule Field. I will discuss Battle Music and specifically *Ocarina*'s implementation in the next section of this chapter.

Other game time systems may not attempt to replicate Day-and-Night changes, but instead function as time limits for players to complete a given task. Sometimes games have a time limit to complete an entire level, and a warning will sound when the timer reaches a certain point. For example, the infamous "Hurry Up!" jingle from *Super Mario Bros.* (1985) depends on the in-level timer, and sounds when players only have 100 "seconds" to direct Mario to the end of a level. This Time System Jingle serves as a musical "bridge" between the current background music — such as the "Overworld" or "Underwater" theme — at normal speed, and the same music played at twice the speed, for the final 100 seconds. The ascending melody, whose tempo lies somewhere between the normal and "2×" speeds of the "Overworld" theme, produces a tension that is then sustained by the faster version of the background music that follows. If this bridge were not present, the increase in tempo would seem much more abrupt, and it might not convey urgency in the same way.

Finally, game developers program other timers for mini-games available to players within the main gameplay. These mini-games typically have their own music for their gameplay, and this music is typically preceded by a Time System Jingle to indicate the start of the mini-game. For example, each mini-game in the *Donkey Kong Country* games for SNES begins with a screen of instructions, set by a Time System Jingle played on horns that readies players for a quick test of one or more of their skills.

Gameplay Music: Battle Music

Battle Music is music that plays during gameplay that involves fighting one or more enemies. Some games, such as fighting games, are composed entirely of battles, and so their Area Music is always Battle Music, too. Fighting game Area Music therefore has the task of simultaneously representing the fighting stage, or environment, as well as the intensity of battle. The latter is structured according to gameplay design factors that are generally fixed across a wide thematic or narrative range of environments. For example, *Street Fighter II: The World Warrior* (1991) (*SF2*) contains stages based on locations around the world and eras across history, such as the character Ryu's home stage, Suzaku Castle, set in Japan in the feudal era; Ken's home stage, the Air Force Base, set in the United States in the present day; or Dahlsim's home stage, Maharaja's Palace, set in a fictional palace of an Indian Maharaja. Each of these stages features unique music by Yoko Shimomura (2014: 16), who explains her composition process for *SF2*:

> When it was decided that I'd be doing *SF2*, it was mostly the planner who explained what kind of songs they wanted. He gave me a kind of list. As far as I can remember, he just told me they wanted theme songs for the characters.
>
> So I got a list at first, and when we were discussing the type of songs I should make, there were different scenes from different countries, but I thought, 'The real India isn't like this.' It's the same way that Japan is geisha and kabuki from the eyes of foreigners. That kind of mysterious, distorted view of the world was funny to me.
>
> We discussed the idea of — rather than character theme songs — maybe making background music with the feeling of each country instead. For example, for India I wouldn't make real Indian music, but I'd make what I imagined Indian music to be like. When I suggested that making some kind of world music with a comical taste might be funny, they said it was fine, and we went with it. For the music when you had ⅓ of your energy left and were struggling, I suggested making the music faster and more desperate.

In game scores for *SF2*, players can expect to find "world music with a comical taste," with some musical features based on their current stage, and some musical features based on

FIGURE 4.7   The Amazon River Basin stage from *SF2* (1991). E. Honda (left) is preparing for an attack from Blanka (right).

gameplay. For example, all of the Battle Music in *SF2* features prominent differential pulse-code modulation (DPCM) percussion samples, and most of it has a very fast tempo, in order to set the violent and frenetic gameplay. Melodic structure and orchestration, on the other hand, are based on each stage's unique environmental features. For example, the music for the character "Blanka," whose stage is the Amazon River Basin, is composed of a wooden flute melody in a minor key, supported by a wooden flute and horn rhythm section playing in a major key. The bright timbre and ascending contour of the melody makes it more compatible with the upbeat rhythm section, though the harmonic clashes between the keys lends it a mysterious, or "strange, broken feeling," as Shimomura (2014: 22) notes. Thus, the rhythmic drive of "Blanka" is compatible with the gameplay of *SF2*, while its melody and timbre set the venue of the Amazon River (pictured in Figure 4.7).

Battle Music also features prominently in Role-Playing Games, or RPGs. RPGs involve the player forming a party of fighters, each with their own strengths and weaknesses, and battling countless enemies, usually in an effort to amass "experience points" and grow more powerful. RPGs typically have long, epic narratives that are lengthened by the many battles the player experiences. In early examples of this genre, the same Battle Music plays for nearly every enemy encounter, and so this is arguably the most important music category for RPG scorers. The first *Final Fantasy* (1987), scored by Nobuo Uematsu, uses the same Battle Music, "Battle Scene," for every single battle in the game, despite having more music than any other NES game at the time. Later RPGs have multiple tracks of Battle Music for different enemies and special encounters, and composers of NES music likely have Uematsu to thank for the space afforded them by developers in the wake of the first *Final Fantasy*. The jump in soundtrack length at the time added to the feeling of epic scale in the game.

"Battle Scene" features a driving bassline and music in G-minor played at 150 beats per minute, or BPM. These features combine with the use of the dissonant tritone interval at the opening of the melody, and throughout, to create the tension necessary for a battle scene. Figure 4.8 is the score for "Battle Scene:"

Figure 4.9 is an example of a battle scene in *Final Fantasy*:

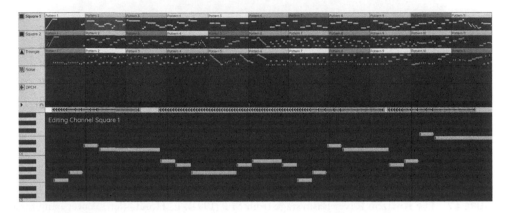

FIGURE 4.8 The beginning of an official piano reduction of Uematsu's "Battle Scene." An opening bassline introduces the tempo and tension of battle, while tritone intervals and punctuated pauses in the melody heighten the intensity of fights for *Final Fantasy* players.

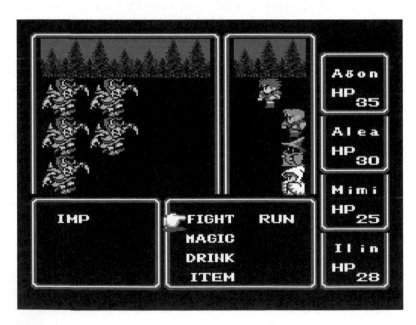

FIGURE 4.9 An early battle scene from *Final Fantasy* (1990). My team faces five "imps," the least powerful enemies in the game. Players have the option with each character to fight, use a magic power, drink a potion, use an item or attempt to run away from battle. I am currently selecting an action ("FIGHT") for my "Fighter."

Strangely, "Battle Scene" does not feature percussion, even though it is a fast tune meant to produce gameplay tension. In fact, none of the music on the score utilizes the NES APU's noise channel (NGC), the primary channel for percussion. Game designer Michael Matlock (2018) theorizes that Uematsu avoided using the NGC for one or more of the following three reasons: (1) he was attempting to produce an "old-fashioned" or "classical" sound in his compositions, and the exclusion of percussive sounds aided this attempt; (2) he was attempting to generate a sound signature to his compositional style, since most other NES game scores heavily feature percussion; or (3) he was simply leaving the noise channel free for sound effects, an explanation that works well in the case of "Battle Scene," since battles in *Final Fantasy* feature many sound effects generated by the noise channel.

Later installments of the *Final Fantasy* series, and RPGs in general, would include different versions of Battle Music for various types of enemies. For example, "Franky," scored by Keiichi Suzuki and Hirokazu Tanaka for *Earthbound* (1995), is a 1950s rock 'n' roll-inspired — it resembles "Johnny B. Goode" by Chuck Berry — piece that plays whenever players encounter either the Frank Fly or New Age Retro Hippie enemies.

While RPGs typically have "announced" enemy encounters, where players definitively transition from exploration to battle, action-adventure games that involve real-time combat have enemies the player may approach and leave at their convenience. These encounters necessitate a smooth transition from "safe" music to "danger" music, because there is no "scene change" akin to the ones from RPGs discussed above. *Ocarina* is largely credited with popularizing game scores that transition seamlessly between "safety" and "danger" states, as I mention briefly above, though it has both precursors and contemporaries of this technique. Table 4.1 is a list of examples:

Game scorers for many gaming genres also recognize that special enemies known as "bosses" require special Battle Music. In action games, bosses are larger and more complex than normal enemies, and typically command their own "gameplay scene." For players encountering important bosses, there may be an introductory cut-scene — especially in 3D games — that showcases the enemy's animations and sounds. Thus, Cut-Scene Music often serves as an introduction to Boss Battle Music, as bosses are often introduced through cut-scenes in action games.

Boss battles in games are designed for very specific gameplay. The skills that players need to learn and master are put to the test in boss battles, and game designers' greatest hope is that many players are successful, because it means they have committed to learning and performing specific controller techniques that have hopefully become less of a chore and more of a dance. The latter analogy works well in the case of action game boss battles, because game designers typically program boss battles to require more dodging and defending than normal enemy battles. If players have become accustomed to "mashing" the attack button and never defending against normal enemies, they will have to learn how to dodge and defend for a boss battle. In other words, players often need to widen their skill repertoire for boss battles. Arguably, it is quite frightening for players to attempt to "defend" for the first time, if they have spent all their time attacking in an action game. Defending involves patience and timing, while attacking often only requires impatient "button-mashing." Thus, players turn their attention to gameplay experimentation in boss battles, as they attempt to find the best strategy to defeat them while surviving.

Game designers often program boss battles in phases. A boss battle may start by demanding the player dodge multiple attacks, and then enter a new phase where the player may

TABLE 4.1 A list of examples of adaptive Battle Music in games

Game and genre labels	Description
Space Invaders (1978) Genre labels: "shoot 'em up," action, two-dimensional, top-down view, arcade.	The Area Music for the game is a simple four-note pattern generated by analog circuitry, and increases in tempo as enemies get closer to the avatar, a laser cannon.
Twisted Metal (1995) Genre labels: Vehicular combat, action, three-dimensional, third-person view, console.	In the "Cyburbia" level, the Area Music transitions between "Cyburb Hunt," an ambient track that sets players hunting for enemies, and "Cyburb Slide," a fast, hard rock track that sets vehicle battles.
Need for Speed III: Hot Pursuit (1998) Genre labels: Racing, three-dimensional, first- or third-person view, console, personal computer.	The race music changes in intensity depending on player position, speed and lap count. In "Hot Pursuit" mode, the Area Music transitions to another, more energetic theme that grows in intensity as police cars get closer.
X-COM: Interceptor (1998) Genre labels: Space flight simulation, business simulation, strategy, three-dimensional, first-person view, personal computer.	Ambient Area Music transitions to Battle Music when players enter a battle, and snippets of music react to players' actions within battle, such as a triumphant melody when players defeat an enemy.
Metal Gear Solid (1998) Genre labels: Action, stealth, espionage, three-dimensional, third-person view.	The Area Music for each level shifts to "Encounter," the "danger state" music, when the avatar, Solid Snake, is noticed by enemies.
The Legend of Zelda: Ocarina of Time (1998) Genre labels: Adventure, action, RPG, three-dimensional, third-person view, console.	The Area Music transitions seamlessly to Battle Music when Link is near enemies, whether because players directed him, or the enemies moved towards him. Each "battle score" is aleatoric; the Battle Music consists of four 8-bar phrases that repeat and transition between each other in a semi-random looping system.

attack the boss, for example. Bosses can also have various forms that each demand different gameplay strategies to defeat, and so boss battles are venues for game scorers to employ adaptive scoring techniques, as gameplay scenarios change during boss battles to demand different kinds of player action and thus, music. For example, the Boss Battle Music for *The Legend of Zelda: The Wind Waker* (2003) varies for each stage of action, such as adding a bass line in "Helmaroc King" when players successfully remove the boss's crown. The Boss Battle Music for sub-bosses in *Wind Waker* also has different music adaptations for battle intensity that are triggered by various gameplay parameters. "Mini-boss" changes to a softer texture and volume when Link's sword is sheathed; changes to a louder, brighter sound when players unsheathe his sword; adds drums when Link is near the sub-boss; quickens in tempo for when Link is low on health; quickens in tempo and lowers in pitch when Link is struck by an enemy; and adds a horn roll every time players perform a "spin-attack." These changes quickly communicate to players the success or failure of their gameplay actions, and "funnels" them toward specific ones for defeating the sub-boss. The music adaptations encourage players to keep their sword unsheathed and perform spin attacks — more difficult but also more powerful sword strikes. The score also adds rhythmic drive to enemy proximity, resulting in an intense combat experience. The tempo changes for low health and successful enemy attacks against Link warn players to fight with greater attention to timing, while providing negative feedback for their performance in the fight.

Gameplay Music: Rest Music

Rest, or "safety state" Music plays when there is zero chance of danger to players in a game, and helps elucidate the sense of relief this situation brings. It is important to note that some games do not even feature danger states — such as many simulation games — so, similarly to the ubiquity of Battle Music in fighting games, "Rest Music" can refer to any music in games of this type. However, Rest Music has even broader contextual parameters than Battle Music. Whereas Battle Music must sound during battles, the designation of Rest Music is not limited to the main gameplay portions of a game. That is, players may interpret any music that accompanies a sense of relief as Rest Music. Even the high-energy "Invincibility" theme from *Sonic the Hedgehog* may signify a "rest" for players who normally have to defend themselves with greater focus. The subjective nature of the definition of Rest Music also means that Pause or Menu Music may serve as Rest Music. Area Music may also become Rest Music in non-quantitative gameplay scenarios, such as one of the "vista" screens from *Gimmick!* (Figure 4.10):

Though it is not an explicit example of Vista Music — a type of Rest Music that accompanies impressive "views" accessible via normal gameplay — the vista by the sea in *Gimmick!* includes special sound programming afforded by the game's extra audio hardware included in its cartridge. The cartridge includes the "Sunsoft 5B" audio chip, which includes several extra synthesizers that were used for the music and sound effects in the game. For example, at the vista by the sea, the Area Music for the level is accompanied by barely audible "squawks" to mimic the animated seagulls in the background — an early example of Ambiences mixed with Area Music.[18] In terms of rest, players might enjoy relaxing at the vista

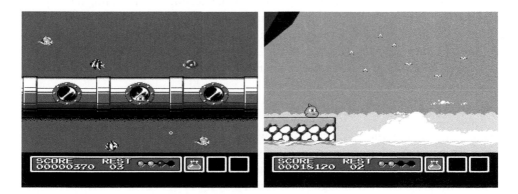

FIGURE 4.10 Two vistas from *Gimmick!* (1992). The underwater vista (left) is a pipe that the protagonist, Yumetaro, must pass through to complete the first level. Players observe the various fishes' graphics and animations as they proceed right. The vista by the sea (right) is an optional screen in the second level, where players may observe the water, sky and birds in the distance.

by the sea and listening to the birds. However, the birds also serve as reminders that players could still direct Yumetaro to fall into the sea and thus lose a life.

Players may also treat Cut-Scene Music as Rest Music, and this flexibility elucidates a key difference between playing a game and watching a film. In a film, the narrative will always progress with or without spectators' input, and so tension is created by the narrative itself. In a game, the narrative may only progress if certain goals are met, and so the progression of narrative is *always* a reward, even if the narrative involves the player's avatar suffering, for example. Thus, there is always relief involved in watching a cut-scene in a game, no matter what the cut-scene actually consists of. Cut-Scene Music might sound extremely gloomy, for example, but it would still perform the function of Rest Music: setting a period of relaxation, after a period of intense gameplay.[19]

"Generative" music applications, such as those scored by Brian Eno, exclude quantitative goals normally found in games, such as high score systems or enemies that must be defeated by players. Instead, generative music applications are meant for relaxing, non-goal-oriented operations. In some applications of this type, users may ascertain the inner workings of the music system through experimentation, and by noting what musical effects are generated by what actions. In others, it is unclear how the music reacts to user input, and the point of the application is for users to "let go" of such concerns, and simply enjoy the fact that they are instigating sound and musical events in some way. Though I cannot fully examine generative music applications in the space I have here, it is worth noting that the latter pleasure is not exclusive to them. That is, game scores do not need to explicitly react to "good" and "bad" events in gaming activity. They can rely on other data from gameplay, internal music system data, or programmed chance operations. From my experience playing *FEZ*, a game that relies on relatively neutral data to generate its music, this type of scoring does not preclude immersion. Nor does a game score based on gameplay value judgments necessarily increase immersion.

That said, there are points in numerous games where players direct their avatars to an explicitly resting state, such as making Mario take a nap in *Super Mario RPG*, for example. As with that game, resting states typically involve some sort of health or power revival, and so Rest Music in these cases would also have to evoke healing. An ascending melody could represent a "life meter" filling up in any number of action games, for instance, though this example is only one of any number of animation possibilities for resting states that game scorers must musically elucidate.

A selection of other types of — or contexts for — Rest Music is available in Table 4.2.

Gameplay Music: Dialogue Music

Dialogue Music is music that accompanies written or spoken dialogue between characters in a video game that occurs outside of a cut-scene. While in a cut-scene players must often cede control over dialogue timings, with in-game dialogue there is typically a level of control over the progression of dialogue that in turn means a level of control over how long Dialogue Music plays for. Composers are usually tasked with writing unique Dialogue Music for dialogue with special characters — typically ones that are more ludally instructive. For example, in *Ocarina*, a guardian-instructor owl named Kaepora Gaebora presents himself whenever players direct Link past certain narrative checkpoints or to enter new, unfamiliar areas (see Figure 4.11). While players (optionally) direct Link to talk to other characters in

TABLE 4.2 Other types of Rest Music

Type	Description	Function
"Town" or "Safehouse Music"	Music that plays when players direct avatars to a town, village or safehouse to gain information, rest and/or shop for items.	Scored to evoke a sense of safety and in the case of populated areas, community. See, for instance, "Hyrule Castle Town" from *Ocarina*.
"Shop Music"	Music that plays in a shop, or to set dialogue with a merchant.	Scored with similar goals to "muzak," as it is meant to play in the background while players shop for items. If composers aim for this goal, they should score their "muzak" with less intensity than — or as a pastiche of — their other compositions. See, for instance, "Crazy Cap" from *Odyssey*.
"Cut-Scene Music"	Music that plays during a cut-scene.	Scored to set and evoke the emotions involved in the narrative of the game, presented in a cut-scene format. Follows similar conventions to film scores.
"Pause Music"	Unique music that plays while the game is paused. Primarily a form of Menu Music, but it remains the case that pausing the game (and even equipping items etc.) is a form of rest from the main gameplay.	Pause Music can interrupt almost any other music in the game, and so it should complement rather than contrast the rest of the score. See, for instance, the interactive instrumentation used for the pause menu in *Super Mario Bros. 2*.
"Vista Music"	The music currently playing, or unique music for "vistas," or generally safe areas where players may observe the game's visuals.	Vista Music should not only complement the vistas it sets, but also excite the player to return to normal gameplay. See, for instance, the Title Motif for *Breath of the Wild*.

the game by pressing "A," each of Kaepora Gaebora's special dialogues are triggered automatically when Link moves to certain areas — an operation similar to location-triggered cut-scenes in games. However, unlike in a standard cut-scene, players have control over the progression of written text from Kaepora Gaebora. This control means that the length for which the Dialogue Music plays is up to players' reading speeds and/or desire to navigate through the dialogue.

With Kaepora Gaebora's Dialogue Music, Koji Kondo expresses not only the owl's wisdom, but also his often indirect and lengthy advice that occurs at points where players are most excited about exploring the world of *Ocarina* — after major narrative action has taken place and while Link enters a brand new area. First-time players and speed-runners alike have complained about Kaepora Gaebora's obstinate presence in *Ocarina*, a frustration that Kondo seems to be already aware of in his composition. The piece repeatedly follows both the dominant chord, as well as B-natural notes, with the tonic, C. While contrasting the dominant chord with the tonic is a routine use of scale degrees to produce tension in music theoretical terms, Kondo applies this technique in a rote, almost academic way to "Kaepora Gaebora." Furthermore, the use of B-naturals as opposed to B-flats, evokes a much earlier

FIGURE 4.11 Link turns a corner after exiting his home village, Kokiri Forest, and glimpses Hyrule Field (top, left). The game stops players from directing Link once he reaches a pre-defined point, the camera tilts up to reveal Kaepora, and the frame is cropped to indicate a dialogue scene (top, right). Kaepora indulges himself in lengthy advice (not pictured), encouraging players to press "A" repeatedly to skip through the dialogue. Unfortunately, at the end of the dialogue, impatient players may accidentally inform Kaepora that they did not "get all that," and he will repeat himself (bottom, right).[20]

form of music theory that strove to omit B-flats, which arguably looks and sounds arbitrary today. These musical features combine to produce a "boring" sound in the piece, to elucidate the impatience players feel while talking with the owl in *Ocarina*.

Dialogue Music case study: the Owl and *Link's Awakening*

Kaepora Gaebora is not the first owl, and "Kaepora Gaebora" is not the first music written for dialogue with an owl, in the *Zelda* series. *The Legend of Zelda: Link's Awakening* (1993), developed for the Nintendo Game Boy handheld video game system, also features music specifically for the un-named "Owl" in the game. The Owl in *Link's Awakening* functions similarly to Kaepora Gaebora in *Ocarina*; he appears after every musical instrument Link finds in each dungeon, each signifying a "chapter" in game and story progression. The Owl also communicates to Link telepathically while he is inside a dungeon, through owl statues, though these dialogues are triggered through a button press, rather than major game progression, and they are not accompanied by unique music. Thus, the Owl's physical presence is a necessary condition for the "Owl" theme to play in *Link's Awakening*.

The Owl — along with his statues that populate both the overworld and dungeons — offers hints about the mysterious narrative of the game, in addition to direct instruction on where to go next, in order for Link to find the next dungeon and musical instrument. According to the game's narrative, Link was shipwrecked by a storm and washed up on the shore of "Koholint Island." The Owl and other characters in the game inform Link of a mysterious being known as "the Wind Fish," who sleeps in a giant egg at the top of the island's single mountain — "Mt. Tamaranch." Link eventually learns that the only way for him to leave the island is to wake the Wind Fish, and the only way to do so is to find eight magical musical instruments. Screenshots of the narrative introductory video to *Link's Awakening* are available in Figure 4.12:

The ending to *Link's Awakening* confirms — while leaving the door slightly ajar to alternative readings — that the events of the game actually take place in Link's dreams; that he did not wash up on shore, and that he remains floating, passed out, and clinging to the wreckage of his ship in the middle of the ocean. Throughout the game, the Owl hints at this possibility, though, if this reading is correct, the Owl must be part of Link's dream as well. The latter reading would mean Link's subconscious structures his own interactions with the Owl, even as the Owl gives him advice on his adventure. Since the Owl seems to be the most knowledgeable about Koholint Island, he is both the best chance for Link to wake up, and one of the deepest parts of the dream.

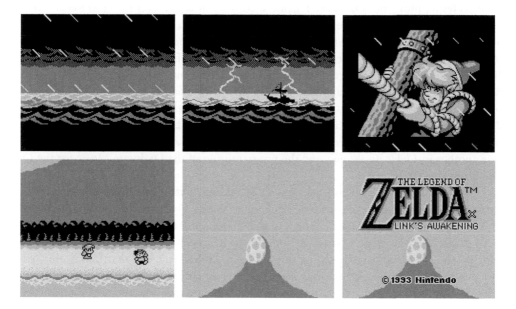

FIGURE 4.12 The introductory video and story to *Link's Awakening* (1993). Booting the game causes a wicked sea storm to appear on the Game Boy screen, and a small boat appears from the right of the frame. Lightning flashes, and the game cuts to Link struggling to hold himself and the boat together. Another flash of lightning occurs, the screen fades to white and fades into the character Marin walking on the beaches of Koholint Island, only to find Link washed up on shore. The screen pedestals upward to reveal Mt. Tamaranch in the background, upon which sits a giant egg.

The "Owl" theme, composed by Minako Himano and Kensuke Tanabe, is a short, re-peating loop split into two five-note ascending phrases that are played by the two pulse wave channels on the Nintendo Game Boy APU. The melody never resolves, though it sounds as if it is close on the fifth and tenth notes. After players conquer any of the dungeons in *Link's Awakening*, they will likely return to the overworld feeling accomplished. The main theme of the "Overworld" music evokes exploration and courage, but the visit from the Owl evokes mystery and a slight urgency. The Owl could thus symbolize Link's main "survival drive" in the real world, beckoning him to wake up as he drifts at sea. The "Owl" theme is a constant reminder of responsibility in the game, and that there is a problem that still needs resolution.

The "Owl" theme only plays while the Owl speaks to Link, except for one important instance in the game. Near the very last gameplay portion of the game, when Link is about to enter the giant egg at the top of Mt. Tamaranch to wake the Wind Fish, the Owl returns for one last dialogue. The "Owl" theme plays as normal, but when the Owl flies away, instead of stopping and resuming to the music for Mt. Tamaranch, the score stays on the "Owl" theme, and players may move Link for the first time while this music plays. Though Link may only move up and down a staircase on this single screen, this simple access to freedom of movement as the "Owl" theme plays is an immense release to players. Finally, it is time for Link to take control of his own destiny, and the "Owl" theme becomes his own theme, perhaps as the Owl is folded back into his subconscious, if the above reading of the narrative is correct.

If, as Jesper Juul (2005) has noted, game worlds are designed according to the abilities of the main protagonist, then the story to *Link's Awakening* is a communication of this central aspect of game design. If everything on Koholint Island comes from Link's dreams, then ev-ery aspect of gameplay is structured by Link's abilities, since he cannot — or must not, much like the real designer — imagine scenarios where he does not have the ability to progress. Whereas the vast number of elaborate puzzles in other *Zelda* games may only be attributed to some imagined villainous mastermind operation, the puzzles, as well as everything else in *Link's Awakening*, may be narratively traced back to Link's "ebb and flow" between survival and slumber. In a narrative sense, then, gameplay and narrative are completely fused with one another in *Link's Awakening*, and the programming of the Dialogue Music for the Owl elucidates this fact.

Link's Awakening also includes an extended ending, with extended music, for players that complete the game without experiencing a "Game Over." While I discuss alternate and multiple ending scenarios for games in the section on Results Music, below, it is worth noting here that the game's "true" ending offers the possibility that another character es-caped Koholint Island, and thus Link's dream. This ending suggests that Link's dream was not purely a "nightmare," that there *was* a narrative goal in the story other than his own survival. Yet, to access this narrative element, and to gain a greater sense of the *meaning* of the game, players must perform well, so, again, narrative and gameplay are always entangled in *Link's Awakening*.

Gameplay Music: Challenge Music

Challenge Music is music that plays when players encounter special challenges, "mini-games" or "bonus areas" in games. As with level hubs, game designers may program challenges separately from the main gameplay, in which case I would refer to them as "mini-games." As I explain in an above section, loading screens are an excellent context for mini-games, though there are few examples of loading screen mini-games outside the Namco Corporation. However, since loading screens involve loading the main gameplay portions of a game in the background, loading screen mini-games are an example of challenges that always contain alternate gameplay. The latter means that different Gameplay Music is necessary for loading screen mini-games.

"Bonus areas," on the other hand, are areas that players may navigate to, usually by uncovering some sort of secret, such as finding a beanstalk in *Super Mario Bros.*, which leads Mario to "cloud land," as players refer to it. This bonus area in particular is quite rewarding; it is filled with coins that Mario must only jump to collect, and contains no danger besides the level's time limit.

To summarize the above, mini-games are discreet games that involve different degrees of skill and luck to obtain a reward, while bonus areas are inherently rewarding and utilize the existing gameplay mechanics of the game. However, the main aspects of mini-games do not completely preclude the main aspects of bonus areas. Mini-games might utilize the same world and controls as the main game, though in a different way from the main gameplay actions. For example, the jump-rope mini-game in *Super Mario Odyssey* requires players to make Mario jump at a rhythm that increases in speed at specific intervals — a skill that is not explicitly required in the main gameplay. Bonus areas, moreover, may be programmed so that players are not punished for attempting them, but still require advanced techniques to be fully exploited. Thus, the line between mini-games and bonus areas is not clear, and the scoring context for challenges varies considerably. For example, finding a well-hidden bonus area in a game deserves a reward of its own, which might include reward items that require very "easy" or non-threatening gameplay to collect. A game score would need to set a sense of surprised discovery, proud accomplishment and an unrestrained — perhaps even self-righteous — collection of rewards. Other bonus areas might not be programmed for such low difficulty, and players might be tested for their skills, even after proving their exploration skills by finding the bonus area in the first place. This scenario would require Challenge Music that encourages players to continue their efforts, instead of promoting a carefree collection of rewards.

Chapter conclusions

Though game scoring analysts might attempt to isolate composers' intentions, the subjective experiences of players, and the music programming itself, all three impact one another in actual gameplay. In this chapter, I have explored the experience of scoring music for and through gaming by examining each of the most common game scoring components in terms of composition, implementation and "performance" — from both the performer and spectator points of view — alike. While in Chapter 2 I examined how game scoring is structured by gaming technology, with a focus on composition, in this chapter I have attempted to bridge the conceptual gap between game scoring as composition and as gameplay. As it turns out, game scorers navigate the very same conceptual gap through software programming. Game scorers program music for games based on specific aspects of gameplay design. While some programming categories relate more to certain gaming genres, I have attempted in this chapter to cover only the most common musical needs for games. However, this taxonomy is not meant to dictate the "proper" ways to score music for each category. On the contrary, my aim is for this taxonomy to inspire game scorers approaching these categories for the first time. I chose each example in order to show the possibilities for each component, and to elucidate how these components are integrated in games differently than music for other media, such as film, for example. Film scorers do not bear the burden of musically representing two different endings for a film, for example.

From my case studies, I have also "stumbled" across a few key observations about gaming in general, and its differences from other media. Importantly, gaming is *mimetic animation*. Games are always animated rather than "filmed," in other words, and their animations correspond in different ways to haptic operation by gamers. Similarly, game scores "sound" according to player input, and so they play a crucial part in gaming as a mimetic technology. Music and sound "mime" different gameplay actions and parameters, such as Koji Kondo setting Mario's transition from swimming in the water to running on dry land in *Super Mario 64*, for example.

Game scores do not simply "set" a narrative. As I have attempted to show with "Kaepora Gaebora," game scores set the "gameplay mood" as well. With that piece, Kondo predicted that *Ocarina* players would skip through the owl's dialogue, and that they would be eager to explore Hyrule Field, and so he wrote repetitive music that had an "academic" thematic content. Similarly, some game scoring components seem to be more open to subjective interpretation in the gaming experience. For example, players may interpret any music that plays during a period of "rest" as Rest Music. Games, like animations, are inherently less "serious" and more playful than film, for instance, and their scores allow for more "playful" interpretation. Even "serious" gameplay such as speed-running often involves breaking traditional rules. For example, speed-runners may find it quicker to let their avatar "die" at a certain point in the game so that the game "re-loads" in a different location, resulting in a "death warp." A "game over" theme would thus remain Results Music, but would signify "positive" results to a speed-runner, contrary to the intended affect of the theme.

In the next chapter, I will examine game scoring through gameplay of one level of the original *Super Mario Bros*. Whereas in this chapter I split game scores into identifiable categories, in the next chapter I examine a single game score, to see how these categories interact with each other in the context of gameplay, and to argue that game scoring is a variant of aleatoric composition.

Notes

1 Shimomura has a uniquely diverse and impressive résumé, as she has composed for multiple major Japanese game development companies and games, including: Capcom (*Street Fighter II* [1991]); Nintendo (*Super Mario RPG* and the *Mario and Luigi* RPG series for handheld systems); Square (*Live a Live* [1994], *Super Mario RPG*, the *Kingdom Hearts* series and *Final Fantasy XV* [2016]); and Monolith Soft (*Xenoblade Chronicles* [2010]).

2 Screenshots of SNES games are taken by the author, using the *Snes9x* emulator written for Microsoft Windows.

3 Demos are non-interactive videos, while "tutorials" involve some kind of interaction, even if it is minimal, such as menu operation, for example. Interaction with a fixed demo video typically interrupts it, and brings players to the game menu. Tutorials may include demo videos, and also opportunities for players to "test out" newly-learned skills. In effect, tutorials may include Demo Music, Menu Music, Menu Sound Effects, Gameplay Music, Gameplay Sound Effects and other game scoring categories, while demos only include Demo Music, Gameplay Sound Effects and perhaps a Menu Sound Effect for cutting the video.

4 For more on this, see Kamp (2009).

5 Hirokazu Ando composes music primarily for the *Super Smash Bros.*, *Kirby* and *BoxBoy* series for Hal Laboratory, and often with his colleague Jun Ishikawa, who works on the same series.

6 Screenshots of gameplay from Nintendo 64 games are taken by the author using the *Project64* emulator written for Microsoft Windows.

7 The success-or-failure aspect of gaming is related to two of Roger Caillois' (1958) dimensions of play: *Agon* (competition) and *Alea* (chance). However, these dimensions are not the only ways to conceptualize gaming activity, as demonstrated by the two other dimensions: *Ilinx* (vertigo) and mimicry (role-playing).

8 Map-level frameworks differ greatly by game, as map screens may be integrated into the main gameplay. For example, in *Breath of the Wild* and many other open world action-adventure games, players have the ability to warp or "fast-travel" to locations they have previously visited, making the in-game map screen once again a kind of area selection screen.

9 Actually, if players access the first secret world from the second normal world, they technically only need to visit three normal worlds and one secret world to complete the game as fast as possible, as exemplified by speed-runs for the game.

10 In film-making, this shot is known as a pedestal shot, because the camera moves up or down but retains the same angle.

11 Control over the camera arguably makes the gamer a camera operator in games, as an analogy to film-making. However, gamers arguably became camera operators in a limited sense the first time they had control over a game's "frame." For example, *SMB* players have limited "trucking shot" capabilities, as the frame "trucks" right every time players direct Mario to the right. In *SMB2* and *SMB3*, this ability was expanded to allow left trucking shots, as players could direct their avatars left and "backtrack." In *SMW*, players could press the shoulder buttons on the SNES controller, which were dedicated camera buttons, to "peek" in one of four directions, allowing for "dollying" and trucking without avatar movement.

12 Of course, Lakitu only becomes the camera operator in a narrative sense. In both ludal and physical senses, the player is the camera operator, as stated above.

13 This jingle's official name is "Toad's Message" because it also plays when talking to Mario's friend Toad.

14 These shapes actually pre-date *Tetris* and are known as "tetrominoes," four-square versions of "polyominoes," which are two-dimensional geometric figures formed by joining equal squares together.

15 This quote is from an interview featured in the Japanese magazine *Game Maestro Vol. 3* (2001), and later translated to English by the *shmupulations* website.

16 Kondo (2014: 32) refers to the "original" version of *Ocarina* for N64 from 1998, as well as the "3DS version," *The Legend of Zelda: Ocarina of Time 3D* (2011), for the Nintendo 3DS handheld system, from 2011.

17 There are also game time systems that are based on real-time, such as several games in the *Pokémon* RPG series.

18 I explore Ambiences, or ambient sound effects, in Chapter 5.

19 Interactive cut-scenes are another story, and so in this case I refer only to "movie-like" cut-scenes that are non-interactive.

20 Sometimes Kaepora Gaebora will ask "Did you get all that?" and sometimes he will ask "Do you want me to repeat what I said again?" so that "Yes" and "No" mean different things in each context. Link's answers may also be listed in different orders, so even veteran *Ocarina* players find themselves asking the owl to repeat himself, even though that is the last thing they want to happen. This occurrence has an upsetting effect for speed-runners, and a comical effect for speed-run spectators.

References

Caillois, Roger. 1958. *Les Jeux et Les Hommes*. Paris: Librairie Gallimard.

Juul, J. 2005. *Half-Real: Video Games between Real Rules and Fictional Worlds*. Cambridge, MA: MIT Press.

Kamp, Michiel. 2009. "Ludic Music in Video Games." Master's Thesis, Utrecht University. http://igitur-archive.library.uu.nl/student-theses/2010-0902-200305/Kamp,%20Michiel%20-%20MA%20Thesis.pdf.

Kondo, Koji. 2001. "Koji Kondo – 2001 Composer Interview." *Shmupulations.* http://shmuplations. com/kojikondo/.

———. 2014. "A Music Trivia Tour with Nintendo's Koji Kondo." *IGN.* https://www.ign.com/ articles/2014/12/10/a-music-trivia-tour-with-nintendos-koji-kondo.

Matlock, Michael. 2018. "The Music of Final Fantasy (An Analysis)." *Weather Gage Workshop.* https:// www.weathergageworkshop.com/articles/2017/2/5/analysis-of-ffi-music-4S8Yn.

Myamoto, Shigeru. 2016. "Nintendo on Zelda 1." *Nintendo Everything.* https://nintendoeverything. com/nintendo-on-zelda-1-miyamotos-inspiration-kondos-all-nighter-molblins-famous-mes-sage-original-hyrule-fantasy-name/2/

Shimomura, Yoko. 2014. "Interview: Street Fighter II's Yoko Shimomura." *Red Bull Music Academy.* https://daily.redbullmusicacademy.com/2014/09/yoko-shimomura-interview.

5
GAME SCORING
Gameplay as performance of aleatoric composition

Game scoring is distinct from other types of scoring, because it is always an at least partially aleatoric compositional activity, given the nature of the gaming medium. Most crucially, video games are *interactive*, meaning that the gamer actively *performs* the gaming experience, though their actions are orchestrated within a set of predetermined possibilities.

This chapter will elucidate game scoring's "aleatoriality" by examining chance operations and "performer freedom" embedded within game scores.[1] This examination will require study of actual gameplay. Given the breadth of scoring possibilities available through even the simplest of video games, I shall only examine one part, or "level," of a game, namely, level 22 of *Super Mario Bros.* I restrict my view to one level to demonstrate how gameplay patterns determine the final game score a gamer hears during each gameplay. I shall compare the game scores I produce for *Super Mario Bros.* to a non-aleatoric musical source, which is the game's "official soundtrack." Video game soundtracks differ from game scores because they are fixed, "idealized" game scores, divorced from gameplay itself. Before I do any of the above, though, I briefly survey the aleatoric tradition in Western Art Music, to provide an historical and analytical context for game scoring. I survey the aleatoric tradition by scrutinizing John Cage's *TV Köln* (1958) in detail. In the last part of this chapter, I offer four final game scoring categories, in order to explore game scoring as a kind of aleatoric composition for "games-as-systems."

Before video games: the aleatoric tradition

While composers such as Henry Cowell, John Cage and Christian Wolff took the first decisive steps towards the creation of an aleatoric compositional style in the early 1950s, there exist many examples of aleatoric music that pre-date the twentieth century. As Antokoletz (2014: 385) explains:

> There has always been some degree of rhythmic, harmonic, and formal freedom for both the composer and the performer throughout earlier centuries, as manifested in

DOI: 10.4324/9781003045465-5

the use of rubato or *ad libitum* indications, fermatas and grand pauses, improvisation in cadenza-like passages, realization of figured bass, and even the elimination of the barline resulting in metric freedom, as in keyboard fantasias of C.P.E. Bach.

In the early part of the twentieth century, composers such as Arnold Schoenberg, for instance, made more radical attempts to "free the performer" from the rigid structures of fixed composition. Antokoletz (Ibid.) notes:

> The use of tone clusters and the elimination of the barline in works of Ives and Cowell resulted in both harmonic and rhythmic indeterminacy, while the use of *Sprechstimme* permitted a degree of pitch and harmonic indeterminacy in works of Schoenberg and others.

Meanwhile, many composers moved toward "integral serialism," an opposing style founded on the idea of total composer control over all aspects of the performance of a composition. From the early twentieth century on, an ever-increasing gap formed between the tenets of integral serialism and the principles of aleatoric composition. These two compositional styles reached their most extreme polarization in the early 1950s, when the American composer John Cage began to compose pieces in which the performer had almost total freedom over the score.

In fact, according to Antokoletz (Ibid.), many of the main principles of aleatoric composition formed specifically in reaction to the principles of integral serialism:

> [Several] distinctions may be observed in the approach to aleatoric composition. These include the elimination of rational composer control over content and/or form in producing a composition that is nevertheless fixed as far as the performer is concerned, use of special indications and notation (either conventional or newly invented) leading to a shift toward performer determination in the generation and ordering of events, and the elimination of both composer and performer control leading to randomness and indeterminacy.

The American composer John Cage was the first to incorporate chance operations fully in his compositions from the early 1950s. Cage was influenced by the improvisational opportunities afforded by certain scalar and rhythmic formulae, namely, *ragas* and *talas*, that he took from Carnatic and Hindustani music traditions. Moreover, his philosophy of music derived from his interest in Zen Buddhism. Cage (1973: n.p.) explains:

> We need first of all a music in which not only sounds are just sounds but in which people are just people, not subject, that is, to laws established by any one of them, even if he is "the composer" or the "conductor." [...] The situation relates to individuals differently, because attention isn't focused in one direction. Freedom of movement is basic to both this art and this society.

Thus Cage advocated both for a relinquishment of control on the part of the composer and a degree of indeterminacy for the performer. In this way, both roles, as we would normally conceptualize them, are problematized by Cage's music from this time.

In 1958, Cage composed *TV Köln*, one of his first works to introduce indeterminacy in the realm of performance. The score for *TV Köln* incorporates both traditional Western notation and a notation system of Cage's own invention. The piece is divided into four sections that Cage explains are of equal duration, though he does not specify their absolute durations.[2]

The instruction sheet accompanying the score provides a legend for four of the capital letters written on the staves:

I = Interior Piano Construction
O = Exterior Piano Construction
A = Auxiliary Noise
K = Keyboard (Numbers = Number of Keys)

Morgan (1991: 317) explains:

> [The] lines [of each section], unlike the staves of traditional piano music, do not separate bass and treble clef, or right hand and left hand, but distinguish the type of sound played or — more accurately — where that sound is produced: on the keys (K), inside the piano (I), on the piano's exterior surface (O), or somewhere other than the piano (A).

Strangely, Cage did not provide an explanation for the letter "P," that appears on the fifth line of the third section. Finally, Cage instructs that a note's proximity to a line may indicate either its relative pitch, duration or amplitude.

TV Köln's score is unique in that it does not instruct performers to play particular sounds, but indicates the way that sounds should be produced. As Morgan (1991: 317) notes, what "is indicated are essentially actions, not musical events." Cage creates a general musical structure for the performer to follow, though he leaves considerable room for that performer's agency. The score for *TV Köln* allows for "freedom of movement," as Cage puts it, meaning that many of its compositional parameters are left to the agency of the performer. For example, the absolute duration of any musical event in the piece is unspecified, and a single notational element refers to three completely independent parameters (pitch, duration, amplitude), thereby leaving those to the performer's discretion. Each letter corresponds to an increasingly vaguely-defined action, from "K" which corresponds to pressing a piano key, to "A" which corresponds to almost any action, to "P" which could signify anything. Finally, the difference between stemmed and unstemmed note heads is also unexplained, leaving performers to interpret it themselves, however they see fit. Yet, as Morgan (1991: 318) suggests, despite all these compositional uncertainties, *TV Köln*

> has a definite "shape," because the events that constitute it have been arranged in a given temporal relationship with one another. This shape even has, however inadvertently, a certain traditional quality. The piece opens with a single isolated event; continues […] with a relatively quick succession of events […] and closes with two more isolated events.

In future compositions, Cage would endeavour to avoid any defined "shape" through various means, all of which granted the performer greater agency, and the score itself greater indeterminacy. Cage's inclusion of "non-musical" sounds in his scores — such as the "auxiliary" sounds he indicates in *TV Köln* — is salient to the current analysis of game scoring, particularly with respect to "sound effects." Cage's score "musicalizes" sounds that would ordinarily register as "extramusical" in traditional musicological analyses. Similarly, as the next section will demonstrate, game scoring includes a recognition, accommodation and even an orchestration of sound effects that ordinarily might also be considered "extramusical" to the untrained ear.

A note on sound effects

Before I investigate examples of actual game scores, I should clarify the role of sound effects in game scores, and the way I intend to conceptualize sound effects in the following case study. One might equate video game sound effects to extraneous sounds heard in the orchestra pit of a ballet recital, for instance, such as the squeaks of chairs or the coughs of performers. This analogy is unsuitable for video game sound effects, however. In the example of sounds heard in the orchestra pit, the composer of the piece does not take these extraneous noises into account. They are considered "extramusical," as it were. The instruments that make "music" are not the same objects that produce these sounds, in this instance.

In contrast, game scorers must consider "extramusical" sounds in a video game as not only an inevitable but a complementary musical device. After all, a game score may only be *realized* through the act of gameplay, a state that contains many more sounds than those programmed as "music" *per se*. Game scorers must be highly aware of these sounds, to the extent that their scoring process is tailored significantly to accommodate them. Moreover, they are "scored" precisely as, say, a triangle-wave bass line would be. Whereas the ballet orchestra composer only tolerates incidental sounds as extramusical accidents, the game scorer thus integrates sound effects into the compositional process. In short, the game scorer *composes* sound effects, and thus they must be fully aware of the parameters under which sound effects "intrude" upon their scores. Koji Kondo (2010: n.p.) explains:

> The thing I consider to be most important is making the game more fun. There are three things I keep in mind. First of all, each game has a unique rhythm or tempo, so I try to capture that and compose music that fits the game's rhythm. Second of all, the balance. For games, it isn't just the music, one also has to consider sound effects, the balance of the volume, the balance between left and right channels, and make sure the sound effects [are] more prominent. Third, putting in variations in the music to fit with the interactivity of the game. For example, speeding up the tempo when time is running out or changing the music that plays depending on the player's location.

Kondo considers sound effects every time he scores a game. They must be louder than the background music he composes, he notes. Even if Kondo does not consider sound effects "music," then, their presence heavily informs his scoring choices. In fact, I would argue that the musical consequences of video game sound effects — that is, how game scorers accommodate these phenomena in the composition of their own "music" — are too significant to ignore in analyses of any game score.

When a player directs Mario to collect a coin in *Super Mario Bros.* (*SMB*), for instance, a satisfying "Ching!" effect sounds. This sound effect is of primary importance to the "fun" of the game, as it serves as an "aural reward" each time players direct Mario to collect a coin. In addition, this sound effect directly affects the orchestration of the background music in *SMB*. It is created by the two pulse wave channels of the Nintendo Entertainment System (NES), and so any melody that utilizes either or both of those channels is attenuated each time Mario collects a coin. For a very brief period, as this sound effect plays, the background music contains only a bass line, provided by the triangle wave channel (TWC), and a drum loop, provided by the noise channel (NGC). In effect, the orchestrations of the "Overworld," "Underworld," "Underwater" and "Castle" themes change each time Mario grabs a coin. This effect was used more prominently for the U.S. version of *Super Mario Bros. 2*, where the pulse channels are muted each time the player pauses the game, leaving only the triangle and noise channels to play bass and percussion on the "pause screen."

The overlap between music and sound effects in game scoring has its precursor in Cage's earlier work, which was influenced by early twentieth century composers who incorporated so-called "noise" in their compositions. For example, Erik Satie orchestrated *Parade* (1916) with the sounds of typewriters, roulette wheels, sirens and airplanes motors, creating a collage of sounds that was intensely related to everyday life, and allowed Cage to incorporate similar sounds in his own compositions. Cage (1961: 84) also credits Satie's contemporary Edgard Varese as an influence, suggesting that he

> established the present nature of music [...] [through an] acceptance of all audible material proper to music. While others were still discriminating 'musical' tones from noises, Varese moved into the field of sound itself, not splitting it in two by introducing into the perception of it a mental prejudice.

Cage's remarks on Varese indicate the importance of music "opening its doors" to noise. While serialist composers attempted to — internally — de-hierarchize the tonal system, then, Cage sees in Varese an — external — de-prioritization of the tonal system in music. To Cage, the very existence of a tonal system inherently carried a prejudice against non-tonal sounds, while Varese represented a truly democratic approach to music, through his incorporation of noise in composition. Cage's inclusion of "non-musical" sounds in his scores — such as the "auxiliary" sounds he indicates in *TV Köln* — is salient to the current analysis of game scoring, particularly with respect to "sound effects," because Cage's score "musicalizes" sounds that would ordinarily register as "extramusical" in traditional musicological analyses.

My aim is not to discard the categories of "music" and "sound effects" altogether. Obviously, they can serve as useful categories for the basic designation of sounds in a given game score. However, the designation of sounds as "sound effects" can sometimes preclude their musical analysis. The designation of some sounds as "music," on the other hand, privileges those sounds as subjects for musical analysis, and lends some sense of their musical merit over others. Ludo-musicologists would do well to broaden their scope beyond those sounds considered traditional "music," and to analyze the musical contributions of sounds normally considered as "sound effects." This would both allow for more comprehensive examinations of game scores, and direct those examinations toward the challenges of composing music that is interactive.

Roger Scruton (1997: 17, emphasis in original) argues that a musical *tone* is a *sound* that exists in a musical "field of force:"

> This field of force is something that *we* hear, when hearing tones. […] It may even be that the transformation from sound to tone is effected *within* the act of hearing, and has no independent reality. But it is a transformation that can be described, just as soon as we forget the attempt to find 'something in common' to all works that critics have described as music.

The ephemeral nature of this transformation resonates with the fundamentally interactive nature of game scoring and the fact that, given minor exceptions, two game scores for the same game are never identical. Accordingly, the musical field of force is determined by gameplay and is thus different for each game score. Therefore, transformations from sound to tone must be described in terms of that particular field of force.

Game scorers work with, and alongside, sound effects to produce a coherent aural world for games. Sound effects must match the music's aesthetic, and vice versa. The analytic categories of "sound effects" and "music" are only useful, then, in the categorization of sounds in a game score, but neither is more central or crucial to a game score. One does not belong to the world of the game score, while the other belongs to the world of gameplay, for instance. A game score is a product of gameplay, after all. To demonstrate this idea, I now turn my attention to the game score for "World 6-2" of *SMB*.

Case study: *Super Mario Bros.* ("World 6-2")

This case study examines the game score for level 22 of *SMB*, namely, "World 6-2." I use *SMB* as the setting for this game score because of its simplicity and relatively recognizable structure. In addition, *SMB* is an NES game, and so Chapter 2's case study of the NES sound hardware configuration will inform this analysis. I shall examine each section of the level, starting with a visual overview of each section. Figure 5.1 is an overview of the "overworld" section of World 6-2 of *SMB*.

In *SMB*, players must navigate Mario through "worlds" or levels by using his basic abilities of walking, running, jumping, "stomping" on enemies and throwing fireballs, depending on whether he has a "Fire Flower power-up." Mario may also travel down "secret" pipes and up hidden "beanstalks," to embedded micro-levels. Enemies such as "Piranha Plants" intermittently block his way down pipes, while "Goombas" (brown mushroom-like creatures), "Koopa Troopas" (turtle-like creatures with green shells) and "Buzzy Beetles" (turtle-like creatures with harder, darker shells), all threaten Mario's survival.

An almost infinite number of game score variations may result from any given "play-through" of World 6-2 of *SMB*. Musically, the beginning of the level is always the same: Mario starts outside the castle from the previous level and the first notes of the "Overworld" theme play. The "Overworld" theme is in the key of C-Major, contributing to its "happy" and "energetic" mood, while its rhythm is perfectly suited to the ludal rhythm of *SMB*. The opening riff introduces the piece with a jazz-like "turn-around" cadence that complements Mario's first — perhaps hesitant — steps in an Overworld level.[3] This riff sets up the main melody, which begins with an ascending section that could set Mario's first jumps in World 6-2. Ascending phrases in the melody become more frequent as the piece plays, and as the player progresses through the level and finds more obstacles to clear.

The game score for the level may conclude at any point in which Mario "dies," an action that triggers the "Death Sound," a comedic descending riff punctuated by what sounds like

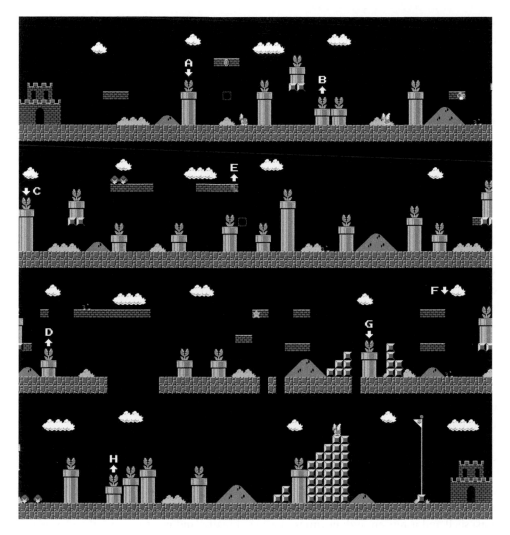

FIGURE 5.1 "World 6-2" of *Super Mario Bros.* (1985). During gameplay, the gamer may only see a small section of this level. The pipe labelled "A" leads to an "underworld" area, while the "B" pipe takes Mario back to the "overworld." The "C" pipe leads to an "underwater" area, while the pipe labelled "D" takes Mario back to the overworld. Point "E" is a secret "beanstalk" that Mario may climb up to a "bonus" area, while "F" is where Mario may fall back to the overworld. Finally, pipe "G" leads to another underworld area that has the "H" pipe as its exit back to the overworld.

bongos from the NGC. A number of actions result in Mario's death: running into any enemy while in "small Mario" form, falling down "pits" or allowing the time limit to expire, which, in World 6-2, is 400 "seconds."[4] A game score can be cut short by any of these occurrences, or it may be extended indefinitely if at any time players press the "Start" button, which pauses the game and silences all of the Audio Processing Unit (APU)'s channels.

If players choose to progress through the level normally, the game score will usually be accented with the "Boing!" sound effect produced when Mario jumps, an action crucial to navigating the game world. This sound effect plays through one of the pulse channels in such a way that it does not normally affect the melody of the theme, as with the "Coin" sound effect. The latter, as noted before, uses both pulse channels of the NES APU, and so the main melody of the "Overworld" theme, also requiring both pulse wave channels (PWCs), is muted every time Mario collects a coin. Koji Kondo seems to have been aware of the "Coin" sound's interrupting effect, because he did not compose it with a single tone, as many other game scorers might have done with the NES APU. Instead, "Coin" is composed of an *appoggiatura* on B, followed by a whole note on E. The *appoggiatura* contributes to the overall satisfying texture of the sound effect, and also makes it a perfect fourth interval that is harmonically compatible with the "Overworld" theme.[5]

In the overworld of World 6-2, there are only three blocks that contain coins. Two of them are invisible and yield one coin each, and they are indicated by the dotted square outlines in Figure 5.1, above. The last of these is a "Ten-Coin Block," indicated by a coin inside a brick block just past the first pipe, accessible only by finding and jumping on the invisible coin block beneath it and avoiding or killing the Koopa Troopa below. A Ten-Coin Block may yield anywhere from one to ten coins, depending on how fast the player can repeatedly make Mario jump into it. Hitting this block triggers both a "thud" sound effect, presumably meant to signify Mario's head or hand hitting the block, and of course the sound effect for collecting a coin. If the player repeatedly hits the block — as they are encouraged to by the "Ching!" sound — this sound effect can significantly change the game score for the level. In that case, the melody of the "Overworld" theme is attenuated, and its bass line is similarly interrupted by the numerous "thuds" of Mario hitting the block, which require the TWC's resources. The sound effect of Mario's jumps will play at this time as well, and so in this instance the score is pervaded by sound effects. Whether or not these sound effects ever sound in Kondo's score for *SMB* is determined completely by each gameplay, as is the tempo and number of sound effects.

One more sound effect is potentially related to Mario's collection of coins in World 6-2: the "1-Up" sound. The "1-Up" sound effect, a quick *arpeggio* in C-Major, plays every time Mario obtains an "extra life" in *SMB*, which can be accomplished by players through several means. First, players may direct Mario to collect a "1-Up Mushroom," a green-coloured version of the Super Mushroom. Alternatively, players can obtain a 1-Up if they kick a Koopa shell and it hits enough enemies in a row. Finally, and most commonly, players obtain a 1-Up if they collect 100 coins in Mario's "wallet," which resets to zero once they do. In World 6-2, only the latter method of obtaining a 1-Up is possible.

In this same area, a Koopa Troopa poses a threat below the invisible coin block. If Mario jumps on this Koopa Troopa, the "Stomp" sound effect plays, and the Koopa hides in his shell. As with the "Coin" sound effect, the "Stomp" sound effect is composed of a perfect fourth interval, though at a semi-tone higher, making it more dissonant sounding in the context of the Area Music.[6] The player may then navigate Mario towards the shell, which makes him kick it and send it sliding across the ground, bouncing off any obstacles and killing any enemies in its path, as well as Mario. Kicking the Koopa shell has varying musical consequences. If I make Mario kick the shell between the first two pipes, for instance, the shell will rapidly bounce back and forth, triggering a "Thud!" sound — a sound louder than the "thud" heard when Mario hits a block — each time it hits a pipe, thereby adding an offbeat percussive section to the score for the duration of this event.

Other sound effects are triggered when Mario obtains a "power-up" like a "Super Mushroom" or "Fire Flower," or if he takes damage while "powered up" by either of these items. Appropriately, the "power-up sound" is an ascending melody, while the "damage sound" is composed of the same notes in the reverse order. Power-ups carry over from level to level in *SMB*, and since World 6-2 is a later level in the game, Mario may already have a Super Mushroom or a Fire Flower, effectively changing the possibilities of such sound effects even occurring. Furthermore, Mario's Fire ability, obtained through collecting the Fire Flower power-up, has its own sound effect that sounds each time Mario throws a fireball, and is a means of killing enemies from a distance.

The "Starman" power-up, an erratically bouncing star that grants temporary invincibility to Mario, is available in the overworld of World 6-2, and is indicated by a star in a brick block after the twentieth pipe in Figure 5.1. When Mario is invincible in *SMB*, the background music switches entirely from whatever theme is playing to the "Invincibility" theme, a fast-tempo piece with a strong percussive element and a repetitive "danceable" melody. As Guillaume Laroche (2012: 108) explains, this melody is played by the NES APU as part of a "ii^7-I^7 chord progression." Variations of the "Invincibility" theme have been composed for many other *Mario* games, but these variations always preserve a ii^X-I^X chord progression, as this minor-Major transition helps elucidate the confidence players feel when they obtain a Starman and become invincible.[7]

Players also have considerable control over if and when the "Invincibility" theme plays in *SMB*. In fact, it is gameplay that dictates if and when Mario collects the Starman power-up, and thus whether or not the "Invincibility" theme ever even sounds. Given the Starman's erratic movements, however, the player may wish to make Mario collect the Starman and fail, in which case whichever theme is currently playing simply continues.

World 6-2 has four hidden areas, accessible to Mario via pipe or beanstalk, each with their own background music. The entrance to the first of these, an underworld area stocked with coins, is the pipe labelled "A" in Figure 5.1. Figure 5.2 below shows this underworld area.

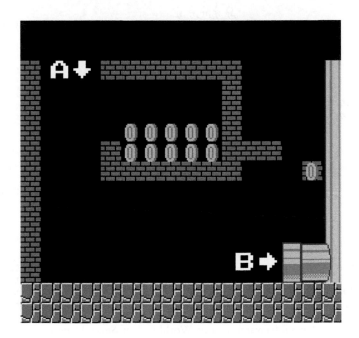

FIGURE 5.2 The secret underworld area of World 6-2 in *Super Mario Bros.* (1985). When the player navigates Mario down the pipe labelled "A" in Figure 5.1, he falls from the top of this screen at the position labelled "A" here. Ten coins and one Ten-Coin Block await Mario in this area.[8]

When players navigate Mario to the underworld in World 6-2, the background music changes entirely to the "Underworld" theme. This piece contains short, punctuated, sporadic-sounding riffs on the pulse channel, each divided by large sections of silence. At the end of each loop there is a longer, descending melody composed of these quick notes, which resolves the tension created by the heavy use of silence. These punctuated sequences evoke the feeling of claustrophobia, aurally complementing the cramped underworld areas in *SMB*. In the first underworld area of World 6-2, the player may make Mario jump on the pipe and hit the Ten-Coin Block for up to ten coins. They may also jump up, run over and jump into the brick structure housing the other ten coins. Again, whenever Mario grabs a coin, the pulse channels sound the "Ching!" effect instead of the melody. Alternatively, players may choose to bypass the coins altogether and make Mario head straight for the pipe, effectively cutting the "Underworld" theme section of the score short. Finally, the player may remain in this area for the remainder of the time limit, which would result in a game score concluding with the "Underworld" theme and finally the "Death Sound." Traversing the "B" pipe leads Mario back to the pipe labelled "B" in Figure 5.1, which once again triggers the "Overworld" theme to play.

If players navigate Mario down the pipe labelled "C" in Figure 5.1, he ends up in an "underwater" area, reproduced in Figure 5.3. Travelling to the underwater area triggers

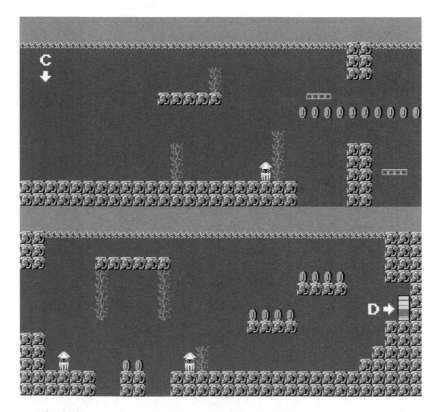

FIGURE 5.3 The hidden underwater area in World 6-2 of *Super Mario Bros.* (1985). Threats to Mario include squid-like creatures known as "Bloopers" and more pits, which in this level include deadly currents that pull him downward. Mario sinks downward from the point labelled "C," if he travels down the pipe labelled "C" in Figure 5.1.[9]

the background music to switch to the "Underwater" theme. The "Underwater" theme, unlike the other themes in *SMB*, is a slow waltz-like melody, perhaps meant to evoke the motion of Mario gracefully swimming past obstacles and enemies. Again, any occurrence of the "Coin" sound effect interrupts the melody line of the "Underwater" theme, as it does with the other themes. Mario has a new sound effect, similar to his "jump" sound effect but shorter, quieter and lower in pitch, that plays whenever he takes a stroke through the water, which he does whenever the player presses the "A" button. In order to avoid being sucked down by the currents, the player must rapidly press "A" to make Mario swim vigorously, whenever he is over the "pits." Naturally, this action produces many instances of the "swim stroke" sound effect. If a player "dies" here, then the game score of course ends with the "Underwater" theme and, finally, the "Death Sound."

The third and final type of hidden area accessible in World 6-2 of *SMB* is the "bonus stage." This area is only accessible if the player makes Mario find the beanstalk hidden in a brick block just above the eleventh pipe of the overworld. If Mario climbs the beanstalk at the point labelled "E" in Figure 5.1, he ends up at point "E" of the bonus stage, pictured in Figure 5.4.

Bonus stages in *SMB* have the same theme as the "Invincibility" theme. The only difference is that while the "Invincibility" theme has a set duration — the duration being the specific period of Mario's invincibility — the "Bonus Stage" theme may continue for as long as Mario is in the bonus stage, a duration that the player has some control over. There are many coins in bonus stages, and so the pulse channels must often rapidly switch between playing the melody of the "Bonus Stage" theme and playing the coin sound effect, as players make Mario jump (triggering the "Jump" sound effect) up and down from the cloud platform.

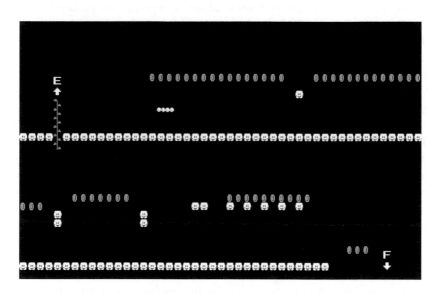

FIGURE 5.4 The "bonus stage" of World 6-2 of *Super Mario Bros.* (1985). In order to reach the coins arranged in the sky, the player must make Mario jump onto a cloud platform that promptly begins moving horizontally to the right, all the way to the end, where it finally leaves the screen. To exit the area, Mario simply has to fall back down to the overworld at the point labelled "F," which returns him to the point labelled "F" in Figure 5.1.[10]

The only way to "die" in a bonus stage is to run out of time, which would result in the game score for this level ending with the "Bonus Stage" theme and finally the "Death Sound."

Players of *SMB* may complete World 6-2 by successfully progressing to the end of the level, marked by a flag that, if Mario touches it, triggers the "flag" sound effect and finally the "Course Clear Fanfare" theme, a triumphant ascending melody. The "flag" sound effect is a slide from low to high frequencies on the two PWCs. This sound effect increases in length and its final pitch increases, the higher the player makes Mario jump onto the flag-pole. Furthermore, if the timer's last digit is a "1," "3" or "6," then the respective amount of fireworks will appear over the castle, which have their own "explosion" sound effect provided by the NGC. In effect, the ending of a level can contain many different arrangements of sounds, all of which depend upon gameplay patterns.

Finally, if at any time during the level the timer reaches "100," the "Hurry Up!" jingle plays and the theme currently playing then increases to a faster tempo. Each theme in *SMB* therefore has a "Hurry Up!" variation that can occur at any physical point in the level. For example, I may choose not to move Mario in World 6-2 until the timer has reached "100," which would produce a fast version of the "Overworld" theme. Similarly, if I am running out of time in the underwater area, the "Underwater" waltz will play at a faster rate. Even the already fast tempo of the "Invincibility" theme doubles when this event happens, resulting in an especially frenetic piece.

Game scores vs. game soundtracks: *Super Mario Bros.* on CD

Despite its ubiquitous and archetypical status, the complete game score for *SMB* may not be found on any single officially-released music album. *Famicom Sound History Series: Mario the Music* (2004) is one of a handful of releases that contain all the background music pieces from *SMB*, though it contains none of the game's sound effects. Those wishing to own an album that contains these sound effects must seek out *Super Mario History 1985–2010* (2010), a booklet and soundtrack CD bundle that is only included with the game *Super Mario All-Stars Limited Edition* (2010) for the Nintendo Wii. Unlike actual game scores, officially-released video game soundtracks rarely contain every sound from their respective games.

The most important difference between game soundtracks and game scores, for my purposes, is that while game scores are inherently interactive, game soundtracks are almost completely non-interactive. Whereas a game score's musical structure is dependent upon gameplay patterns, a game soundtrack exists as a fixed sequence of audio information. One listens to game soundtracks, while one *performs* game scores. Table 5.1 is a partial track list for *Famicom Sound History Series: Mario the Music*:

Each *SMB* background music track on *Famicom Sound History* is composed in a similar manner. The "normal" version of the theme plays at its normal tempo, then, after it has looped a few times, the "Warning" sound plays, and the so-called "Hurry Up!" variation on the theme plays at its faster tempo. Each track thus includes sounds that one might hear when playing the game, though the compositional structure of each track never changes. While I may navigate Mario to die after five seconds of playing World 6-2 of *SMB*, resulting in a brief game score, the tracks contained on *Famicom Sound History* are always the same compositionally, each time I play them.

Aurally, the most obvious difference between playing *SMB* and playing *Famicom Sound History* is the lack of sound effects in the latter. Game scoring involves a recognition and

TABLE 5.1 Tracks 4–11 of *Famicom Sound History Series: Mario the Music*, which includes all of the background music from *Super Mario Bros.*, as well as the "Death Sound," that, arguably, may be considered a sound effect

Track no.	Title	Length
4.	Aboveground BGM ~ Warning ~ Aboveground BGM (Hurry Up!)	5:17
5.	Course Clear Fanfare ~ Scene Change BGM	0:13
6.	Underground BGM ~ Warning ~ Underground BGM (Hurry Up!)	1:07
7.	Bonus Stage / Invincible BGM ~ Warning ~ Bonus Stage BGM (Hurry Up!)	0:46
8.	Miss ~ Game Over	0:14
9.	Underwater BGM ~ Warning ~ Underwater BGM (Hurry Up!)	1:55
10.	Koopa Stage BGM ~ Warning ~ Koopa Stage BGM (Hurry Up!) ~ Koopa Defeated Fanfare	1:04
11.	Ending BGM	0:37

integration of sound effects into the musical process, and game scores contain many instances of sound effects that are triggered as a direct result of gameplay patterns. A game soundtrack typically contains musical themes unaccompanied by the usual sound effects heard in-game, for a more "pure" presentation of the music. If a game soundtrack offers a game's sound effects at all, they are typically bunched together under one "Sound Effects" track, or, as with *Super Mario History*, they are offered as individual tracks. Table 5.2 is a partial track list of *Super Mario History*.

The sound effects of *SMB* are offered on *Super Mario History* unaccompanied. Oddly, the game score for *SMB* is unable to even produce sound effects in this manner. Background music is always playing during gameplay, which is the only state that may produce such sound effects in-game. Not only is a game score capable of orchestrations not possible on a game soundtrack, then, a game soundtrack may similarly contain orchestrations not possible in a game score.

TABLE 5.2 Tracks 11–20 of *Super Mario History 1985–2010*, which include most, but not all of the sound effects in *SMB*

Track no.	Title	Length
11.	*Super Mario Bros.* — Coin	0:05
12.	*Super Mario Bros.* — Small Mario Jump	0:05
13.	*Super Mario Bros.* — Power-up	0:05
14.	*Super Mario Bros.* — 1-Up	0:05
15.	*Super Mario Bros.* — Pipe Travel/Power Down	0:05
16.	*Super Mario Bros.* — Hurry Up	0:05
17.	*Super Mario Bros.* — Lose a Life	0:05
18.	*Super Mario Bros.* — Game Over	0:06
19.	*Super Mario Bros.* — Course Clear	0:07
20.	*Super Mario Bros.* — World Clear	0:07

Case study conclusions

Game scoring deserves classification as a new type of aleatoric composition, because of its dependence on chance operations and gameplay. In the above sections, I have examined game scoring on its own terms, by analyzing actual game scores, resulting from my own gameplay of *SMB*. Just as John Cage wrote rules for how sounds are to be produced in his scores, game scorers like Koji Kondo are cognizant of, and in many cases determine, the parameters under which sounds and music are triggered in gameplay. For example, during one playthrough of World 6-2, I had directed Mario to the bonus stage with less than 100 seconds left on the timer. The "Bonus Stage" theme was triggered by my entrance to the area, and it played at a faster tempo because of the current state of the timer. As I proceeded to collect as many coins as possible, the background music only played the frenetic TWC bass line and NGC drum loop, both PWCs' resources exhausted by numerous instances of the "Coin" sound effect. The creation of this strange soundscape is only possible through my own gameplay patterns.

Game scoring's "moment of reception" occurs as an active state of performance. In fact, game scores are only ever materially realized by gamers, through gameplay. Game soundtracks, as I hope I have shown, are simply fixed sequences of audio information, unresponsive to anything resembling gameplay. In fact, the aforementioned game scoring example is impossible to hear on any soundtrack for *SMB*, because game soundtracks lack the interactivity involved in game scoring. Game scoring exists as part of gaming, *per se*, a medium that is inherently interactive, and so it follows that game scoring itself is interactive.

In the final sections of this chapter, I offer the four remaining game scoring categories in my taxonomy, namely, Menu Sound Effects, Menu Music, Status Music and Gameplay Sound Effects, in order to extend my discussion of game scoring as aleatoric composition. I include these categories here because they contain many opportunities for performer freedom, as well as chance operations, in the context of game operation.

Game scoring taxonomy: Menu Sound Effects

As an introductory video loops endlessly, gamers will soon become ready to play a game, which involves pressing a button, such as the "START" button on a PlayStation 2 controller in *Gran Turismo 3,* for instance. Players cut the introductory video at its playback point through this interaction, and the Introduction Music typically fades to silence or crossfades to another theme, unless it is the same as the "Title Music." Besides these audio transitions, the button press itself may trigger a "confirmation" sound — an example of a "Menu Sound Effect." Menu Sound Effects are sounds triggered by interaction with text, such as cursor navigation tones and menu select sounds. Below, I explore in detail the latter two examples, which I would argue are the most common Menu Sound Effects in game scoring, though there are many more types of Menu Sound Effects that are also common, and especially in certain gaming genres. Moreover, some Menu Sound Effects affect other parts of game scores, such as the above example of Introduction Music muting to give way to a "confirmation" sound.

Mario menus: a case study of Menu Sound Effects in two *Super Mario* games

The title Menu Sound Effects are the first audible sounds of *Super Mario Bros. 3* (*SMB3*) (1988 in Japan, 1990 in North America), a game that has an introduction video many gamers consider memorable (Figure 5.5):

FIGURE 5.5 The introductory video, title screen and demo for *SMB3* (1990). Powering on the NES results in a silent screen with a black and white checkered floor, and red curtains that begin to raise gradually to reveal the title logo and the Mario Bros., who perform various gameplay actions such as jumping, and grabbing and throwing "Koopa shells."

There is no Introduction, Title or Demo Music for *SMB3*, and this is somewhat surprising, since the game's score contains much more music than any *Super Mario* game released before it.[11] The first sound of any player's *SMB3* score will always be one of two Menu Sound Effects: either (i) the cursor navigation tone, the same sound used to accompany Mario or Luigi navigating the map screen by one space; or (ii) the menu selection sound, the same sound used to indicate Mario or Luigi collecting a coin. The cursor navigation sound will only play if the cursor is moved from "1 PLAYER GAME" to "2 PLAYER GAME," and so the order of these sounds in any particular game score is dependent on this action. It is significant that while operating the title screen is nothing like actual gameplay in *SMB3*, players "preview" sounds that they can expect to hear many times over the course of playing, though without background music accompaniment.[12] In the case of experienced players that return to play the game again, the coin/menu selection sound effect could serve as a familiar aural reintroduction to gameplay, as they will have heard this sound many times while collecting coins in previous play sessions.

While the start Menu Sound Effects in *SMB3* are the same as two of its Gameplay Sound Effects, the pause Menu Sound Effects of the much later *Super Mario Odyssey* (2017) reference music used in another *Super Mario* series game, *Super Mario Galaxy* (2010). When players of *Super Mario Odyssey* select an option in the main pause menu, they will hear two notes of the "Comet Observatory" theme from *Super Mario Galaxy*, a piece of Hub Music for that game, and a sub-menu will appear. If players select an option in this sub-menu, another two notes will play from the same theme, and the third and final level of menu will appear. Figure 5.6 shows these three levels of menus:

The first two-note quotation of "Comet Observatory" will play if players select "Action Guide," "Save" or "Options" on the first level (top). If players select "Action Guide," they

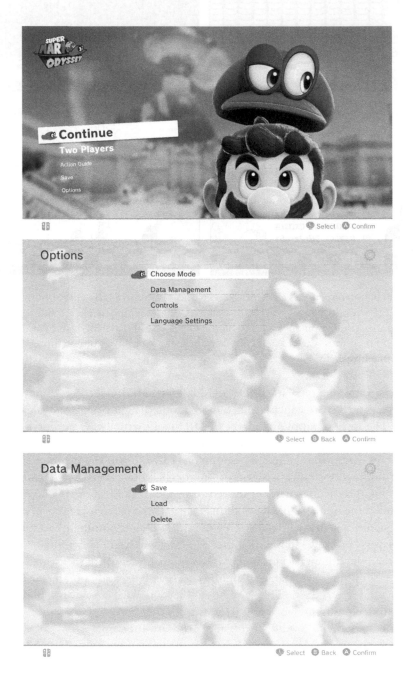

FIGURE 5.6 Three levels of menus in the pause menu for *Super Mario Odyssey* (2017).

navigate to a screen where the second quotation is unavailable. Selecting "Save" will save the current game file, and the menu will stay on the same level. If players select "Options," they go to the second menu level (middle), where the second two-note quotation may be triggered by navigating to one of four third-level sub-menus: "Choose Mode," "Data Management" (bottom), "Controls" or "Language Settings." In the third pause menu level of *Odyssey*, players can only trigger cursor navigation tones and menu select sounds that do not contain this "Easter Egg" reference to *Galaxy*. The only way for players to play the Easter Egg again is by navigating "back" to previous menu levels, though this operation also triggers the "Back" Menu Sound Effect. In effect, players may not reproduce the full four-note Easter Egg repeatedly, without interruption by the "Back" sound effect. Moreover, the menu structure prevents the "Comet Observatory" snippets from ever playing in the wrong order, as the first snippet is only playable from the first level of menus, and the second is only playable from the second level. This example illustrates how sound effects may function musically in a game score, and even in a more "program-like" gaming context.

The *Odyssey* Easter Egg example also helps elucidate the primary limitation inherent in game scoring, namely, that musical ideas must be *programmable*, since games are technically programs with a finite set of options and features.[13] In the case of the pause Menu Sound Effects in *Super Mario Odyssey*, Koji Kondo had to score a pause menu with a limited range of options and depth, and chose to reference a game he had previously scored, thus creating a musical relationship between the two games, and also arguably canonizing "Comet Observatory" as a "multi-game piece" in the *Super Mario* series.

It is worth noting the differences between *Odyssey*'s reference to, and *Galaxy*'s version of "Comet Observatory." Though these differences may seem obvious, they will be helpful in reaching my goal of determining how game scoring's various contexts affect musical composition for video games:

1. *Unity*: The Menu Sound Effects of *Odyssey* do not form a complete melody, let alone a full musical piece. *Galaxy*'s version is a full and repeatable theme.
2. *Interactivity*: The Easter Egg in *Odyssey* may be performed at any point where the player may pause the game, as well as the title menu. Furthermore, the four-note phrase is split into two two-note sound effects, and the timing of these is up to players — though, without the use of the "Back" button and its sound effect, the order is not. In *Galaxy*, "Comet Observatory" functions as background music for the Comet Observatory area, and so players must enter this area for it to play, while pausing in this area or directing Mario to talk to another character will partially attenuate it. The instrumentation changes according to player progress at three levels, as instruments are added to the mix twice over the course of the game. In *Odyssey*, the instrumentation of the Easter Egg never changes.
3. *Significance*: Neither instance of "Comet Observatory" needs to be recognized or even heard by players to complete either game. That said, the context of each instance, along with players' experience with the *Super Mario* series affects the musical significance of the score. For example, the instrumentation of the "Comet Observatory" theme in *Galaxy* denotes game progression, effectively rewarding the player with more instruments as they progress, and thus producing a less direct form of ergo-audition. In *Odyssey*, the significance of the Easter Egg depends on whether players recognize it as such — which depends on familiarity with the theme and/or *Galaxy*. Otherwise, it only denotes to players that they have selected a menu option.

Menu Sound Effects, cont.

As I have stated above, Menu Sound Effects encompass any sound triggered by interaction with text elements onscreen, and so the above examples of cursor navigation tones and menu select sounds are only two of many. Below is a list of other common Menu Sound Effects in games, with a brief description of each (Table 5.3):

The operation of menus can also have an effect on other parts of a game score, such as the attenuation of background music for the pause menu of many games. While I am tempted to call this attenuation another kind of Menu Sound Effect, I will instead categorize it as a Menu Music operation, in the section below.

Menu Sound Effects have a natural corollary in personal computer operating system sound effects. For example, Brian Eno's infamous start-up chime for the *Microsoft Windows 95* operating system functions in a manner similar to "Start Game" sound effects. "Start Game" menu select sounds are special sound effects because they are the last sounds players typically hear in game title menus, before plunging into the main gameplay. In *SMB3* the "Start Game" sound effect is the same as its most important Gameplay Sound Effect, the "Coin" sound, and so these two contexts are aurally linked. However, "Start Game" sound

TABLE 5.3 A list of other common Menu Sound Effects in games

Name	Description
Dialogue navigation sounds	Sounds that accompany the navigation of text-based dialogue in games. This includes sound effects for continuing to the next line of dialogue and often, sounds for the dialogue itself to be "written" gradually on the screen (usually in a dialogue box). In games there may also be sounds for starting, skipping or cancelling dialogue with non-player characters (NPCs) or reading in-game signs. If there are multiple responses possible for the player, each response may have its own sound effect, such as an ascending phrase for "OK," or a descending phrase for "No."
Text entry sounds	Sounds that play when players enter text into a game using a virtual keyboard with a cursor. Possible sounds include keyboard cursor navigation tones, letter confirmation sounds and deletion sound effects. For instance, a game score could be programmed to mimic the sounds of a typewriter as players write the name of their save file.
Save sounds	Whether a "save point" is accessible during normal gameplay or via the pause menu, the act of saving a game may have its own "Saving" and/or "Successfully Saved" sound effect. These sounds reassure gamers that their progress is successfully saved — that their games are reliable programs that can back up and store their unique gameplay data.
Password screen sounds	Most home console games before the 1990s and many before the mid-nineties lacked a save system, and instead "passwords" were used to jump back quickly to a level in a game, for instance. Password screens may have their own unique keyboard or letter/number system for password entry, and this input may have its own sounds, such as those for "Wrong Password" notifications, for example.
Equalization test sounds	In many games, players may set the volume of both, "background music" and "sound effects" through a settings menu. For the "sound effects" volume setting, a sound will typically play each time players increase or decrease the level. This sound might be an existing Gameplay Sound Effect or could be a unique Equalization Test Sound.

effects have arguably become even more important in modern gaming, due to the introduction of "load times" to games. As I have shown in the section on Loading Music in Chapter 3, there typically is no sound to a Loading Screen, and so "Start Game" sound effects are often followed by a period of silence in modern game scores. Thus, while scorers for many older games opt to use a pre-existing sound effect for "Start Game," scorers for many newer games compose a unique jingle, or design a unique sound for this operation. For example, the "Start Game" sound effect for *The Legend of Zelda: Breath of the Wild* (2017) — a single percussive tone that is followed by a long, metallic-sounding ambient decay — is not present in any other part of the game.[14] It is a sound that players may hear many times as they return to their progress in the game, and signifies their "re-entering" the world of *Zelda*. The percussive tone confirms their selection, while the long decay functions to ensure a smooth transition to the Loading Screen, and helps elucidate a slow "falling back" into this world.

It is worth noting one of the differences between the two different console versions of *Breath of the Wild*, namely, the version for the home console Nintendo Wii U and the version for the hybrid handheld-home console, the Nintendo Switch. Since the Switch is also a handheld device, it includes a "Sleep" function, where players can turn off their console temporarily while the console saves their exact state in memory, and are able to resume at any time. The Wii U console does not have this feature, and so players of this version can expect to hear the "Start Game" sound effect much more, as they begin each play session in the traditional "home console" manner.

Modern game consoles also have their own operating systems that require design of Menu Sound Effects and Music. I will discuss the latter in more detail in the section on Menu Music, below.

Game scoring taxonomy: Menu Music

Menu Music is music that plays while players navigate the menu system of a game. Much of the significance of this type of music therefore depends on the game's amount of set-up required in pre-game menus, before players "enter" the game world. For all games, it can be assumed that developers wish for players to successfully navigate the menu, and reach gameplay as soon as possible, though different genres might require more set-up than others. For example, single-player *Zelda* games typically require little menu navigation before actual gameplay — players simply choose their existing saved file or start a new one. That said, returning to a *Zelda* game can be a bit overwhelming, as there are many items to amass, and many "side-quests" in addition to a longer main quest. In short, the "player repertoire" can be quite extensive in a *Zelda* game. Thus, the file screen for most *Zelda* games is set by the "Fairy Fountain" theme, the music that plays when players direct Link to a Fairy Fountain — a healing space where his health can be recovered. Figure 5.7 shows the file screens for a selection of games in this series:

The "Fairy Fountain" theme is a descending melody that loops forever, and evokes relaxation and relief through repetition and a soft, smooth texture. The latter varies according to the sound hardware used to produce the theme, which varies between most *Zelda* games, and especially between those for different consoles. However, the piece was originally scored for *The Legend of Zelda: A Link to the Past* (1992) for the Super Nintendo Entertainment System, or SNES, which contained sound hardware particularly suited for producing a rounded-off texture. Specifically, the SNES APU contains a built-in filter that eliminates

FIGURE 5.7 The file screens, from left to right and top to bottom, for the following *Legend of Zelda* games: *A Link to the Past* (SNES, 1992); *Ocarina of Time* (N64, 1998); *The Wind Waker* (GameCube, 2003); *The Minish Cap* (Game Boy Advance, 2004); *Twilight Princess* (GameCube, 2006); and *A Link Between Worlds* (3DS, 2013). Each game's file screen uses a different variation of the "Fairy Fountain" theme, first scored for *A Link to the Past*.

both high and low frequencies, pushing the sound toward the middle range of frequencies, resulting in a "smooth" sound signature.[15] Later versions of the "Fairy Fountain" theme, such as those for Nintendo 64 and GameCube, are produced with similar textures in order to retain its relaxing, meditative mood.

Some games' menu screens are scored to evoke excitement, and may contain many more options than those for single-player "long form" adventure games, such as those in the *Zelda* series. Multiplayer "arcade-style" games, for instance, have menus for many more options, including character selection, "stage" or "level" selection, and various customization options depending on the game's genre. Some games of this style have scores that change as players navigate to different levels of menus, somewhat similarly to the *Odyssey* Easter Egg mentioned above (though in these cases it is the Menu Music that changes, rather than the Menu Sound Effects). For example, in the arcade-style battle-racing game *Mario Kart 8* (2014), the starting Menu Music includes interactive instrumentation. Specifically, the short loop of Menu Music that sounds as the player navigates car and race selection screens incorporates a drum track only once the player has finished selecting and customizing their racing "kart." At this point, the player has only to press "A" to enter the silent loading screen and start the race, and so the addition of drums is effective in building rhythmic "drive," and hence anticipation of the main gameplay.

Similarly, the Menu Music for the multiplayer *The Legend of Zelda: Four Swords Adventures* (2004) fills out its instrumentation as players navigate "Game Mode Selection," "Player Set-Up" and "Level Select" screens. As with many *Zelda* games, the Menu Music for *Four Swords Adventures* is a variation on the "Fairy Fountain" theme, though it is the most upbeat version, perhaps due to the game's ability to be played with 2–4 players. A selection of games with interactive instrumentation for their Menu Music is available in Table 5.4:

As I briefly mentioned in the section on Menu Sound Effects, above, game scorers also compose Menu Music for gaming console operating systems. Console operating system Menu Music is scored similarly to Menu Music for games, in that it usually repeats

TABLE 5.4 Interactive instrumentation in Menu Music

Game (year — composer, platform)	Description
Super Mario Bros. 2 (1988 — Koji Kondo, NES)	The instrumentation for the Area Music changes whenever players activate the in-game pause menu. Specifically, the pulse channels in the NES APU stop playing, leaving only the bass line (TWC) and percussion (NGC). Interestingly, this happens no matter what music is playing, such as the "Invincibility" theme.
Diddy Kong Racing (1997 — David Wise, N64)	Each character on the character selection screen has its own instrument that each plays a unique part over the bass and percussion. For example, selecting the character Banjo-Kazooie causes a banjo to play the main part of the Menu Music.
Pokémon FireRed and *LeafGreen* (2004 — Go Ichinose, Junichi Masuda, Nintendo Game Boy Advance)	The music for the tutorial menu screens at the beginning of the game builds in instrumentation as players progress through the text. First, only percussion plays, then bass, counter-melody and harmony are added, with the main melody only playing at the final screen.
The Basement Collection (2012 — Danny Baranowski, PC)	The Title Music is a pared-down version of the Menu Music for game selection. When players navigate past the title screen, electronic drums and accents are added to the ambient pads that make up the Title Music.
Super Mario Maker (2015 — Koji Kondo, Nintendo Wii U)	The main gameplay consists of a menu system used for players to create their own "Mario level." Whenever players pick up an item to place on the level screen, the music includes vocals that sing the name of that item along to the melody, which depends on the type of level created: Overworld, "Underworld," "Underwater" or "Castle."

indefinitely, though its musical content does not set specific gameplay, but represents a console's "sound" in general. For example, the Nintendo Wii U's operating system Menu Music consists mainly of synthesizer sounds designed to have airy, smooth and ambient timbres. These synthesizers play gentle, undulating melodies at slow and deliberate tempos to create a "comfortable" atmosphere for the end-user. The Wii U is also unique in that it has a second screen built into its main controller, known as a "Gamepad," that also has speakers. For the operating system Menu Music, Nintendo composers decided to take advantage of this second sound source, and wrote different musical parts for the television speakers and Gamepad speakers. For example, the "Parental Controls" theme, written for the "Parental Controls" Settings Menu, has different parts written for each sound source that players may "mix" however they want.

Finally, one form of game console operating system Menu Music that deserves special mention — and special attention from game scorers — is Digital Game Store Music. Digital Game Store Music is music meant to set real shopping activity in a digital game "store" program, usually built into a console's operating system. While Digital Game Store Music is not to be confused with Shop Music — music that sets an in-game "shop" that sells items for in-game currency, to aid gameplay in a particular game — or physical store "muzak," all three types of music tend to serve the same function. That is, Digital Game Store Music, Shop Music and real-life muzak all serve to create a more comfortable, perhaps more rewarding shopping experience. Only Shop Music differs in motivation, because in-game shops do not deal in real-life currency, and so it more often draws attention to the act of shopping itself. Digital Game Store Music and muzak, on the other hand, are composed to distract shoppers from the seriousness of spending real money.

Game scoring taxonomy: Status Music (Gameplay Music, cont.)

Status Music is music that plays to convey a change in avatar status that players initiate either directly or indirectly. This change in status is independent of factors external to the avatar, such as a game's time system or environment, for example. Avatar status changes may be temporary, and may require new gameplay strategies to accommodate. For example, many games in the *Zelda* series have continuous warning tones for when Link is low on health, and these tones only cease when players recover enough health to bring him back to "normal" status. Appropriately, the "low health" status tone for the first *Legend of Zelda* sounds similar to a hospital heart rate monitor (though it always plays at the same tempo). Moreover, the "low health" status tone requires the pulse channels of the NES APU, and so it does not just "play over" the existing theme; it integrates itself with the existing background music by replacing notes. For whatever music is playing, the pulse channels will still attempt to play their parts, while the "low health" signal interrupts them at a steady rate. This fact might provide another reason why Kondo scored the "Underworld" theme's melody with the channel normally reserved for bass parts: the triangle channel. In *Zelda*, "Underworld" areas are typically more dangerous than overworld areas, and so players are more likely to lose health and hear the "low health" signal over the "Underworld" theme, where it is arguably less intrusive. This reasoning is supported by the fact that if players successfully direct Link through a given dungeon, their health is fully replenished before returning to the overworld. Thus, it is impossible to hear the "low health" status jingle over the "Overworld" theme after successful completion of a dungeon, thereby ensuring that exhilarated players experience the full theme, inspiring them to explore the open overworld, after traversing one of the claustrophobic dungeons of the underworld.

The "low health" status jingle is also notable for its aleatoric relationship to game design and gameplay in *Zelda*. *Zelda* is designed to be navigated one "screen" at a time, and the environments in these screens are largely static while players move Link around to battle enemies and hunt for secrets. Each time players move Link to one of the cardinal edges of a screen, the game will perform a "wipe" edit to the next screen in the chosen direction. Due to technological limitations in the NES CPU and APU, the "low health" status jingle may not sound during this transition, and will only resume once it is complete. Meanwhile, whatever background music is playing will continue, resulting in the status jingle exiting and re-entering the mix at various points in the rhythm. Since the status jingle monopolizes one of the pulse channels of the NES APU, it will thus attenuate this channel's part at different points in the game's background themes, resulting in different and ever-shifting compositions for *Zelda* players who find themselves in need of a health pick-up.

Status Music may consist only of changes or effects applied to an existing theme, or it may be an entirely different piece. "Invincibility" themes in two-dimensional platformers and arcade games are common examples of the latter. For example, games in the *Super Mario*, *Sonic the Hedgehog*, *Kirby* and *Adventure Island* series have dedicated "Invincibility" themes. Common musical features amongst these themes are easy to recognize. They all feature fast tempos, driving basslines, bright timbres and short, looping melodies designed to evince excitement and encourage a kind of "carefree" movement within the game.

Other Status Music may be a variation on an existing theme in a game score, in order to elucidate the shift from a "normal" status to an altered one. The score for *Yoshi's Island*, for example, includes Status Music as a variation on the Area Music for a special level called "Touch Fuzzy, Get Dizzy." In this level, Yoshi faces a new type of enemy, namely, "Fuzzies," who do not directly hurt him, but transform the way he and players perceive the world of the game. Specifically, if Yoshi touches one of the Fuzzies — that resemble white dandelion spores and float through the air, unimpeded by walls and platforms — the level becomes hazy, colours shift and platforms become dynamic with a slow "wobble" effect (Figure 5.8):

Similarly, when Yoshi touches a Fuzzy, a special sound effect plays to evoke the perception transformation, and the background music, "Above Ground," plays in an altered form. Specifically, the music's tempo is cut almost in half and the entire piece is "de-tuned," meaning that the pitches are bent in an attempt to produce a "warped" quality to the sound. The melody, in this altered form, does not follow any tonal logic because the pitch bends make it stray too far from traditional notes.

It is an enjoyable activity in its own right to direct Yoshi to touch a Fuzzy, though players may find that the altered perception causes them to run into other enemies, lose their balance and fall into a pit, or simply run into other Fuzzies, which re-initializes the — unseen — timer for the effect. Since the effect makes gameplay considerably clumsier for most *Yoshi's Island* players, it is likely that the latter will happen, thus increasing the length of time for which the "Above Ground" theme plays in its Fuzzy-status version.

A simpler, less intrusive example of adaptive Status Music is in *Super Mario World*, where any Area Music includes a bongo track whenever Mario or Luigi ride Yoshi. Since many levels feature opportunities to find Yoshi, and every level features opportunities to lose him, the bongos in the score for the game are added and subtracted from the mix in an aleatoric

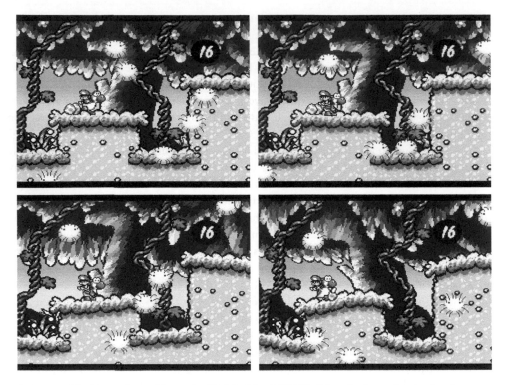

FIGURE 5.8   Yoshi touches a Fuzzy in *Yoshi's Island* (1995). The platforms in the level are normally straight (top, left), though when Yoshi touches a Fuzzy they become curved
and wobbly (top right, and bottom row). Yoshi's eyes widen and the screen shifts
in hue. Players will also find Yoshi less responsive and difficult to control in this
scenario.

manner. It is important that Yoshi is an optional aid in the game, and that he can be easily
lost, as he runs away when players direct him into an enemy. This design makes his bongo
accompaniment one of the clearest examples of the combination of performer freedom and
chance operations in game scoring through gameplay. Players have performer freedom to
find and ride Yoshi, who grants them extra abilities. By chance (or, again, performer freedom), players may lose Yoshi, especially because riding him makes the player's avatar twice
as big, making it more vulnerable to enemies. Fortunately, the bongos fade in and out of the
mix seamlessly, and complement each of the pieces of Area Music for the game.

Game scoring taxonomy: Gameplay Sound Effects

Gameplay Sound Effects are sounds that serve as auditory effects for gameplay actions. As
with Gameplay and Area Music, this category is quite broad, and the need for sound effects
varies considerably according to gameplay genre. Car racing games such as those in the *Gran
Turismo* and *Forza Motorsport* series require sound effects of car engine noises, tire squeals
and collisions, to name a couple examples. While analysts may have no problem identifying
these as diegetic, sound effects in other genres, such as puzzle games, are more difficult to
contextualize. Puzzle games such as *Tetris* often contain sound effects that do not refer to

anything "real," and the "diegetical" nature of these is as unclear as it is for Menu Sound Effects. The sound effect for rotating a block, for instance, does not pertain to any real-world sound. Nor does *Tetris* include a stable avatar for players to control, as discussed above, and so it is difficult to take any "in-game" perspective on the action.

I argue that it is necessary for ludo-musicologists to take a primarily ludal stance towards game scoring, because, unlike a primarily narrative stance, it is not limited by the conceptual world that some, but not all games clearly present. A ludal approach to game scoring involves thinking about gameplay in a technical sense, though thinking in this way does not rob games of their creative value. For example, in any game, sound effects may refer to one or more of the following three game design factors: (1) movement; (2) terrain; and (3) collision. Again, car racing games provide clear examples of each. Movement sounds are sound effects generated by movement of any element onscreen. For example, the engine sounds of a car accelerating in a racing game are movement sounds. Terrain sounds are sound effects generated by "natural" events such as weather systems, or from the combination of movement and collision factors. For example, acceleration in a car racing game will produce collision between the tires and the road, thus necessitating terrain sounds for rubber hitting pavement. Finally, collision sounds are sound effects generated when collisions between two or more objects happen in gameplay. For example, a crash in any racing game requires a multitude of collision sound effects.

While car racing games offer clear examples of movement, terrain and collision Gameplay Sound Effects, I should note that I refer to these aspects in the broadest physical sense. Thus, in *Tetris*, there are movement sounds for rotating a block, movement and terrain sounds for dropping a block, and collision sounds for when a block hits the ground or another block.

Ludo-musicologists have compared sounds that relate directly to visual movements onscreen in games to the same use of sounds in animation, also known as "Mickey-Mousing." Not just any sound is required for "Mickey-Mousing" though; the sounds used in this technique are either stylized versions of sound effects or musical gestures. Stylized sound effects are another example of a game scoring category that complicates the diegetic status of sounds in games. For example, can Mario hear the ascending synthesizer slide that accompanies his jumps in *SMB*? This example, as well as many other examples similar to it, seem to operate similar to animation, in that *exaggerated* sound effects are simultaneously meant for both enhancing viewing pleasure and developing aesthetic coherence for the "worlds" that animators and game designers create. It simply does not matter whether characters in games may conceptually hear their own exaggerated sound effects, since either way the "world" continues to operate in the same fashion.

"Musical sound effects" are another example of "Mickey-Mousing" in games. These are sound effects, in that they react directly to player actions, but use musical gestures to do so. For example, in the score for *The Legend of Zelda: The Wind Waker* (2003), Link's successful sword strikes produce "stabs" of notes played by a piano and string instruments. If players direct Link to successfully strike an enemy two or more times in a row, they trigger a melody composed of the amount of strikes. Thus, *Wind Waker* players encounter musical sound effects in combat, and are encouraged to perform successful combinations of sword strikes, not only to defeat enemies, but to experience the pleasure of *ludally* generating a melody. It is significant that this technique was employed in the first "Toon Link" *Zelda* game, or the first game in the series to utilize an explicitly "cartoon" or animation graphical style, pictured in Figure 5.9:

FIGURE 5.9 A gameplay screenshot of *The Wind Waker* (2003). In the game, Link holds a conductor's baton known as the "Wind Waker," that he uses to control the direction of the wind, to navigate the ocean in his boat.

In this stylistic context, the composers, Kenta Nagata, Hajime Wakai, Toru Minegishi and Koji Kondo opted to "Mickey-Mouse" the sound effects in order to create a more presentational effect, since the game's graphics were developed in the same way. Of course, many games with "realistic" graphic styles also contain "Mickey-Moused" sound effects, and so this example is more of a creative choice than the rule for game scores.

Some games go so far as to reward musical gameplay within the context of non-musical gameplay, thus encouraging players to play "musically." For example, *Mother 3* (2006, Japan) is a role playing game (RPG) that contains optional rhythm gameplay in its many battles.[16] The game's score contains different Battle Music for different types of enemies, and each piece of Battle Music contains a rhythm that represents an enemy's "heartbeat." Players may deduce this rhythm from the music itself, or, if they are able, they may put the enemy to sleep, which makes the heartbeat audible over the Battle Music. If players press "A" along to this rhythm, they can hit an enemy up to 16 times, as opposed to only once, and so music gameplay is advantageous to destroying enemies faster. Each time they press the button in rhythm, a short riff plays on an instrument that corresponds to whatever character is attacking, thus adding small musical accents to the background music. It bears mentioning here that speed-runners might find using this technique to be faster in completing the game, and so their "runs" will have scores that feature these accents. While music gameplay is somewhat of an anomaly in the context of normal gameplay in non-musical games, *Mother 3*'s score is an instructive example of it, because music gameplay is optional, yet actually *aids* traditional gameplay.

At the other end of the realism spectrum, some developers even take the time to explain the diegetic status of notification sounds from the game's user interface. For example, the stealth-action game *Metal Gear Solid* (1998) for PlayStation contains an early cut-scene of dialogue between the game's avatar, a special-operations government agent named Solid Snake, and his commanding officer (CO) (Figure 5.10):

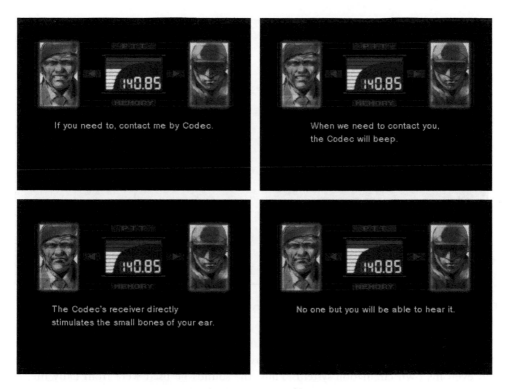

FIGURE 5.10 An early cut–scene from *Metal Gear Solid* (1998).

Snake's CO identifies the "Codec" sound as diegetic by indicating that Snake can hear it, though he also notes that "no one else can hear it," an important factor for a stealth game's diegesis, where the player directs their avatar with the goal of performing in–game actions while remaining undetected by enemies. In this instance, sounds that players would ordinarily identify as part of the game's User Interface, may occupy the game's diegesis, thanks to the CO's explanation early in *MGS*.

Akash Thakkar (2017: 13m45s), the sound designer for *Hyper Light Drifter* (2016), a multi-platform 2D action-RPG, notes that he wanted to have his sound effects "grounded in reality, but 'stylized out from there,'" and explains the sound recording technologies he used to create this aesthetic: "For sound design I decided to go with 'weird tech' to get the sound […] distorted, crunchy, nightmarish […] and kind of 'otherworldly.'" See Figure 5.11 for a screenshot of *Hyper Light Drifter*:

The "weird tech" Thakkar refers to consisted of an early magnetic recording technology, a wire recorder that he not only used to record sounds with, but also contained historical sounds from when the technology was last used, the 1950s. For example, Thakkar recorded his own voice with the wire recorder to create all the monster enemy "vocals" for the game. By using his own voice recorded onto an analog audio storage medium, he kept the sounds "grounded in reality," though they were "stylized" through the later addition of digital effects and processing. Similarly, Thakkar recorded the sounds for each weapon in the game through the wire recorder in multiple layers. For example, the "diamond shotgun" in *HLD* contains nine different layers of sound recorded by wire and then digitally processed.

FIGURE 5.11 *Hyper Light Drifter* (2016) gameplay screenshot.

Thakkar also attached a medical stethoscope to a microphone, in order to record normally inaudible sounds such as the lower frequencies of refrigerator and freezer motors, and even his own circulation system. Thus, the sounds he used were from daily life, but they achieved an "otherworldly" aesthetic through obsolete and unconventional recording practices.

Rich Vreeland (2017), the composer for the music in *Hyper Light Drifter*—as well as *FEZ*—notes that he too desired to use analog recording technology, namely tape recording, for his compositions, in order to take advantage of the unique timbre of tape. Unfortunately, this timbre is owed in large part to fluctuations in the rate at which audio is recorded and played from tape. For Vreeland (2017), the sound of tape was desirable for his compositions, but he ultimately moved onto digital recording for *Hyper Light Drifter*, because the speed fluctuations made his tape recordings too unstable for dynamic music. Dynamic music requires exact audio timings to transition between sections properly. In the next section, on Ambient Sound Effects, I explore Vreeland's approach to the music of *HLD* in further detail, and specifically how the category of Ambient Sound Effects may overlap with the more "musical" components of game scores. For now, I will simply note this crucial difference between sound effects and music in game scoring, namely, that sound effects are not required to interact *rhythmically* with other scoring elements, such as background music (though they still may). Gameplay Music, on the other hand, needs to transition seamlessly between sections, and so it requires a stable, steady beat, as with a DJ making a "continuous mix" with a digital audio workstation (DAW) or turntables, for instance.

Game scoring taxonomy: "Ambiences" or Ambient Sound Effects

Ambient Sound Effects, or "Ambiences," as Vreeland (Qtd. in Thakkar, 2017: 24m15s) refers to them, are sounds used explicitly to elucidate the ambience or "feel" of a physical space in a game. In traditionally-recorded music, the ambience of the recording venue determines certain "spatial" characteristics of sound, such as echo and reverberation timings. Similarly, in digital music production, producers may artificially create echo and reverberation effects to emulate a specific room size or space. The same recording techniques may be used to elucidate the sense of space in a game, particularly important in modern 3D games.

Whereas NES game scorers must "scheme" the NES APU to achieve even basic echo effects, modern game scorers are limited only by their own DAW's range of echo and reverberation plug-ins. This change in game music technology affects how game scorers approach the problem of setting uniquely designed game environments. For example, Koji Kondo elucidates the claustrophobic spaces of the "Underground" levels in *SMB* by composing short melodic phrases separated by long rests. Since he did not have a "cave" or "dungeon" echo plug-in preset to select in a DAW, he had to represent this space via musical phrasing.

In Vreeland's process for composing Ambiences for *HLD*, on the other hand, he was only limited by the programming system he used, as he was for *FEZ*. Vreeland (Qtd. in Thakkar, 2017: 47m00s) notes that the development team for *HLD* relied entirely on YoYo Games' 2D game development software, *Game Maker Studio*. This development scenario meant that he (Ibid.: 47m23s) had to "mix [solely] via scripts," and that there was no "middleware" music system as with *FEZ*. Vreeland (Ibid.: 47m27s) asked the developers of *Game Maker Studio* to add memory support for multiple streams of audio, as well as "positional Ambiences," or Ambiences with a specific locational source in the game.[17] Positional Ambiences change in content and volume according to player position. However, just like any other element in a game, Positional Ambiences do not have to react *realistically* to player position — they simply need to react *consistently*. For example, an in-game boombox could grow quieter as players direct their avatar towards it, and grow louder as they move away. Positional Ambiences, similar to Thakkar's vision for the sound effects of *HLD*, can exhibit realistic, as well as "otherworldly" characteristics, depending on the game. For example, Vreeland programmed an Ambience for the computer modules found in most areas of *HLD*, though he programmed it to play at the *same* volume no matter how many were in the player's vicinity. Thus, while Vreeland requested the *Game Maker* developers to add support for Positional Ambiences, he opted not to use this feature for the computer module Ambience, as he wanted a less realistic, and perhaps "otherworldly" sound.

Vreeland (Ibid.: 25m20s) also notes that he wanted his music to "mimic the real world" and offers the example of the very low and distant-sounding bass drum that plays occasionally in the score for *HLD*. Similarly, players may notice a distant-sounding "electrical" white-noise sound that occasionally plays over the music. These Ambiences, Vreeland notes, are meant to function as sounds, and also complement the music's aesthetic. He also notes that another Ambience, a low-resolution texture of swarming birds, plays as textural support for the background music, as well as on its own, to represent the birds in the northern region of *HLD*, whose "cult" behaviour resembles the crows in Alfred Hitchcock's *The Birds* (1963). The music for this area contains a heavily-processed "hoo-hoo" sound that mimics an owl, and that pairs well with the ominous swarming sound of the birds.

As modern game environments become larger and more complex, Ambiences have arguably grown in importance in game scores, due to their ability to elucidate and enhance the sense of space players visualize and inhabit. Ambiences also seem to occupy the middle of the music–sound effect spectrum, as indicated by Vreeland's involvement in creating them for *HLD*. It appears that they are traditionally the sound designer's domain, as Vreeland notes that he asked Thakkar if he could compose Ambiences before he did so. Nevertheless,

Vreeland also points out the potential for integration of Ambiences in music, such as the above example of the birds, and musical instruments in Ambiences, such as the above example of the distant bass drum.

Chapter conclusions

As both my case study of *SMB*, and the remaining categories of my game scoring taxonomy demonstrate, game scoring is always an at least partially aleatoric compositional activity, the final score being determined as much through user input as traditional composition. In addition, some gaming contexts have more potential for, and already exhibit recurring techniques of, aleatoric musical gestures. For example, game menu screens have identifiable structures that game scorers may set with corresponding musical structures, as in the case of interactive menu music, or in the case of the music quotation Menu Sound Effects for *Odyssey*, to name two examples. Aleatoric composition depends on non-musical structures and patterns to determine musical operations, and menu screens are ideal frameworks for such activity.

Gameplay Sound Effects and Ambiences, too, serve important functions in game scoring as aleatoric composition, and may be responsible for some of the most important differences between game scores and video game soundtracks, as demonstrated in my case study of *SMB*. My exploration of these game scoring categories has also shown the blurred line between game sound effects and music, another defining aspect of the aleatoric tradition. Game scorers compose music and sound effects together in an aleatoric style, and expect the two types of sounds to overlap with and complement each other in the flow of gameplay and user inputs. Since game scorers are tasked with writing music for ostensibly non-musical activity that is shaped by both competitive and performative decisions, they undertake a uniquely aleatoric form of composition when they compose music for games.

Notes

1 Roig-Francoli (2007) coined the term "aleatoriality" to designate the degree of chance in a composition.
2 In effect, the piece can be of any duration, similar to a game score, as noted above.
3 For more on this riff, see "Super Mario Melodies" (2010).
4 One "second" in *Super Mario Bros.* is equal to 0.4 seconds in real life, so the actual time limit for World 6-2 is 160 seconds.
5 "Super Mario Melodies" (2010).
6 Ibid.
7 For more on consistent elements across different *Super Mario* game variations of the same theme, see Laroche (2012).
8 "World 6-2," The Mushroom Kingdom.
9 "World 6-2," The Mushroom Kingdom.
10 "World 6-2," The Mushroom Kingdom.
11 *Super Mario Bros. 3* had the benefit of a larger memory space than *Super Mario Bros.* (1985), *Super Mario Bros.: The Lost Levels* (Japan, 1986) and *Super Mario Bros. 2* (North America, 1988), which allowed for more music to be programmed for it.
12 This situation is not reproducible once the game starts. That is, gamers may only trigger these sound effects in *SMB3* alongside background music during actual gameplay and past the title screen.
13 Of course, just as loopholes and workarounds exist in software programs, "glitches" or bugs exist in every game. Gamers locate and exploit glitches for two main reasons: (1) to find information about game programming, in order to preserve it in an archival or historical manner, and (2) to find ways to complete games faster, in the interest of "speed-running."

14 *Breath of the Wild* was scored by Manaka Kataoka, Yasuaki Iwata and Hajime Wakai.
15 The sound hardware design and resulting texture of the sound of the SNES APU contrast heavily with the design and sound of the NES APU. The NES features a bright and sometimes harsh sound that the SNES, in fact, cannot match. The SNES features its own distinct sound, structured by the SNES APU, though I do not have time to cover it in detail here. For now I will note that it utilizes a unique sampling technique that involves playing many iterations of very short samples in a row, to produce a continuous sound that can be further modified by various types of modulators.
16 *Mother 3* is the successor to *EarthBound*, known as *Mother 2* in Japan. However, as with *Mother* (later released in North America as *EarthBound Zero*), it was only released in Japan, and so there is no "EarthBound 2."
17 It is strange that Vreeland had to request support for multiple streams of audio. This example speaks to the current range of technological limitations that the modern game scorer faces. In short, game scorers must collaborate with programmers to develop audio systems that meet their needs, even as established composers.

References

Antokoletz, Elliott. 2014. *A History of Twentieth-Century Music in a Theoretic-Analytical Context*. New York and London: Taylor & Francis.

Cage, John. 1961. *Silence: Lectures and Writings*. Cambridge, MA: MIT Press.

Cage, John M. 1973. *Writings '67–'72*. Middletown, CT: Wesleyan University Press.

Kondo, Koji. 2010. Special Interview – Koji Kondo. Interview by Shinobu Amayake. http://www.glitterberri.com/ocarina-of-time/special-interview-koji-kondo/.

Laroche, Guillaume. 2012. "Analyzing Musical Mario-Media: Variations in the Music of Super Mario Video Games." Master's Thesis, McGill University. http://logical.ai/make/music/Analyzing%20musical%20Mariomedia%20%20variations%20in%20the%20music%20of%20Super%20Mario%20video%20games.pdf.

Morgan, Robert P. 1991. *Twentieth-Century Music: A History of Musical Style in Modern Europe and America*. New York: Norton.

Roig-Francoli, Miguel A. 2007. *Anthology of Post-Tonal Music*. New York: McGraw Hill.

Scruton, R. 1997. *The Aesthetics of Music. Oxford Scholarship Online*. Oxford: Oxford University Press.

Thakkar, Akash. 2017. "The Sound and Music of Hyper Light Drifter." GDC Vault. https://www.gdcvault.com/play/1024135/The-Sound-and-Music-of.

6

GAME SCORING

Conclusion

In this book I have examined an emerging compositional mode that I call "game scoring," that is, composing music for and through gaming. As I hope I have shown, game scoring involves a host of technical and aesthetic priorities, values, obstacles and concerns that do not influence scoring for other media. Most fundamentally, game scorers must accommodate unprecedented levels of interactivity in their compositions, as game scores are only ever *realized* through gameplay.

In Chapter 2 of this book I considered game scoring's context in gaming through a discussion of interactivity's bearing on the broader experience of game scoring through gameplay. I conducted a case study of music for *The Legend of Zelda*, to elucidate how "large-scale" gameplay patterns shape game scores, in terms of both reception *and* composition.

Game scorers also compose for particular sound hardware configurations and so their scoring process is structured entirely by gaming technology. I demonstrated the technological structure of game scoring in Chapter 3 of this book, through a case study of a particular gaming sound hardware configuration: the Nintendo Entertainment System Audio Processing Unit (NES APU). Just as a game scorer would approach this sound hardware technology, I examined the APU for its musical abilities. As Koji Kondo suggests, the NES sound hardware configuration structures NES game scoring in its own peculiar way, which is different from other gaming sound hardware configurations. For example, the NES APU offered only five discrete sound channels, while the later Super Nintendo Entertainment System (SNES) sound hardware had eight.

As it turns out, NES game scorers developed unique and innovative compositional strategies in order to program musical ideas into the APU (that in many cases would be impossible otherwise). After examining the NES APU's musical possibilities and limitations, I surveyed well-known examples of NES game scorers "scheming" within this sound hardware configuration's abilities and limitations. These examples were meant to demonstrate both the technological structure of game scoring, and the broader point that this compositional activity resembles software programming more than any traditional compositional mode.

DOI: 10.4324/9781003045465-6

In fact, a fundamental argument of this work is that game scoring *is* software programming, though this constitution should not be taken as indicative of game scoring's "unmusical" nature. Programming, coding and gaming are involved in game scoring, and these activities are no less musical than writing notes on a staff. I forego the outdated distinction between programming and composition, and instead suggest that game scoring comprises a unique compositional mode that is characterized by the activity of software programming itself.

In Chapter 4, I extended my discussion of gaming technology to game design, in order to discuss the various gameplay contexts that game scorers compose for. This discussion resulted in a "taxonomy" of game scoring categories that applied to contexts in all, or at least most, gaming genres. These categories often overlapped with one another, and these overlaps were useful in discerning the correct language to conduct game scoring analysis, and to discuss music's role in the gaming experience. As it turns out, music and sound form the aural component of gaming as a mimetic technology. Gaming — specific mimetic experience that is afforded by gaming technology, envisioned by game designers and facilitated by programmers — is experienced by gamers in part *through* game scoring. Thus, "mimesis" in gaming and game scoring does not require a narrative component. Even in games with clearly defined narratives and "roles" to "play," players' subjective gameplay experiences often take precedence over traditional means of producing affect in narrative media, such as musical gestures to "set" a "mood." Since gaming is a mimetic technology, game scorers instead attempt to set "player action," conducted through a controller and represented visually on a screen.

In Chapter 5, I demonstrated that game scoring is ultimately only realized through gameplay (the duration of any game score, for instance, is always determined by the duration of a given gameplay session), thereby making it an inherently aleatoric compositional activity. I began by providing a brief case study of a canonic aleatoric composition by John Cage: *TV Köln*. I used *TV Köln* to define aleatoric composition in a simple and accessible manner, and to demonstrate the main principles of the aleatoric tradition. To my unexpected benefit, Cage composed "sound effects" for this piece that would normally be considered "extramusical" in traditional musical composition. Similarly, game scorers expect, integrate and even compose sound effects into their scores. I used this similarity between game scoring and aleatoric composition to suggest that the distinction between "music" and "sound effects" is irrelevant to the game scoring analyst. Game scorers program video game sound effects just as they program video game music, and so I considered both as "game scoring" in this research.

I then performed an in-depth case study of World 6-2 of *Super Mario Bros. (SMB)* to elucidate game scoring's aleatoric nature. While I expected to find a breadth of musical consequences for my gameplay choices in World 6-2, I did not expect to find so many. Even in an early game for the NES (an earlier home gaming technology by today's standards), Koji Kondo had to program numerous musical ideas for numerous gameplay states in *SMB*. For example, when I direct Mario to collect the "Starman" power-up, the game score switches entirely to the "Invincibility" theme. I outlined all the ways in which my gameplay could affect the game score for World 6-2, in an effort to show that the realization of any game score is ultimately dependent on gameplay itself.

In order to elucidate game scoring's aleatoric nature, I then compared my game scores for World 6-2 to a non-aleatoric musical source, namely, officially-released soundtracks for *SMB*. This comparison highlighted both the "fixed" nature of video game soundtracks, as well as the "unfixed" nature of game scores. Game scoring is aleatoric because the gamer presents "chance" and a degree of "performer" freedom to the final composition. As expected, the video game soundtracks for *SMB* were only "idealized" renditions of game scores, and were even impossible to produce by gameplay itself. This comparison thus revealed game scoring as an inherently aleatoric compositional activity.

Future directions

With this book, there are many directions for game scoring researchers to take in their work. The interaction between the game scorer (and the gamer)[1] and gaming technology, for example, is most fascinating, since it is a wholly unique interaction. The game scorer devises compositional strategies in response to the abilities of particular sound hardware configurations, just as the gamer develops ludal strategies in response to the world, rules and mechanics of a game (that are only experienced through gaming technology). In fact, game scoring may affect the latter in a peculiar way. Beyond greed, my motives for directing Mario to repeatedly collect coin after coin — especially in the bonus stage — stem from a "circular causal" relationship generated by the system of visuals, haptics and most importantly for my purposes, sound of *Super Mario Bros.* In this case, the "Coin" sound effect exists as both a feedback and control mechanism, because it is both a reward and a motive for my gameplay patterns.[2] I am, in effect, involved in a kind of "closed signaling loop" that constitutes my experience of the game.

Similarly, the act of game scoring, that is, scoring in a traditional sense, by a video game music "composer," involves a circular-causal relationship with gaming technology. For example, Koji Kondo composed the score for *SMB* in a music editor program he wrote himself in *Family BASIC*, a dialect of the *BASIC* programming language[3] that is used to program the Famicom. As such, his written "score" for *SMB* exists as code in the *Family BASIC* language that he could make changes to, in order to effect various musical outcomes (one of which is the realtime re-orchestration of APU channels in the event Mario collects a coin). Kondo's feedback and control mechanisms are the sounds he is able to produce from the NES APU through this code, as they constitute his motive and reward. As such, this "closed signaling loop" is indicative of a "cybernetic system," which is any system that involves this kind of "circular-causal" relationship.

Future directions for game scoring research could involve discussing the "closed signaling loop" involved in the cybernetic systems of gameplay and game scoring. This discussion would build upon the examination of the technological structuration of game scoring I performed in Chapter 3, and the discussion of gameplay as performance of aleatoric composition I conducted in Chapter 5 of this book, thus making it an ideal avenue for future research.

In the modern gaming landscape, game scorers often work with game audio "middleware," or audio workstation software that includes functionality for assigning interactive musical operations to game engine events, such as *FMOD Studio* and AudioKinetic's *Wwise*. These programs are designed with "visual" programming languages, or programming languages that incorporate graphic representations of coding operations. Beginning and aspiring game scorers, for example, may use these programs to create interactive music systems without any programming experience or knowledge, and so they are significant for "democratizing" game scoring practice, though programming experience remains crucial to utilizing them to the fullest extent. More research is necessary to determine how approachable these programs are to composers, and where their limitations lie, especially in regard to where programming knowledge could unlock their full capabilities. One more future direction for this research could involve surveying the gaming industry for its use of audio middleware, development of proprietary audio engines or hybridization of both. I would expect this research to reveal that while audio middleware applications are accessible entry-points for composers to adapt music to game engines, game scorers still benefit from intimate collaborations with software programmers and game designers, and these collaborations could in turn lead to the development of newer versions of middleware applications, thus providing an up-to-date case study of the "closed signaling loop" in game scoring technologies that I note above.

Significance

Though this research contributes to ludology, ludo-musicology and interactive media studies in kind, its most significant contribution is within the field of ludo-musicology. As stated, ludo-musicology is still forming as a field, and so there is much work yet to be done on game scoring *per se*. This book is relatively unique in that it concerns itself with video game music from a "scoring" perspective. Indeed, recent studies of interactive media have tended to overlook the act of game scoring itself, fixating instead on the product of that process. Most fundamentally, then, this book is significant simply because it focuses exclusively on a form of musical activity that, though culturally significant, remains conspicuously absent from the lion's share of research on modern scoring activity.

The ludo-musicological analysis of game scoring I have performed here, i.e., a ludology informed by musicological scholarship, revealed that current analytic approaches to film scores are unsuitable for studying game scoring. Despite attempts by scholars to make terms and concepts from film studies fit in studies of game scores, such as "diegetic" and "non-diegetic," for instance, it is my opinion that concepts developed to analyze other media map clumsily onto the video game medium, and may even work to obfuscate the affect of certain game scoring gestures.

Moreover, analysts, non-academic writers and gamers alike often confuse video game soundtracks with actual game scores. In this book I drew a technological distinction between these two media: a video game soundtrack is a record, realized by playback functions of audio technology, and produced by recording technology, while a game score is only realized through gameplay, and produced by gaming technology. This work is an analytic model designed to examine game scoring vis-à-vis concepts drawn directly from gaming rather than borrowed from other cultural forms (such as modern record production), and so it is significant simply for this distinction.

Implications

The act of game scoring can be analyzed through a multitude of theoretical lenses. I intended for my book to be an attempt at constructing a broader theory of this activity, and its result is a working methodology for analyzing game scoring via a ludo-musicological research framework. More specifically, one of the outcomes of this book was a methodology for analyzing any particular game score. While I chose to analyze the NES APU for its relative simplicity, and my scores for *SMB* for my familiarity with its "world," my research methods may be applied to all gaming technologies and game scores, regardless of their complexity. As I have shown, game scores must be analyzed first-and-foremost in terms of their technology, and then through the gameplay used to realize them. The methodology I developed in this book allows for such an analysis.

One undeniably major force in gaming at present is the proliferation of mobile devices that, with advancements in handheld technology, are fully capable gaming machines in their own right. Mobile gaming is growing more and more popular each day, though very little research has been conducted on the process of "mobile game scoring." Mobile devices present yet another technology for the game scorer to orchestrate, though they present very different aesthetic challenges than, say, the NES APU. Most significantly, mobile video games are developed for numerous different devices, and so their game scores are structured by numerous different sound hardware configurations, and realized by numerous different gameplay scenarios. Even the choice of wearing headphones has its effects on the realization of a mobile game score. My methodology allows for an analysis of this peculiar type of game score, too, since it approaches game scoring from a broad perspective, and certainly includes scoring for mobile games.

Sociological and psychological research on video game music may also benefit from my analysis of game scoring. For instance, many studies from these fields on video game music focus on the widespread use of electronic gambling machines.[4] These studies tend to analyze sounds and music used in these machines, as "feedback" and "control" mechanisms that encourage playing (and spending). As noted, the nature of these mechanisms is dependent on the nature of the game scoring process, which itself is structured entirely by gaming technology. Just as gaming consoles vary in musical ability, the sound hardware configuration is often unique to a particular electronic gambling machine, and thus structures the game scoring process in a unique way. Since music is posited by these researchers as a crucial element in encouraging play, they may use a ludo-musicological analysis of game scoring to better understand how these machines, and their games, are scored. This understanding may reveal more aspects of game scores that facilitate more explicit capitalistic intentions than do "regular" game scores.

Research from psychology, sociology, media studies and cultural studies alike has begun to address the extremely "gendered" identity of the average gamer.[5] While the proliferation of mobile gaming may have increased the amount of female gamers in recent years, the gender identity of gaming remains predominately masculine. Moreover, this phenomenon was much more pronounced in earlier gaming eras. How has game scoring affected, facilitated and/or resisted this phenomenon? My methodology allows for analyses of gender politics in video game music to be grounded in an understanding of how that music is created in the first place, thus allowing for a more thorough examination.

Conclusion

To be sure, "video game music" differs from game scoring, in that the former is a "thing," while the latter remains an ongoing *activity*. While video game music may be analyzed as an ontologically terminable, or "fixed" product, game scoring remains ontologically "open." In this book, I have attempted to develop a working methodology for the study of game scoring as such.

Notes

1 By now it should be clear that the gamer is, in fact, part game scorer.
2 Whalen (2004).
3 Beginner's All-purpose Symbolic Instruction Code, or "BASIC," is a family of general-purpose, high-level programming languages.
4 For significant examples, see: Collins et al. (2011); Noseworthy and Finlay (2009); and Dixon, Trigg and Griffiths (2007), among others.
5 For example, see: Brown, Hall and Holtzer (1997); Eden, Maloney and Bowman (2010); Feng, Spence and Pratt (2007); Chess (2011); Ferguson, Cruz and Rueda (2008); Greenberg et al. (2010); Jantzen and Jensen (1993); Homer et al. (2012); Behm-Morawitz (2014); Dietz (1998); Cruea and Park (2012); Scharrer (2004); Miller and Summers (2007); Perry (2011); Hamlen (2011); Williams et al. (2009); Ogletree and Drake (2007); Gailey (1993); Ivory (2006); and Soukup (2007), among many others.

References

Behm-Morawitz, Elizabeth. 2014. "Examining the Intersection of Race and Gender in Video Game Advertising." *Journal of Marketing Communications* 23 (3), 220–239.

Brown, Ralph M., Lisa R. Hall, and Roee Holtzer. 1997. "Gender and Video Game Performance." *Sex Roles* 36 (11): 793.

Chess, Shira. 2011. "A 36-24-36 Cerebrum: Productivity, Gender, and Video Games Advertising." *Critical Studies in Media Communication* 28(3): 230.

Collins, Karen, Holly Tessler, Kevin Harrigan, Michael J. Dixon, and Jonathan Fugelsang. 2011. "Sound in Electronic Gambling Machines: A Review of the Literature and Its Relevance to Game Sound." In *Game Sound Technology and Player Interaction: Concepts and Developments*, edited by Mark Grimshaw, 1–21. Hershey, PA: IGI Global.

Cruea, Mark, and Sung-Yeon Park. 2012. "Gender Disparity in Video Game Usage: A Third-Person Perception-Based Explanation." *Media Psychology* 15 (1): 44–67.

Dietz, Tracy L. 1998. "An Examination of Violence and Gender Role Portrayals in Video Games: Implications for Gender Socialization and Aggressive Behavior." *Sex Roles* 38 (5): 425–42.

Dixon, Laura, Richard Trigg, and Mark Griffiths. 2007. "An Empirical Investigation of Music and Gambling Behaviour." *International Gambling Studies* 7 (3): 315–26.

Eden, Allison, Erin Maloney, and Nicholas D. Bowman. 2010. "Gender Attribution in Online Video Games." *Journal of Media Psychology* 22 (3): 114–24.

Feng, Jing, Ian Spence, and Jay Pratt. 2007. "Playing an Action Video Game Reduces Gender Differences in Spatial Cognition." *Psychological Science* 18 (10): 850–55.

Ferguson, Christopher J., Amanda M. Cruz, and Stephanie M. Rueda. 2008. "Gender, Video Game Playing Habits and Visual Memory Tasks." *Sex Roles* 58 (3): 279–86.

Gailey, Christine W. 1993. "Mediated Messages: Gender, Class, and Cosmos in Home Video Games." *Journal of Popular Culture* 27 (1): 81–99.

Greenberg, Bradley S., John Sherry, Kenneth Lachlan, Kristen Lucas, and Amanda Holmstrom. 2010. "Orientations to Video Games Among Gender and Age Groups." *Simulation & Gaming* 41 (2): 238–59.

Hamlen, Karla R. 2011. "Children's Choices and Strategies in Video Games." *Computers in Human Behavior* 27 (1): 532–39.

Homer, Bruce D., Elizabeth O. Hayward, Jonathan Frye, and Jan L. Plass. 2012. "Gender and Player Characteristics in Video Game Play of Preadolescents." *Computers in Human Behavior* 28 (5): 1782.

Ivory, James D. 2006. "Still a Man's Game: Gender Representation in Online Reviews of Video Games." *Mass Communication and Society* 9 (1): 103–14.

Jantzen, Gitte, and Jans F. Jensen. 1993. "Powerplay — Power, Violence and Gender in Video Games." *AI & Society* 7 (4): 368–85.

Miller, Monica K., and Alicia Summers. 2007. "Gender Differences in Video Game Characters' Roles, Appearances, and Attire as Portrayed in Video Game Magazines." *Sex Roles* 57: 733.

Noseworthy, Theodore J., and Karen Finlay. 2009. "A Comparison of Ambient Casino Sound and Music: Effects on Dissociation and on Perceptions of Elapsed Time While Playing Slot Machines." *Journal of Gambling Studies* 25 (3): 331–42.

Ogletree, Shirley M., and Ryan Drake. 2007. "College Students' Video Game Participation and Perceptions: Gender Differences and Implications." *Sex Roles* 56 (7): 537–42.

Perry, Stephen. 2011. "Top MCS Downloads for 2010: Sexual Content, Video Game Violence, and Gender Studies Grab Attention." *Mass Communication and Society* 14 (4): 403.

Scharrer, Erica. 2004. "Virtual Violence: Gender and Aggression in Video Game Advertisements." *Mass Communication and Society* 7 (4): 393–412.

Soukup, Charles. 2007. "Mastering the Game: Gender and the Entelechial Motivational System of Video Games." *Women's Studies in Communication* 30 (2): 157.

Whalen, Zach. 2004. "Play Along – An Approach to Videogame Music." *Play Along – An Approach to Videogame Music* 4 (1). http://www.gamestudies.org/0401/whalen/.

Williams, Dmitri, Nicole Martins, Mia Consalvo, and James D. Ivory. 2009. "The Virtual Census: Representations of Gender, Race and Age in Video Games." *New Media & Society* 11 (5): 815–34.

INDEX